T0284995

NEIL YOUNG ON NEIL YOUNG

Other Books in the Musicians in Their Own Words Series

Bowie on Bowie: Interviews and Encounters with David Bowie
The Clash on the Clash: Interviews and Encounters
Cobain on Cobain: Interviews and Encounters
Coltrane on Coltrane: The John Coltrane Interviews
Dolly on Dolly: Interviews and Encounters with Dolly Parton
Dylan on Dylan: Interviews and Encounters
Fleetwood Mac on Fleetwood Mac: Interview and Encounters
George Harrison on George Harrison: Interviews and Encounters
Hendrix on Hendrix: Interviews and Encounters with Jimi Hendrix
Joni on Joni: Interviews and Encounters with Joni Mitchell
Judy Garland on Judy Garland: Interviews and Encounters
Keith Richards on Keith Richards: Interviews and Encounters
Led Zeppelin on Led Zeppelin: Interviews and Encounters
Lennon on Lennon: Conversations with John Lennon
Leonard Cohen on Leonard Cohen: Interviews and Encounters
Miles on Miles: Interviews and Encounters with Miles Davis
Patti Smith on Patti Smith: Interviews and Encounters
Springsteen on Springsteen: Interviews, Speeches, and Encounters
Tom Waits on Tom Waits: Interviews and Encounters
The Who on the Who: Interviews and Encounters

NEIL YOUNG ON NEIL YOUNG

INTERVIEWS AND ENCOUNTERS

ARTHUR LIZIE

Published by Chicago Review Press Incorporated
814 North Franklin Street
Chicago, Illinois 60610

ISBN 978-1-64160-463-5

Library of Congress Control Number: 2021942199

A list of credits and copyright notices for the individual pieces in this collection can be found on pages 345–346.

Interior layout: Nord Compo

Printed in the United States of America
5 4 3 2 1

For my parents,
Arthur and Mary

CONTENTS

ACKNOWLEDGMENTS

Assembling this book was a pleasure, but, like Neil, I didn't do all the work myself. I'd particularly like to thank:

All of the contributing authors. Without them there literally would be no book.

Carleen Loper and Mary Ellen West from Bridgewater State University Library Services for research help and document delivery.

Dr. Andrew Holman and the Bridgewater State University Canadian Studies Program for funding and support.

Neil fans extraordinaire Scott Sandie, Tom Hambleton, and Thrasher for guidance and encouragement.

Marc Mamigonian for proposing the idea and Ric Dube for being a sounding board and general reference-chaser.

Kara Rota, Senior Editor at Chicago Review Press, for commissioning the book and fielding my endless queries.

Finally, Susan, Eloise, and Orson for convincing me to spend some time away from the keyboard every afternoon for some fresh air and exercise.

PREFACE

Although *Chrome Dreams II*'s centerpiece, "Ordinary People," begins with an evocation of Fred Zinnemann's 1952 Western classic *High Noon*, it's a quote from a decade later in John Ford's *The Man Who Shot Liberty Valance* that better captures the essence of Neil Young: "When the legend becomes fact, print the legend." This quote applies not only to the musical stories Young tells, which often traffic in the magical transition between dull fact and golden myth—a point alluded to on 2012's *Americana*/Alchemy tour with Crazy Horse—but also in the stories we tell about him.

Perhaps the biggest legend perpetuated about Young is that he doesn't talk to the press, that he's a hippie hermit in a hair shirt who barely opens his mouth. As recently as 2018, a major publication promoted a "rare interview" with Young. This "rare" interview was published during a week in which more than half-dozen other publications offered their own "rare" interviews. Print the legend.

What seems true is that Young doesn't like talking to the press. Unless, that is, he has something he really wants to promote, such as Pono, or LincVolt, or his Archives, or his view on Canadian tar sands, or his latest (don't call it a) comeback. It's then that his chat amp goes to eleven. At these times he can be quite generous and, increasingly with age, quite personable.

To be fair, interviews were rarer during the first decade of Young's career. But, after an initial flourish of minor interviews, he pulled away, suffering shell shock from both his "sudden" fame with CSNY and *Harvest* and the typical recreational pitfalls of rock-star celebrity. Over the second decade he built back slowly and, after 1985 and *Old Ways*, it was rare for much time to pass when he wasn't regularly meeting with the press, always available to promote his new creative project. And to answer the same questions—about Buffalo Springfield and Crosby, Stills, Nash & Young reunions, about *Trans*, about supporting Reagan, about cerebral palsy, about the Archives, about audio technology—over and over again (to coin a phrase).

But this seeming contradiction is part of what makes telling *the* Neil Young story so difficult—or rather, so much fun: he's a study in opposites. He is the infrequent interviewee who can't stop talking to reporters. He's the sensitive acoustic guy who can make your ears bleed. He's the counterculture hero who supported Reagan. He's the leave-the-bad-notes-in guy who'll talk your ear off about digital audio bitrates. He's the ordinary dude you'd smoke weed with who dated Hollywood actresses. Back and forth: he is the ocean.

Another legend we tell about Young concerns his fierce individualism. While there is no denying he has always pretty much done what he's wanted, and you'd be hard pressed to say he's not his own person, he doesn't always do what he does on his own. He's not only The Loner, but also The Leaner, resting against a vibrant network of creative support. From the Mynah Birds to Buffalo Springfield to Crosby, Stills & Nash and countless backing bands, including the Stray Gators, Promise of the Real, and, of course, Crazy Horse, Young has more often than not relied on other musicians to help make his music. And this spreads beyond guys with instruments (let's face it, he mainly works with guys) to other collaborators, such as producer David Briggs, manager Elliot Roberts, engineer John Hanlon, and directors Jim Jarmusch and Jonathan Demme. And, in this volume, cointerviews with R.E.M.'s Peter Buck and producer Daniel Lanois. Another contradiction.

That being said, this volume avoids group interviews: too little Neil Young is covered in too many words. This is particularly true of CSNY interviews, which are their own beast and well collected in Dave Zimmer's *4 Way Street* reader. Likewise, while *Rolling Stone* was a major early Young supporter, the magazine's 1994 compendium ably covers that material.

But this is about all the sense I want to make of Neil Young in this introduction. The point is to let Young's own words tell his story. To that end, the chronological chapters—culled from press conferences, magazines, radio appearances, and online interviews, from sources famed, fleeting, and forgotten—were selected with an eye toward both telling the overall Neil Young story and illuminating key events, ideally with little repetition from chapter to chapter (although some creeps in—sorry). Each chapter includes a brief contextualizing introduction, especially important at times when there's a big gap between years. Let's roll: here we are in the years.

THE BUFFALO SPRINGFIELD MESSAGE

Jeffrey C. Alexander | September 17, 1967 | *Los Angeles Times*

Buffalo Springfield began playing Los Angeles gigs in early 1966. They released their eponymous debut album in early December, followed by their only top-ten single, "For What It's Worth." This interview took place after the summer 1967 release of the stalled single "Bluebird" / "Mr. Soul," just prior to October's *Buffalo Springfield Again*.

Young responds to a perpetual predicament: being asked to explain a song's meaning. He's more effusive than later but still prefers to discuss circumstances rather than meaning.

This omits a short discussion with Stephen Stills. –Ed.

"Just because I wrote a song doesn't mean I know anything. I don't know very much about all the things that are going on around here, all the scenes, all the questions. All I know is just what I'm writing about. And even then I don't really know. I'm just trying to convey a feeling. The only things that I really know very well are the things that are at my house, the people I work with."

These gentle and modest words come from Neil Young, lead guitarist and songwriter for a rock 'n' roll group named the Buffalo Springfield.

The Springfield ranks among the best of the West Coast groups. Its melodies are simple, almost commonplace, but its musicianship is tight, and they write lyrics with more wisdom and poetry than anyone else round.

Neil Young wrote its first hit song, "Nowadays Clancy Can't Even Sing," released in August, 1966. It tells, in a bewildered fashion, about the tension between living and loving freely and functioning with success in today's constrained society.

"Many people, I know, tell me they don't understand 'Clancy.' They can't figure out all the symbols and stuff. Well, I don't think it's possible at all for them to know who he really is. For listeners, Clancy is just an image, a guy who gets come down on all the time.

"He was a strange cat, beautiful. Kids in school called him a 'weirdo,' 'cause he would whistle and sing 'Valerie, Valera' in the halls. After a while, he got so self-conscious he couldn't do his thing anymore. When someone as beautiful as that and as different as that is actually killed by his fellow men—you know what I mean—like taken and sorta chopped down—all the other things are nothing compared to this.

"In the song I'm just trying to communicate a feeling. Like the main part of 'Clancy' is about my hang-ups with an old girlfriend in Winnipeg. Now I don't really want people to know my whole scene with that girl and another guy in Winnipeg. That's not important, that's just a story. You can read a story in Time magazine. I want them to get a feeling like when you see something bad go down—when you see a mother hit a kid for doing nothing. Or a frustration you see—a girl at an airport watching her husband leave to go to war."

NEIL YOUNG ON

Picking Out the Buffalo Springfield Name

"So we just got out by the side of the road with our instruments and started doing the do. A big steam roller came by and somebody said that it would be really groovy if the group ever got as big as that steam roller. That night we 'acquired' some of the signs from the roller; we made sure we chose a variety of colors so as not to offend anyone."

—from an interview with Pam Fourzon, *TeenSet*, January 1967

NEIL YOUNG ON

Planning and Fears

"I never think more than three weeks ahead, and I can't remember more than a week back, except for certain things that stick out of the general mass of experiences. I never worry about what will happen because I know I can do certain things now, I've proved myself. My only insecurity, I guess, is a fear of not being able to talk or sing or not being able to use my hands."

–from an interview with Judith Sims, *TeenSet*, April 1968

NEIL YOUNG ON

This Year's Model

"Maybe some group will come along and be big, but, you know, who cares? It's just happened so many times now, it's like a 1969 car. Who cares? We all know it's not going to be any better than a '68 car.

–from an interview with Pete Johnson,
Los Angeles Times, October 28, 1968

NEIL YOUNG . . . ON HIS OWN

January 24, 1969 | *Ann Arbor Argus*

This interview took place during Young's gigs that ran November 8–10, 1968, at the Canterbury House, where the radical newspaper *Ann Arbor Argus* was published. These shows were his first official headlining gigs; *Sugar Mountain—Live at Canterbury House 1968* (2008) features show excerpts.

The publication of this article coincided with the release of *Neil Young*. The interview loosens up when manager Elliot Roberts jokes that Young's performance "stank." From there, Young raves about a little-know band, the Rockets (that is, Crazy Horse), slags off the Beatles (surprisingly) and Eric Clapton (less surprisingly), and after claiming to not be politically involved, argues about the inevitability of revolution—anticipating the Kent State tragedy by a year and a half. —Ed.

Q: Well, how does it feel to be playing without a group?

Young: Great. I really like it much better.

Q: Why?

Young: Because it's less hassle. I went through two and a half years of that with the Springfield and then three years without the Springfield before and there was about a month between those two periods when I was a single, and I just dug being a single. I can't wait until I start doing concerts when the album comes out.

Q: When's that?

Young: Sometime in February. It's already finished. We are just now putting it together.

Q: Is any of it live stuff or all done in the studio?

Young: No, there's nothing like that on it, but there's one song with no instruments—just guitar and voice.

Q: All the rest of the songs are backed up?

Young: Yeah.

Q: We have this great fantasy, that the Springfield broke up to start five new groups. Is there any chance of groups coming from any of the other guys?

Young: From the Springfield?

Q: Like Stills or anyone?

Young: Stills is starting a group, but you really can't say it'll be coming from the Springfield, because it's coming from two other groups, too. It's coming from the Hollies and the Byrds. Graham Nash and David Crosby.

Elliot Roberts: (Young's manager) You can't print it, though, or it'll get a lot of cats in trouble.

Young: You can't talk about that? Oh well, shit, that is ridiculous—everybody must know. Print it.

Q: But you're gonna stay like you are?

Young: Oh, yeah, no more groups.

Q: What do you think of the Supersession idea that Stills has been doing? Would you ever do anything like it?

Young: No, but it's a good idea, though.

Q: Why specifically did the Springfield break up? Did you all decide you all wanted to go your own ways, or what?

Young: We all got tired of it, and just couldn't hang in there. And as far as our inter-relationships were going, they were hurt because of the group, you know—the group was becoming bigger than us. And it was hanging us all up, and whatever we had for each other was disappearing, because the group was getting too much.

Q: So this is the first gig you've done on your own?

Young: Yeah.

Q: Where are you going to play, at the coffee houses?

Young: Well, yeah, I'll be doing quite a bit of them.

Q: Are you going on nationwide tour now?

Young: No, I'm just sort of poking off into different areas just to try myself out. I'm not making any money now—'cause I'm just flying out here and then flying right back when I finish.

Q: Why did you decide to accept Canterbury House?

Young: Well, cause this is a groovy place. It's got a good reputation, and it's crowded, really good crowds, and it's the best place to start, because the crowd is receptive.

Q: I can't believe you're, like you say, nervous performing alone. I mean, all the stuff you've done.

Young: It's different when you're by yourself. With a group you can do almost anything. I imagine after a while I'll get to the point where I can relax. But I'm really nervous now.

Q: It doesn't show.

Young: If I relax, I don't know how many things will begin to happen.

Q: You don't seem very neurotic performing.

Young: I didn't seem very neurotic?

Q: Not at all.

Elliot: I don't want to impose on you, Neil, but you STANK.

[laughter]

Q: Aside from that you were great, though. You gonna play ballrooms and stuff, or just coffeehouses?

Young: I don't think I'll be doing any ballrooms. I don't think I'll be doing any dances. Nobody'll ever dance while I play.

Q: There's not much you could dance to.

Young: I mean, something like the Fillmore, or something with some groups coming on playing and then me coming on all by myself, I'll never do that. All I want to do is play some concerts.

Q: Are you writing different kinds of songs now that you're not writing for a group? Do you think about it at all?

Young: Well, I'm writing more. That's all I can say. It's just I relax more. I'm writing different now because now I know the songs will be done. You know. Like before I wasn't sure, you know, if it would get done. You know, like there was always the thing about material. And now that I'm sure, you know, that I'm the one who makes the decision about my own material, then naturally I'm writing more. I'm less inhibited.

Q: You were inhibited before?

Young: Well, sure, I was sort of restricted. It was restricted, I mean, I couldn't, well, do a song by myself. It wasn't basically what I wanted to do anymore. As great as the group seemed, or was, you know, it just was not my bag. It could have been much bigger than it was. And I just sort of dropped out.

Q: What kinds of groups do you listen to?

Young: The Rockets.

Q: The Rockets?

Young: Yeah, they're from L.A.

Q: Do they have an album out?

Young: Yeah, it's on White Whale Records. And White Whale is doing an awful job for them.

Q: Why?

Young: They're just not pushing them. Not distributing.

Q: I guess not—not many people ever heard of them.

Young: They're the best new group we've heard in the last two years.

Q: Anybody well-known in it, or all new?

Young: No, all new guys, all new songs. A complete new thing.

Q: Too bad they aren't played around here.

Young: They are really good.

Q: Are they on tour?

Young: [long pause] Well, I don't just . . . it's not my bag. I'm not into it. I've seen too many groups better than the big groups to be in with the big groups. Because the real groups never really get heard.

Q: Like the Rockets.

Young: You know the Rockets are better than the big groups; I'd rather listen to them than to any other group. And that makes them better. Because I mean that . . . all music is . . . I think the best thing now happening is Jimi Hendrix, and not because of his guitar playing, or not because he's, you know, of that movement of guitar players . . . and I don't like that kind of—how can I say it . . . Jimi Hendrix is good, you know—he's really great. Whereas the Cream is the spearhead of a movement, you know. The Cream aren't . . .

Q: The Cream aren't what?

Young: The Cream aren't good. The Cream are good, but there are two types of good, if you know what I mean . . . There is an artistic good—I can't even say that.

Elliot: The Cream are a good Steppenwolf.

Young: Yeah, you know? And Steppenwolf is a fine group, but not like Hendrix. Sure the Cream is fine, but Hendrix is where it's at. And I don't dislike Cream because I like Hendrix . . . Do you know what I mean? It's like comparing Herman's Hermits to the Stones.

Q: You're not saying you like Herman's Hermits?

Young: No, though I did like their first records, "I'm into Somethin' Good."

Q: Earl Jean did a better job.

Young: Yeah, I'm sure somebody did it better, but they did it pretty good. I liked it: I didn't like "Mrs. Brown You've Got a Lovely Daughter."

Q: Well, who else would you put with Hendrix, you know, in the greatness group?

[long pause]

Young: Well, uh, there isn't anybody that impresses me that much. I tell you there is only one other guy that turns me on as far as listening to his music goes, and that's Stephen Stills.

But any of the other people . . . they're good, but they're not great. There is, you know—I can't get excited about anybody but Hendrix and Stills. Not Stills as a guitar player . . . Stills just as he is. He's great. He writes great songs and he sings all right. And he puts nice groovy records together. About every third or fourth one has a magical thing, you know?

Q: Are you into anything politically?

Young: No.

Q: What do you think of the Beatles song "Revolution?"

Young: I don't like it.

Q: Why?

Young: I don't dig it. It doesn't sound nice. I just don't dig it. It doesn't turn me on. It's not as good as "Walrus."

Q: What is.

Young: The Beatles aren't nearly as good as the Stones.

Q: I'll agree with that.

Young: I don't even listen to their latest stuff, like "Hey Jude."

Q: What do you think of their album?

Young: One of the songs, I couldn't believe it was the Beatles, it was so bad.

Q: Which one?

Young: I don't know. There are just so many of them . . . First time I heard it, I said, God, it can't be them. But it really sounded like them. And then I—like I always do—I listened to the lyrics, you know, and they just weren't good enough. The album isn't good enough to be the Beatles.

Q: What about the awful lyrics in "Revolution."

Young: Well, man, this shit, man, everybody knows the revolution's coming. That's all that has to be said. You know, there was one good song written about it—there were other good songs, but one really made it big, and that was "For What It's Worth." And that's not because I was in the Springfield, that's just because that was the song that made it big about that. We don't need anymore—we've already heard that once, you know. It comes out, and it comes out—the Stones' song "Street-Fighting Man," you know—they all come out and do this thing. Now the Stones song, let's face it, is fifty times better than "Revolution." That sounds like a poor rock group track—that fuzztone guitar doesn't have any taste.

Q: Yeah, the beginning sounds like an early Chuck Berry . . .

Young: Yeah, well, that's cool—Chuck Berry's really good.

Q: Yeah, but then they completely break it . . .

Young: It's too obviously a Vox fuzztone, you know. It's too obviously what you can hear anyhow. I don't know—the Stones play . . . I like the way they sound. I heard *Beggar's Banquet* first in London, unmixed, and it's just incredibly good. The Stones are just incredibly talented—they're my favorite group.

Q: What about Donovan?

Young: I don't think he's very good. He started off pretty groovy, and he made one good album, and there was one great song on it—I can't remember the name . . . Elliot?

Elliot: "Guinevere?"

Young: Yeah. That album [*referring to* Sunshine Superman —*Ed.*] was great. After that he just got to be a phony. And that flower kick, man, that was sick. I mean sick. The big picture of the Maharishi on the back of the album, you know, holding hands. What a sick, sick scene. I have no respect for him.

Q: Is there a chance the Springfield will get together for one last album?

Young: No chance. You'll know if another Springfield album comes out that I won't be on it. You'll know it's stuff that we didn't want used, but had stored[,] and was released by the company without our permission.

Q: Do you want to talk about the political situation? I can't think of any other questions to ask about.

Young: Oh, don't worry. You're asking good questions—I want to answer them.

Q: You mentioned something before about everybody knowing the revolution's gonna come. I wasn't quite sure what you were talking about. It doesn't seem to be all that inevitable, and it's not going to be accomplished by everybody singing about it and writing about it . . .

Young: Oh, it's inevitable, and I think—it's just inevitable. When you have such a dissatisfaction among such a majority—not a majority, but such a great amount of the people—and then dissatisfaction with those people among the majority—there's gonna be a clash. And the groups of people are so big, that it has to be a revolution. And it's not gonna come right away, but it's gonna come. We all know it's coming—it isn't gonna come next year, you know. We're gonna have a few riots, and I just don't know when it's coming. But everybody knows it's coming, like everybody knows it's gonna rain again.

Q: You really think that it's inevitable?

Young: It's that inevitable, it is. I mean, can you imagine us going on without this coming to a head.

Q: You don't think the forces of law and order will try and smash us—bash our heads in?

Young: Yeah, but you see that won't happen, because law and order is gonna come and try to do that, but it won't be over with because there'll be enough people . . . it just won't work—they can't just completely remove a thing like that. You can't just take it and snuff everybody out. Cause they'll miss some. And those ones will—you just can't get rid of it. You can't get rid of the hippies, you can't get rid of long hair, you can't get rid of—well, whatever this is, man. In three years we may all be bald, who knows. Anyway, there's definite differences happening, and they're gonna come to a head. There's more people every year. Everything's going to come together and clash. Soon. We see more of it 'cause we're from L.A. Whatever happens in NEW York, and whatever happens in L.A. eventually happens everywhere else. You know, music is that way, styles are that way, fads are that way. Everything's that way. New products come out—they come out in New York and L.A. They test 'em in L.A. And then this new thing of dissention has come out. It started in L.A., and it's gonna spread.

Q: Yeah, who elected Ronald Reagan governor?

Young: Well, you know, L.A. and California.

Q: Okay.

Young: Who elected Richard Nixon. The United States—I didn't elect him. The voting power isn't in the youth, but the manpower is. It's not gonna happen easy. It's not gonna go away. It's just inevitable. That's all I can say.

Q: Okay. Let's talk about your opinions of some people. Like, what do you think of Janis Joplin?

Young: I have no feelings about her.

Q: You don't think she's the greatest white soul singer of all time or something?

Young: I wouldn't know. I'm not that interested in white soul singers.

Q: How about Aretha, then?

Young: I've heard better. And I'm sure you have, too. How many colored people do you think there are who're better than Otis Redding, man, you know, that'll never make it because they're colored?

Q: It's ironic—he made it. His death was the greatest thing that happened to his career.

Young: Well, no—I disagree with you. No.

Q: Okay, well, it's been groovy talking with you.

Young: Okay, take it easy. It was out of sight talking with you. Send us a copy of the newspaper.

NEIL YOUNG ON

Being the "Indian" in Buffalo Springfield

"Everybody thought I was an Indian. That was when it was cool to be an Indian. I was wearin' fringe jackets and everything. I really loved these fringe jackets I used to have with the Springfield. I dug wearing them."

–from an interview with Elliot Blinder, *Rolling Stone*, April 30, 1970

RADIO INTERVIEW

B. Mitchel Reed | September 1973 | KMET

In February 1969, Neil Young transitioned from solo performances to fronting an extensive tour with Crazy Horse that lasted until the end of spring. In May, the joint LP *Everybody Knows This Is Nowhere* was released. In August, Young joined Crosby, Stills & Nash to form the supergroup that toured summer and fall 1969.

Young flip-flopped between the two bands for most of 1970 before releasing *After the Gold Rush*, his second solo LP, in September. He then played periodic solo gigs from November 1970 through February 1971. A Toronto show surfaced on *Live at Massey Hall 1971* (2007) that producer David Briggs originally argued for as the *Gold Rush* follow-up.

April 1971 saw the release of CSNY's live LP *4 Way Street*. Young followed that mega-popular LP on Valentine's Day 1972 with *Harvest*, his laid-back talisman recorded with the Stray Gators. *Harvest* would prove to be his bestselling LP and the lead track, "Heart of Gold," his only gold number-one single.

After these successes, Young threw the first of his career curveballs. While recording *Harvest*, he started the *Journey Through the Past* project. The first three sides of the double-LP, released November 1972, serve as an eclectic career overview, with the fourth being mostly soundtrack filler. The *Journey Through the Past* movie, the first production to use Young's filmmaking pseudonym Bernard Shakey, is, in Young's words, "an experimental film" and "a new form." The "new form" failed to find even Young's desired college audience and barely snuck into theaters in May 1974.

The *Harvest* material didn't get a band workout until 1973, during the January–April 1973 *Time Fades Away* Stray Gators tour. While the shows birthed the *Time Fades Away* LP, comprised of new, unreleased songs recorded live, the tour—the celebrity, the schedules, the pressure—was an exhausting and unpleasant experience for Young. He disliked the LP so much that he refused to release it on CD until 2017.

To compensate for all this, Neil "headed for the ditch." (Congratulations! You get to take a drink or put a marker on your Neil bingo card when this phrase appears.) "The ditch" included late-summer California clubs shows, backed by the Santa Monica Flyers (part Stray Gators, part Crazy Horse), and the rapid recording of the *Tonight's the Night* album. Although this interview, which took place shortly after the last of the club dates, touts it as the next LP, *Tonight's the Night* was not released until June 1975, following *On the Beach* (another "ditch" LP).

By 1973, Young was rarely talking with the press. KMET disc jockey B. Mitchel "Mitch" Reed was part of Young's circle of friends, though, which explains his ability to secure an interview at a time Young was refusing requests from major publications.

The overall theme of the interview is transition, with Young contemplating a culture moving on from the 1960s to the 1970s–to megaconcerts, to freer attitudes about harder drugs and homosexuality, to transitional artists like Lou Reed and David Bowie. He returns to his abiding concerns with recording technology and, like Michael Corleone, claims he's out of the politics game before being pulled back in. As a function of Mitch's concerns, there's a lot of CSNY talk, including details of the group's attempts at recording in 1973 and a somewhat granular analysis of CSN's solo work. The DJ's hope for "a live thing based upon maybe good vibes" would half come true–the group reunited in 1974 for rock's first large-scale stadium tour.

This interview has been lightly edited for clarity, mostly to eliminate Young's ever-present "you know," which would disappear from future conversations as he grew more comfortable with the interview process. –Ed.

B. Mitchel Reed: I'd like to start with your new album *Time Fades Away*, which was recorded live on the last tour, and you were riffing with me before we sat down in our studio to talk about this whole thing, that you had done your album in a different way. Would you like to describe that to me? I'd appreciate that.

Neil Young: You mean technically?

Reed: Technically, the new kind of things you came up with.

Young: Ahh, what we did is we eliminated the tape copy, the generation of, like, a two-track master; we didn't use one, we went directly from the sixteen-track to the disc through a computer.

Reed: And the computer was set up as I recall to make everything possible for helping you mix down, so you could remember all the different tracks that you used.

Young: Yeah. The computer, what the computer does is, instead of you making a mix of the record that they usually use as a master—like you move all the faders and make it sound the way you want it to sound—it remembers all that stuff so you don't have to make a copy of it anymore to know that you got it. That's the principle, that instead of making a copy to capture what you did, this thing remembers what you did and then you can use your original master, the sixteen-track, connect this thing to it, and connect the other end of that to the disc maker, and then you just run it, and it goes right off of the sixteen-track right onto the disc, which brings all the people who buy a record one step closer to the real sound.

Reed: In other words, you save a generation.

Young: Yeah.

Reed: Fantastic. Uh, you're into—

Young: I doubt if this album will save a generation, but . . .

[*Laughter.*]

Reed: All right.

Young: Hey, pretty fast . . .

Reed: The generation was lost, right—sorry about that. It was potentially a funny line. OK, so did you like it as a good representation of your live performance?

Young: Definitely. I think it's really an accurate representation of where that tour was at and the kind of thing I was trying to do on it and where my head was at when I was out there.

Reed: By the time people are listening to this, the show, you might have another album out at the same time, which would be released, what, six weeks after the first, if it goes down, right?

Young: Well, it's not a definite thing that it will come out that fast. It's finished right now, and I feel very strongly that it should come out as soon as it's ready, rather than waiting for other reasons. But I can't guarantee it'll be out in six weeks from now—when *Time Fades Away* comes out—but it *is* ready, and it'll be coming out as soon as we can get it out.

Reed: And that's called *Tonight's the Night.*

Young: Yeah.

Reed: OK, let's go on to other things. Are you satisfied with the songs that you're writing today, such as out of the *Journey Through the Past* or "Love in Mind" or "Don't Be Denied" and "Last Dance"? Are you happy with the things you're doing now as were last year or a year or so back, or two years or three?

Young: Uh . . . well, I'll tell ya, it's kinda hard to say whether I'm *happy* with them or not. Some of them really say how I feel and then some of them are like my viewpoints on other things that don't personally connect to me too directly. Some of the songs aren't super personal, and some of them are. So it's hard for me to say whether I feel satisfied with them or not. The vibe of when I was doing them and when I wrote them and when I recorded them is, ah, I was moving real fast at the time and seeing a lot of people and everything, and I sort of more remember that. I remember more of the *experience* of making the album and everything that surrounded it more than I do the actual performances of the songs on it, on the record. So I don't, what I'm trying to say is, I don't have an objective viewpoint on this particular record like I do on some of my others, because it reminds me so much of the tour and the speed that we were going out and the number of people that I had to confront every night. It puts my head in a different place.

Reed: Different place, right.

Young: Yeah. Other than where the music was.

Reed: Is there something else that you'd like to be doing in music, say from this moment, as we're sitting here, or maybe in your personal life? Is there some other direction? I know about the film, but maybe expand upon that, expand upon that a little bit.

Young: Right now, let's see . . . well, I just finished *Tonight's the Night*, this other album, that was just like, it was sort of an *explosion*. I don't know how that happened, but . . . I feel very happy with that music, but I feel really good about where I am right now. The film, I hope that turns into something for me because I definitely, I think you need something else, other than . . . you can't do the same thing all the time, just make records.

Reed: Yeah. Are you as politically motivated as you were maybe in the early part of your career? I mean, can you separate politics from you as an artist?

Young: Yeah. Before, at the first part of my career or whatever, I wasn't really into politics, and then all of a sudden, I just sort of got into it, because of what was going on around me. I couldn't ignore it, it's just too obvious to me. So I started singing about that for a while and, you know, I got into that and really heavily got into that, and now I think I've come out the other end of that awareness. I'm not as aware of that, I feel like most people are, like most people feel that—the ending of the war, per se, whatever that means, and the Watergate trip and that whole thing—that we are in a different era now than we were then. I think politics plays a different part in this era than it did in the last, in the era, say, of the revolution and the . . . I'm not saying that—ah, well, I guess I *am* saying that the revolution of the '60s is definitely not with us anymore.

Reed: The revolution of the '60s no longer, the revolution [*indistinct*] . . .

Young: It's just different now. I'm not as politically oriented as I was, I don't think, because it doesn't get my heart, what's going on now. It just doesn't, like when—there's nothing happening that would spark a song for me . . .

Reed: Gotcha.

Young: . . . right now. I mean, I'm sure there's a lot of heavy things going down, but I'm just thinking of something else. There haven't been four students killed or eight students killed somewhere else. That kind of thing isn't happening. We've sort of changed, maybe. I don't know.

Reed: Well, I will, then I'll jump away then, if we've changed. Before we went on the air, we were riffing about the fact that the Byrds and the Springfield were latter day—latter '60s, I should say—latter '60s that carried over into the '70s, and we're just beginning our '70s now, is that correct, as far as music?

Young: Yeah, I think so. Insofar as music, I think the last couple of years have just been latent '60s, just—things overhang and everything, and I feel now that the change into the music of the '70s is starting to come, with people like David Bowie and Lou Reed. People like that are really starting to come into their own as writers and performers now. I think there's some really good things there.

Reed: What do you think of Alice Cooper?

Young: I kinda like Alice Cooper. I think that's pretty far out. I think it's a whole other trip, and I enjoy it, it's part theater and everything. I've never seen one of the concerts. I only go by the vibe that they give people and that I've related to, that—I've heard people talking about them, and I see their advertisements, and I hear their records. One was called "School Is Out Forever" or something?

Reed: Yeah, "School Is Out Forever," last year . . .

Young: [*Laughs.*] I don't know, I kinda like that, you know.

Reed: Mmm . . .

Young: It's sort of a gay abandon sort of thing, you know.

[*Laughter.*]

Young: I dig it. I like it.

Reed: Earlier this year, the four of you got together again—I mean, I'm actually putting the cart before the horse. The four of you got together in July: Crosby, Stills, Nash, and you. And, as I understand it, you rehearsed a lot but never put anything down. But maybe you did put some things down on track. Did you?

Young: Yeah, we recorded a little, we recorded a little bit at my ranch. Ah, we, we played a lot, and we got back together again musically . . .

Reed: You did.

Young: . . . which was really nice, when we laid off for a while—we worked at it for quite a while—and we laid off to all do our own things again and we actually didn't produce anything that, during that time we were working together, that anyone will probably ever hear. Although we learned some songs, and . . . we didn't make any finished records or anything during that time, though. We learned a lot of songs, and we learned about each other a little more, about where we're at now, 'cause we haven't seen each other really in a couple of years except, you know, talking on the phone and just keeping in touch, making sure everything's cool and everybody's all right, you know.

Reed: Where are you vis-à-[vis] . . . in reference to the guys, where are they in reference to you? In other words, when you say you've touched base finally after a couple of years, um . . . the question I'm about to ask is—[*indistinct interjection from an unidentified speaker*] . . . Oh, hold on a minute, OK.

Young: OK.

Reed: Um, stop tape for a minute please and start it when I tell you to?

Voice: They can splice that. They can splice tape without any problem.

Reed: Ah, you don't know our techniques. No problems at all. We go *chhh!* and it's spliced.

Young: [*Laughs.*] That's the first time I've ever seen that.

Reed: The first time I ever saw it was when Teddy showed it to me this morning. It's interesting. I'm surprised as hell.

Young: Mitch, you should see the cover itself. This is much smaller.

Reed: Do you have control on your album covers?

Young: Yeah.

Reed: You do?

Young: Yeah.

Reed: You and . . . Joni was the first one I ever knew who had complete control.

Young: Yeah, well, you gotta have it.

Reed: I got a question about Jack Nitzsche, if I get to it. We'll get to it.

Young: We'll get to it.

Reed: We're doing well.

Young: We'll cover 'em all.

Reed: We'll cover 'em all, baby.

Young: That's right.

Unidentified: Thanks, fellas. Again, my apologies.

[*Indistinct discussion.*]

Reed: Start tape, please. We had covered the fact that you all had gotten together, but I wanted to ask this question as a follow-up to that. How did your joining, well, let's see—how different is it now from the first time you did join David and Steve and Graham, um . . . no, I'll ask that question later. Let me start again. You're four divergent personalities.

Young: Mm-hmm.

Reed: Yet you click; you were the supergroup of all supergroups, of all the supergroups of supergroups. I don't think anybody has had the product, A, or the name, B, that you had. There were supergroups such as Cream or what have you—or, no, the other one that was started after Cream, uh, Blind Faith. It was an attempt to do a supergoup, people from other . . .

Young: Mm-hmm.

Reed: You know, the homogenizing, where there's cross-pollination.

Young: Yeah, right.

Reed: But, the thing, Neil, about you four people was very unique, that you came from, you loved each other a lot, I mean, you admired each other's music. . . . I'm actually saying what I'd like to have you say.

Young: Yeah, well, it's true, it's true. We love playing together. We had a lot of past together. We all came from—we had a lot of memories of each from a long time ago, watching each other grow up and watching each other really put out music that has blown each other's minds, over a long period of time. And that, we have that relating point, we have a relating point from the past. Now the thing is, is that, is that still, is that relating point, still going to be sparkling now like it was then, is the thing?

Reed: I see.

Young: That's what we got together to find out and to get it going and see what was happening. And when we did stop playing, we had reached a point that we all felt that we were really together and that we could *do it*. It takes a while, you can't just sync into something like that, you can't just turn it on and everybody walk in the room, and there it is, because we all, we stay away from each other for a while and we get preconceived ideas of different things, and everybody changes; you have to learn to meet everyone again.

Reed: All right, that was July of 1973 and right at the moment of this, as we're taping this show, Graham is on the road with the group that he and David went on the road with, and David is going on the road with that same group, and Stephen, Stephen is off with Manassas. So, this is the fall of 1973. Are you committed to delivering an album, say, February of next year or anything?

Young: No. We have no commitment to do anything, because I think that would make us crazy if we had to. We're trying to stay away from having a commitment to do anything because it seems whenever we have the people that are expecting us to do something is when we start to get shaky about it, it's when we start to get . . . When you start feeling the pressure, I think that's what, ah, you feel the pressure of everybody thinks it's gonna have to be some kind of a great thing. And [we want] to get through all of that and get right down to having a good time playing together in the studio and forgetting about who we are and about who everybody thinks we are and about what the album's gonna be like and whether we should go this way or whether it should be that way—forgetting about everything except the basic songs and the feeling behind the songs and still having all four of us in the same room at the same time; [that] is what we're gonna try to do. And it takes a while to get this when you're in our positions; it takes a while to get that way, together. I hope we can, I sincerely hope we can, because I think it would be great. I heard us singing. In July we sang. It sounded better to me than it ever has. And I certainly hope we can get it on record so that people can hear us.

Reed: Phew. In other words, that which was joined again in July will—conceivably, that good feeling will carry over.

Young: We certainly hope so. No reason why it shouldn't, actually. We all really want to do it; everybody's super into it. We plan to get together in late November or December and start playing again, feel the vibe and do whatever we feel is right. If we feel like playing before we make a record, maybe we should go out and actually see the people as a group of, as a group, going to see the people and get the vibe before we do an album. Maybe we should do that. It's hard to . . . You see, we really don't know what to do exactly, whether we put out an album first or go out and feel it out and just see how things feel, how the *vibe* is, and how the people who are interested in music are feeling, just how things are going and try to put that onto a record, try to *relate* to that and put it onto a record.

Reed: Possibly a live thing based upon maybe good vibes.

Young: Yeah, it would be real nice.

Reed: Was it difficult, Neil, starting your career as a solo artist after you left the Springfield? Was it hard getting together, personally in your head, or musically?

Young: No, I don't think so: I loved it. When I started out playing alone, I really loved it. It was real easy and super simple. I was doing, I guess in '69 was when I started doing, a tour by myself. It was real easy for me. And then I did another one like that in '70, or '71; I can't remember—'71—yeah. And, that was great, too, we did a tour of about thirty places, just alone and everything. It felt really good. Being a solo performer, or whatever, is, ah, it's real easy, if you can just *feel* things and let it out.

Reed: Then, how did you feel about when you, all your four people got together—have I asked this question? I don't know if I did. I sidetracked myself, so I'll go back to it. It was first Crosby and Stills, Stephen had left the group, had left Springfield at the time, David had left the Byrds, then Graham came over leaving the Hollies, and then you were the solo person, and your divergent managers—who, for the moment, were not partners at the time, [David] Geffen and [Elliot] Roberts—put you together, or at least. . . ah, that's a mistake, OK, *you guys* got together, of course. . . .

Young: Yeah, I think it started with Stephen and Ahmet talking to each other. . . .

Reed: Ahmet Ertegun of Atlantic [Records]?

Young: Yeah, I think Crosby, Stills, and Nash had finished their album, and they were thinking about going out on the road to promote the album, to show people what they were. But when they started thinking about it, they realized that to have me there would be just another, another addition, I guess, I guess just another step. And they wanted to do that, to carry that Springfield thing that Stephen and I had going over into their thing, which was a really great vocal sound, and I guess that's why they asked me to join. At that time, I was really excited, because I hadn't been doing really well. I had a couple of records out and neither one was really too successful; it was *Neil Young* and *Everybody Knows This Is Nowhere*. . . .

Reed: Yeah.

Young: Neither one of them were doing super good. Then I joined Crosby, Stills, and Nash and did that tour with them, and my records started taking off. *Everybody Knows This Is Nowhere* started doing better and better and hung in there for a really long time. And so I guess it helped me, on all levels, joining them. Beside making what I felt was really great music that was really getting me off, I mean, more people were getting to know me as an artist and to get interested in what I was saying, so it was a really good thing for me. It was a good thing for everybody, I think, because I think I added a lot to them, too, as well as them helping me.

Reed: Very true. Could you discuss, Neil, the Springfield in retrospect? I mean I asked you about *four,* maybe, diverging questions, but it's all based upon [looking] to discuss the Springfield, particularly how you felt about the group when you were with it, the original with Richie and Bruce, that crazy—

Young: That crazy bunch.

Reed: Crazy Bruce. Crazy bunch of dudes.

Young: Well, I tell you, I felt like I was, I felt—myself and the other guys in the group and maybe about twenty or thirty other people thought that we were fantastic, we thought that the group had a feeling, and we felt real about it. Nobody had ever done it before. I mean, other groups had done it, but *we* had never done it as a group. It was our first try, and we felt like a group, we felt like a unit. And we felt that if we'd've gotten, I'm sure that if we'd've gotten *any* kind of recognition at the beginning for our first two or three albums . . . I mean, we put all our albums out and everything that's ever been out plus anything that they're gonna put out, it all was recorded in two years. And we didn't really get any recognition at that time. If we'd've gotten some, we thought we would have stayed together, because I loved it then.

Reed: You really believe that? Because being on the end as disc jockey, being on this end, the one who plays the finished product that comes out, I remember those exciting days; I was talking about them before the show began, about you running up with dubs of the *Buffalo Springfield Again.*

Young: Ah, yeah.

Reed: The dubbing and the coming from the pressing plant and bringing me dubs, to be the first one to be played on the air.

Young: Yeah, I know.

Reed: And it was exciting, and you were—this town, Los Angeles—I couldn't speak for the rest of the country, I never watch record sales or anything like that—but it was *your town,* it was the Byrds' town. There has been talk for many, many a year that probably the best kind of a nostalgic kind of show they'd want to put on at the Hollywood Bowl would be to put you and the old Springfield . . .

Young: Mm-hmm.

Reed: . . . the old Byrds, the original—I mean, everybody original—and the original Lovin' Spoonful from the East Coast . . .

Young: Phew.

Reed: . . . because that would the music of those late '60s, wouldn't it?

Young: Yeah, that would be great.

Reed: Wouldn't that be great? In one show at the Bowl?

Young: That would be a trip.

Reed: I'd love it.

Young: Boy, I—phew!

Young: Man, that would be something. But that's in the past.

Reed: That is the past, right.

Young: That sort of puts us all in the Bill Haley category . . .

Unidentified: Art Laboe.

Young: . . . when we're Perry Como, trying—[*laughs*] art nouveau?

Reed: Art nouveau? I thought you said Art Laboe.

Unidentified: I did say Art Laboe. [*The California DJ credited with popularizing the term "oldies but goodies." —Ed.*]

[*Indistinct cross talk, laughter.*]

Reed: When you wrote "Nowadays Clancy [Can't Even Sing]," as opposed to what you write now, did you consider yourself a competent writer?

Young: Ah, I didn't have any idea what I was at that time. I was just writing. I wrote the words in a corner and wrote 'em all down so that they looked . . . I'd write twelve lines of poetry and then look at it, and I'd go, "Wow, what a trip that was—nowadays Clancy can't even sing," and then I sat down and wrote the second verse and the third one, just so that they looked the same graphically on the paper. It was weird, just to get the shape of the paragraph the same. And then I wrote a melody to it. I don't write like that anymore. I'm not nearly as analytical.

Reed: Was Stephen, as compared to you, a more competent writer then?

Young: I think he was more prolific than I was at that time, he wrote a lot more songs than I did. He wrote, what was that song, "For What It's Worth," and everything. That was really a spontaneous thing after the Sunset Strip riots and everything. That was probably the best thing, contribution, Buffalo Springfield made on a political level, on a contemporary music contribution to a feeling-of-a-generation or something level. I don't know what I mean by that really, but, ah . . .

Reed: I think I know what you mean by it. I understand it. There was a time when he was frightened he was going to be known as a political writer, at the time of "For What It's Worth," people . . .

Young: Yeah.

Reed: Yet, four years later you wrote an activist song of a nature, a politically motivated song of a nature, that's '66 and '70 you write—was it '71? I forget when [the] Kent State [shooting] was—you write "Ohio." Yet you were not afraid of that kind of conversation being placed in your head.

Young: No, I didn't care because I figured by then people didn't think I was gonna do that, so I didn't feel that I would be typecasting myself as a political person, although I don't really care. I just think that writing that song was just a pure reaction to the cover of *Time* magazine which was sitting there. I never really thought about it any other way.

Reed: What picture?

Young: Picture of Allison What's-Her-Name [*referring to Allison Beth Krause —Ed.*] sitting there with that dead kid lying on the sidewalk. It was kind of a . . . And now all this stuff, it's Segretti [*Richard Segretti, who worked on Richard Nixon's Committee to Re-elect the President and served prison time for his work for Nixon —Ed.*] and all, that whole thing that Watergate brought out about the actual people that went to the demonstrations and provoked these things to happen to make the hippies and all the people to look like a bunch of Communists, make them look like a bunch of radicals that would shoot and kill people and everything, trying to smear that whole trip, that revolution trip and make it a bad name, that's what those cats were trying to do. And that bugs me, I mean, that still bugs me. I can't forget that. And that gives me a reason to sing a song again, because I know that there must have been some connection there, more than what we know about. The investigation and everything was all ludicrous and the whole thing is just like the Kennedy assassination. We never really found out what went down.

Reed: Mm. No, we didn't.

Young: The people who are trying to investigate it are the people who got the whole thing together in the first place. It just doesn't work that way.

Reed: Were you ever that tight with David Crosby, or David, when he was a Byrd? Did you guys hang out?

Young: Not too tight. No, as a matter of fact, we were not the best of friends at that time. Stephen and David were really very good friends, and when I quit the Springfield, the first time I quit the Springfield, I could—both Crosby and Stills and all the other guys in the group thought I was nuts.

Reed: I did too.

Young: I think I was probably.

Reed: [*Laughs.*]

Young: But I got back on the track a couple of months later. Around then, David told me that he thought . . . he didn't have any respect for me, because I quit, and later on I could dig what he was saying, because he thought the group was really good and everything. And then later on we got to be *really* good friends, once we got to know each other. To me he was always David Crosby of the Byrds; that was like, he was this big thing, and I really took a long time before I could relate to him or Graham as anything else. I listened to Hollies records for years. 'Cause to me it's like meeting McCartney or Lennon or something like that. I felt the same way about those guys, because they just really put out. So it took me a while to get over the flash of who they were and really get into meeting them as people.

Reed: You knew Stephen and you didn't know Graham. My next question was going to be if you knew Graham as a Hollie.

Young: No.

Reed: But you just liked his music from afar.

Young: Yup.

Reed: [*Whistles.*] Dynamite. Which of Stephen's songs has impressed you the most?

Young: His songs, ah, let's see now. Let's see now, which . . . there's so many of them. What's that one . . . now, he has one called, he has one called "Love Story" that isn't out yet. That's a really beautiful song.

Reed: Is it with Manassas?

Young: Ah, no, he's never done it.

Reed: Ahh.

Young: It's a great song, though. Beautiful song. And I really liked "Hung Upside Down." I thought that was a fantastic song. "Sit Down I Think I Love You" I thought was a great song. What was that other one he did . . . ? "Bluebird." That was great. And, ah, what was that one, oh, ah, what the heck is that song? The one about old times, good times, um, it's on his first solo album.

Reed: The first solo album . . .

Young: Yeah, he's done some really great stuff. "Black Queen." I like "Black Queen." That was great—I mean, you know, all through his whole career he's had gems that just keep showing up. And sometimes you don't get to hear them the way I get to hear 'em. I just get to hear *him* and the song, so I don't have the same relating point as probably hundreds of thousands of people do, 'cause they don't . . . they buy the record, and the record sometimes doesn't sound like what the song sounded like the first time I hear it. There's another song called "Pretty

Girl Why," which is really a great song that he did, and a couple of other ones. "My Angel" was an early song. Really early. Some beautiful songs that he wrote, really.

Reed: David is not as prolific a writer as perhaps you or Stephen or Graham. Which of David's songs—he writes sad things—"Triad."

Young: "Everybody Has Been Burned." "Triad." "Laughing." "Wooden Ships." You know David's just—"Guinnevere"—he's just, he's had—"All Along the Lee Shore." He's had so many songs that I, that I really like.

Reed: You just made me think about it; he has written more than I thought.

Young: He's written a lot of songs, man. He's, I mean, he's a heavy writer, he just doesn't—personally I think he should record his songs quicker, because he'll get a couple of songs together and then he'll hold on to them for a long time waiting for the right way to do them, and I think, if anything, that's why he doesn't write more, because he doesn't get, he doesn't get it out right away, get it down on tape, and get it out of his system, in order to leave room for something new to come in. And that's probably why we haven't heard more from him than we have. I still think that he's written some of the most *feeling* songs . . .

Reed: Mm.

Young: . . . that I've ever heard. Like "Almost Cut My Hair" was a very crude song, a very crude recording and everything, but it was so real. If you know Crosby, you can believe that what he's telling you in that song is *true*, that he looks in his mirror and sees a cop and gets paranoid is a reality for Crosby. You know that. You know him. Other people listen to that song, they couldn't believe it. They thought it was a little exaggerated, maybe a little obvious, "'I almost cut my hair,' what is that, a joke?" But the thing is that he lives it. At that time he was living that. And that's what I love about David. If he believes it—he believes what he's saying, so he can't do it.

Reed: David is organically alive in the moment.

Young: Yeah. Very, very much into the moment itself and a very emotional person and for sure he was the heartbeat and whole spark of Crosby, Stills, Nash & Young, there's no doubt about that. Crosby was the one who kept it together and the one who keeps it together on stage, although he is probably, in many ways, the shakiest one of all of us. We all go through a lot of changes together, but it's his immediate emotions and his sort of a search for a reality that he can live with at the very time that he is there—[that] is what really keeps it alive.

Reed: He's got a sense of theater, then.

Young: He has a, he just has a sense of, uh, he has a sense of emotions.

Reed: Emotions.

Young: He just lets it out. Whatever it is. And whatever extreme it is.

Reed: [*Quietly*] Dynamite. . . . OK, then I, to be perfectly honest, and I covered all—we'll get around to you in a moment. Which of Graham's song do you like?

Young: Ah, let's see. I like "Our House." I think it's the best one, I think, of his.

Reed: It's so pretty.

Young: It's a great song.

Reed: Yeah. Do you like "I Used to Be a King?" He's a bleeder.

Young: Oh, yeah. Yeah, I love "I Used to be a King." And he's got the new thing, he's a got new song called "Sleep Song" which is on his new album which will be out in about six weeks. He's got some great new songs on that album.

[*Tape cuts, then conversation resumes.*]

Young: Which ones do I like?

Reed: Yeah, overall. Continuously, and which ones have you rejected? Maybe.

Young: [*Sighs.*] Well, they go all the way back. The early Buffalo Springfield stuff I guess I've rejected almost everything from the first album and, ah, "Expecting to Fly" is hanging in there as a record, from the second album, and the third album, the song "I Am a Child" was pretty nice, but I don't think the recording was very good. And then on my first album, I like "The Loner." Felt like I was getting into something different there. Starting to, anyway. And some of the other stuff, "The Old Laughing Lady" I think was probably the best record on that.

Reed: Yeah, it's one of the most requested things on my show.

Young: Yeah, that's really a good one. Although we did some other things on that I really got into; that was a personal album. The second, *Everybody Knows This Is Nowhere*, I don't think there's anything on it that I didn't like.

Reed: You do like it all.

Young: Yeah, I like it all.

Reed: Mm-hmm.

Young: That's when a change came over me. Right then I started trying to just do what I was doing and just trying to be real instead of fabricate something and show people where my head was at. I just wanted them to know where I was at. Since then, I've just been striving to get it realer and realer on the record. . . . As in, more real.

Reed: [*Laughs.*]

Young: My English teacher, man, I can't shake 'im.

Reed: What part of Canada are you from?

Young: Ah, Winnipeg.

Reed: Winnipeg.

Young: Yeah.

Reed: Joni Mitchell is from where?

Young: Saskatoon.

Reed: Is that nearby?

Young: It's not far away . . . about five hundred, six hundred miles.

Reed: [*Laughs.*] That's Canadian, right?

Young: Yeah. [*Chuckles.*]

Reed: That's interesting. You're a woods person, you've carried that over. You're a ranch person and Joni is to a certain extent, too. She likes woodsy things.

Young: Mm-hmm.

Reed: She told me one time—or I don't know if it was part of a riff I heard her do live, when she was doing it—"The Circle Game," that she wrote it for you. Is that true?

Young: Yeah, she wrote it for me. She heard "Sugar Mountain," a long time ago. I wrote "Sugar Mountain" around the time when I first met Chuck and Joni. Chuck was her old man at the time, and they were doing an act together in folk houses, and I wrote that, I was writing that song at that time. She really liked it so she wrote like a sequel to it, which was "The Circle Game." If you listen to those two tunes back-to-back . . . out at The Corral—you should have been at The Corral—Joni and I sang "Sugar Mountain" with an electric band. Joni's into electric guitar now, which is kinda far out. Nobody's heard it yet, but she's been jamming with our band and with Dave, with Graham's band. And she's getting really funky. I think it's gonna surprise a lot of people.

Reed: Yeah, well she started getting funky in this last album of hers.

Young: Yeah.

Reed: A real side trip.

Young: Yeah. "[Cold Blue Steel and] Sweet Fire" and those things.

Reed: Yeah, right.

Young: But, yes, that's *clean* compared to what she's into now. [*Chuckles.*]

Reed: [*Laughs.*] I can't wait. Well, we mentioned Joni. Are there any other musicians, other than yourself, other than the boys, other than Joni, say, that interest you or influence you or have?

Young: I have to say that Lou Reed is probably . . .

Reed: At this moment?

Young: Yeah. I have really only heard one of this albums, and I've heard one of his songs on the air a lot, that one about, uh—

Reed: "Walk on the Wild Side?"

Young: "Walk on the Wild Side." I thought it was a very fresh approach. I thought it was a significant . . . you know. Between him and David Bowie and Alice Cooper, I think that that is a new direction. There's something theatrical about that that wasn't happening in the music of the '60s. And I personally, although I haven't seen any one of those people, I haven't seen any of those people—although I might have met Lou Reed, maybe five years ago in a motel on the East Coast. *Might* have been. He said he used to be in the Velvet Underground.

Reed: Right. He was in the Velvet Underground.

Young: And I can't remember, but I really like his record, the one he made; "Walk on the Wild Side," I thought, was really fresh. That's the freshest thing I've heard recently.

Reed: That's interesting. That music, of course—I mean, the Velvet Underground—was such underground music for so very long, and at times it used to be called transvestite music, and it's not actually. And now he has sprang, as you say, full-grown into the public consciousness.

Young: Transvestite music! [*Laughs.*]

Reed: Transvestite music, it is called that.

Young: Well, maybe it is. It's that and everything else. It's *good music*, is the thing. He's telling a story of, street stories, and that's a reality that we've just been, that's a reality in the '70s. I mean, heroin and the whole way of life that those people are into, or some of them are into, speed or whatever they're into, it's a very—compared to the '60s, this is much more of a dope generation that we're in now, only it's almost taken for granted, and that's what the approach a lot of these people have toward making records is that homosexualism and heavy dope use and everything is a way of life to a lot of people, and they don't expect to live any more than thirty years, and they don't care.

Reed: [*Whistles.*]

Young: They don't care. They're in the '70s. It blows a lot of people's mind that there are people like that, but I understand it. I'm not that far out myself, but I can certainly dig where they're at. I think it's really a good, it's a great reaction to the world, the way the world is now. What these people are doing is, it's an offspring of what we've done to *them*. I think it's valid, and I think it's new. I really—

Reed: What do you mean it's an offspring of what we've done to them?

Young: It's like an offspring of what the establishment or whatever you want to say, you know, *us*.

Reed: Right.

Young: 'Cause we're moving out of where we were into another place, and these people are just coming in. And *now*—we were crazy before, we figured if we ever get grass to be legal it'll be out of sight and now it's not legal, but it's, you know . . . Now, five years ago we were so paranoid that you'd hide in your trunk and smoke grass or whatever. *Now* it's just different. Things that we thought were gonna be breakthroughs now are taken for granted, and people are trying to get further. That's the way it always is, I guess. But anyway, what I'm trying to say is that these people like Lou Reed and David Bowie [*"Boo-ie" —Ed.*], or Bowie, or however you pronounce it, those folks are . . . I think they got something there. [*Laughs.*]

Reed: OK. In that case, I want to ask . . .

Young: [*Singing; Reed joins in for the last couple words.*] "Take a walk on the wild side."

[*Laughter.*]

Reed: In that case, I was going to ask you about—if you think that's the direction—there's a certain kind of jazz [that] is coming down now soft and pretty, maybe you've been listening to that as well. Also, I've been told, and I've been feeling some vibrations about it, but you disagreed with me before when we talked about it, about country having reached a full, well, having [be]come full-grown and maybe crossing over the so-called pop lines and that kind of thing, or bluegrass, and you disagreed. You still feel that way? I mean, look, this is only a few hours ago, of course.

Young: Yeah, right, right. For *me* anyway, I love country music, and I play a lot of it. I've got a lot of country songs that I'm still writing. But I don't, I don't think that country music is a new, is a new—I don't think it's a new form. I think what we're doing is taking an old form and adapting it, changing it, putting the vibe that's happening now into country music and trying to use 1970s words and talk about things people can understand. Now, if they can get to that point, without people trying to sound like they're singing country music, people—for country music to make it, I think you have to forget that you're singing it and just live it. It has to be a real part. You can't be trying to use phrases that people used in the '50s because that's when country music was happening; you gotta be talking about something that people can relate to now, and then it becomes a real, real music. Real country music or whatever. I think country is like the American White blues form, and that's it.

Reed: Exactly, it is that.

Young: It's the roots. But, I think it was really heavily gone into in the last five years and I . . .

Reed: You think it's been . . .

Young: Well, it's been *done*, you know.

Reed: Mm-hmm.

Young: It's been *done*. You hear a lot of steel guitars, you hear a lot of everything. That's not to negate it at all; I love playing it, and I will continue to play it, because I get off doing it. But I don't think it's gonna be a major force. Not to me anyway, 'cause it's nothing new.

Reed: Unless it's done, as you say, like the Eagles' style, as the Eagles do it or something like that. There's a question I wanted to ask you—and that's not true country, they're just getting a little twangy with the steel guitar.

Young: Yeah.

Reed: This question I wanted to ask you: There's a thing that took place. You were out, you weren't out, I mean, you were doing what you were doing. . . . But do you feel the group America, for example, came in—and boy, they sound so much like you—to fill a void that said, "We need a Neil Young at this particular moment"?

Young: No, I think they just came along with a good record; they had a catchy tune. I think that there's so much music out today that if people don't get one thing they'll take another. That's funny saying that after what you just said, now that I listen back to it. But I think that was a valid record, that "[A] Horse with No Name." I've made a lot of jokes about it to my friends and everything, a lot of them have to me. As a matter of fact, once I called my father up on the telephone and he told me he really dug my new record.

Reed: [*Laughs.*]

Young: I said, "Which one's that?" He said, "You know, the one about the horse and the desert." I said, "Wow, that isn't me, that, ah, that's America." And he said, "Oh, well it must have been another one or something like that." That was an interesting time. That was an interesting experience. But I feel, I feel, I'm not grossed out behind it at all; I feel like it's a good thing. I think they were just making music that was reflective of their influences. It was really valid. I actually got more of a buzz out of "Ventura Highway" than I did out of "A Horse with No Name."

Reed: Yeah. So did I, actually. Yeah. The question, um—I'm jumping around a lot, but that's OK. What about accusations, like when Bill Graham [*the famed rock promotor —Ed.*] quit, when he gave up Fillmore East and Fillmore West [*his venues —Ed.*] and of course went back into it right away, practically right away. Bill Graham said he was tired of dealing with superstars and the fact that they came off with the lines—I may be taking it out of context . . .

Young: I think he did it all for the publicity.

Reed: I think so, too.

[*Laughter.*]

Young: Can't blame him, man.

Reed: He says that "I can't stand superstars that rip me off for a lot of bread and then run away from the audience to their boats or their ranches." And of course, I right away relate it to, ah . . .

Young: Was he on his boat or on his ranch when he was talking about that?

[*Laughter.*]

Reed: I don't know, but that answers it right there. Ah, rich musician's lifestyle. That was his riff.

Young: Mm-hmm.

Reed: You recently completed your first movie, *Journey Through the Past*, and—which I haven't seen yet as a matter of fact, although I was—

Young: It hasn't been out yet, but I'll get—when I screen it in L.A., I'll definitely invite you.

Reed: I'll like to.

Young: To see what you think of it.

Reed: It's long overdone, long overdue

Young: Long overdue.

Reed: Long overdue, long anticipated. Would you like to continue making film, or would you like to—

Young: Yeah, I really want to. I think that that's—everybody's starting to get into film now—and I really think it's a good way to go. I wish my film was already out, but it's coming out now. Took a long time to get it out. We had a lot of legal problems we didn't anticipate. Obviously we put out the soundtrack album a year before the movie's coming out, and the movie's only coming out in one market, in Boston. It's sort of an experimental picture in some ways; it's a new form. We're gonna start it off where we think people will be able to relate to it, college-oriented people that can relate to what the film is about. It's not just a rock and roll film. I tried to make it like an album so that you can go and see it over and over again and get something out of it every time you see it. So in that case it doesn't have three major characters and a drama and a shooting at the end or anything like that. It's a different kind of—it's a different kinda thing.

Reed: Mmm.

Young: I can't talk about it too much, because it speaks for itself. It's just a vibe.

Reed: Do you like television for you or the group?

Young: Nope.

Reed: No? You don't like it as a medium.

Young: No, every time I see it, it reminds me of *Shindig!* [*the old musical variety show —Ed.*] or something.

Reed: Gives you that inconsequential feel—

Young: I think those shows are great; I see people up there gettin' off and having a great time. Maybe someday I'll do that too. But I'd rather make a film and give it to them and let them show the film. I'd rather make an eight-minute short or something and edit it together at home in my studio and do that rather than make a live TV appearance, because I hate to let my music into the hands of people who, of people who just don't understand it. I purposefully have worked with certain people through my time as a recording artist that have, in my opinion, made my sound better, and that's what I'm basing my whole trip on and everything is the sounds and the words and the melody of my music. And I just can't put it on TV with a couple of other cats who've never done it before and send it out through a four-inch speaker, even though it may be reaching millions of people and everything, eating TV dinners watching it. I really don't know. . . . I don't think I need that. I don't think it's for me. I feel the same way about those huge concerts and everything. I did it, and it was great for my head to know that I could do that. I guess that's, to be quite honest, it was a good ego fulfillment for me to do that tour. But, even as much as I tried every night to get everybody in those barns off, I couldn't. I couldn't because I couldn't even see them, man, and I knew they couldn't see me. I had to cut off all of the subtleties of my music and just project it out to eighteen thousand people. I was having a hard time doing it a lot of the time because it, my music is basically subtle, and that's why I've gone back to just playing clubs like The Roxy . . . and The Corral in Topanga, and other clubs. We've gotten a thing together now, we've got arrangements with certain clubs in the country, that if I give them a day's notice, they'll drop their acts that they have and I'll just fly in and play for two or three days. Now we got that set up in three or four or five different clubs around the country, which I won't—

Reed: Right.

Young: But when it happens, it'll happen. That way I can play those places, people can see me, we can have a great time. It goes down so fast. There's no scene, nobody's worried, and it gets me off, it makes me feel like I'm still a musician and not in a circus. I mean, I think some other groups, like Led Zeppelin and Elton John and people like that can do it, because Elton's out there with his glasses and—his huge glasses—and that whole trip, and I think that's outta sight, but that's not me. And I think those other big groups, like the Allman Brothers and everything, they put forth that hard sound, man, and they're great, the Allmans and Led Zeppelin and those groups. They're great for those big events, but you take a guy like me and put me in those circumstances; it's just not right, I just don't belong there. I tried to do it. I know I'm not right for that, and it's just a different thing.

Reed: Yeah. When you were recording *4 Way Street* and you did it at three different locations, I think—they took the tapes were from three different locations: here in L.A., I think Chicago, I think New York—I think David Crosby remarked to me, David said one time, he said, "The fabulous Forum is a great indoor blimp." And that was, that really says it. You really cannot communicate when the people are up there in the rafters near where the lights are.

Young: Yeah, unless you're playing the kinda music where you don't have to listen to the words and you just listen to the feeling—and I think that's a valid thing, too. That's like getting together for a war dance or something, and whatever it is, it's a very primitive thing. It's a very primitive thing; it's bunch of people with a bunch of things that make real loud sounds and another bunch of people that are just shaking and boogying to those loud sounds and having a great time getting drunk and taking reds and downers and ODing in the audience. I mean, let's, let's, I mean, I've been to those places. I know there's an ambulance behind the stage and those wheelchairs just fly back and forth all night, man. That's what's really happening. That's where it's really at, man. To me, I went around and looked, and it blew my mind to see that that's where those things were at, and now I know that I have to play smaller, smaller halls just in order to give the people a fair chance to see the real person that they came to see, even if as many of them don't get to do it.

Reed: Earlier on you said, something about, that people will buy what they want to buy, they'll find the music they want, is actually what you said.

Young: Uh-huh.

Reed: And so, it was in reference to the void, about America, et cetera, et cetera—but in line with that, there's Graham, let's get back to him for the moment, who put together, or at least booked/helped book that big, big thing at Watkin's Glen recently in which three hundred thousand or four hundred thousand folks turned out for what the establishment commentators would like to say it as a second Woodstock or a son of Woodstock or daughter of Woodstock [*Reed is referring to the 1973 Summer Jam at Watkins Glen. —Ed.*].

Young: Yeah.

Reed: And three hundred thousand folk for *one day*. It was amazing, or four hundred thousand, whatever that figure was an astronomical—

Unidentified: Six.

Young: Six hundred thousand.

Reed: Six hundred thousand? See, I was being conservative. And that's astronomical, and there's the Allman Brothers, and there's—

Young: The Band.

Reed: The Band. And the Grateful Dead.

Young: The Dead, yeah. That's great that the Dead have made it to that place. I think that's fantastic.

Reed: I think so, too. And they now've got their own label.

Young: They truly deserve it. Now, I've never seen a harder working unit of people than those people. They really worked hard for a long time, when it looked like they weren't going to be—

Reed: Accepted.

Young: Really successful. They kept on at it, and they just concentrated on the quality of their sound and their vibe, and it's come across, I think. I'm really happy to see them where they are now.

Reed: Since they're—we talked about America, OK—the Poco. Poco is spinoff of the Springfield. Burritos were a spinoff of what?

Young: Byrds, I guess.

Reed: Byrds, yeah. What about spinoff groups? You created a style with your group, the Springfield, and David Crosby created a style. No one has ever done a spinoff on the Hollies, however, that's a different riff entirely. But . . . [does] that kind of sound still hold forth, I mean, that great harmony? I mean, you guys harmonize so well, but that great harmony of the—is that disappearing off the scene? The [Flying] Burrito Brothers, of course, have split up. Poco I don't think is any longer, 'cause Jim Messina split away to go to Loggins and Messina.

Young: Mm-hmm.

Reed: Do you like Loggins and Messina?

Young: I never have heard—I wouldn't recognize them if I heard them, I have to be honest with you. I have never heard them, I don't think, on record. I don't follow very closely. I've been making this movie and everything, and I haven't really had a chance to hear them.

Reed: Um, OK, you've answered a lot of questions in the same way. . . . I wanna ask you if—

Young: Should just run through 'em again, man, I'll probably give you a totally different answer.

[*Laughter.*]

Reed: I don't doubt it.

Young: Stay tuned.

Reed: Could you discuss Manassas as a band, Stephen's group?

Young: I don't really know them well enough to discuss them, I—

Reed: You had certain guys work with you on when the four of you were together.

Young: Just Dallas [Taylor].

Reed: Dallas, right.

Young: Yup.

Reed: But you haven't heard them, huh?

Young: And Fuzzy [*referring to bassist Calvin "Fuzzy" Samuels —Ed.*].

Reed: And Fuzzy, right.

Young: That's right. I've never heard them live—no, I did. I heard them live at the Berklee Community Theater, and I was mostly watching Stephen. Just 'cause I didn't—I was listening to him playing the guitar.

Reed: There was talk at that time—of, of the time when you fellas split away, when you went solo, and David and Graham teamed up, and Stephen formed Manassas—that there was inner turmoil or inner tension within the group, because Stephen wanted to take the group in *that* direction, whereas you had your individual ideas about being intimate, as you just expressed.

Young: Mm-hmm.

Reed: And Graham and David like to harmonize a lot against each other.

Young: You mean this last time we got together?

Reed: No, just before this last time you got together. In other words, when Stephen formed Manassas, that's the—

Young: Oh, yeah, right. Well, I think we all just did our own trips for a while there, and we still are, we're still totally different directions. . . . I don't know. Manassas, I think, is a good band for Stephen, inasmuch as Crazy Horse was a good band for me.

Reed: Good. Do you feel that interviews such as this one—I know how grateful I am that we're able to get together because everybody in the media's been after you, particularly the printed media, and you never have given interviews. I think you even turned down a *Time* magazine article, if I'm not mistaken. Is that correct?

Young: Yeah, we turned down a couple of those, but only because I can't, I just can't relate to what happens when you say something and then you read it and it isn't what you said. And the less you say, the more people take stock in what you do say, so, if it gets misinterpreted, it's a pretty important thing. I care what people think about what I think, if they're interested. It makes a difference to me and lately I'm just starting to get loose enough where I don't care that much, where I feel that if I just go and talk and just have faith that it'll get cut together or something in a way so that it represents what I was saying. I figure in a situation like this with somebody like you, who I know very well, enough to communicate with, and have known you for a number of years and have gone through some changes with you that, that, you know me. But just a regular cat, it's very hard to, it's very hard to get into it, because I don't know where they're coming from, and I don't know if they are interested in really reproducing where I'm coming from or whether they just want to get an interview with me or something to make them important at their paper or even if they give a damn what I say or whether than make it up themselves. I mean, I've seen that happen so many times that I . . . you know.

Reed: Do you feel that's—

Young: It doesn't matter. It just doesn't matter anymore anyway. It used to matter to me, but I don't care now. Whatever happens.

Reed: OK, then you're able to—this is probably my last one or two questions, maybe more, but this is it: are you really able to lead a private life, now that you're internationally known? I mean, can you, when you go up to the ranch in Northern California, able to really shut it out?

Young: I don't try to shut it out anymore. I've given up trying to shut it out. I got a ranch with locked gates and everything and that shuts out a number of people who come down. But that doesn't happen anymore so much, because that whole thing, it seems to be ending, where people would relate to your songs and come down and say, "Man, I know you've been singing to me for four years, and here I am, and I'm here, and I got my sleeping bag, and I'd like to stay on your ranch."

Reed: Hmm.

Young: And people came down, a lot of people like that. And I can understand it. Some of them were, some of them were just plain crazy and other ones were honestly trying to make a communicating point with me. And were hip to the fact that I am, that they were invading my privacy, and didn't want to put it on me for too long. All different kinds of people would come down like that to my place, but now, I'm not so much into it. I've been in L.A., as a matter of fact, for the last month, recording and messing around, and I got a studio in the woods. But I'm not there, I'm here, because I want to be with people. I want to see what people, what's happening, and I want to be able to reflect off what's happening, 'cause I see that that as my—that *has been* my—place, where I reflect what I see. And other people feel that they maybe reflect the same way as I do off what they see and they identify with the recording, or whatever. But I know that my mind has changed now from wanting to be secluded and wanting to be alone and everything; I've—I feel more *outward* now than I did before. I feel much happier. There's something, something much freer about me now than there was before. I don't really know, maybe it's my old lady and everything. Having a kid.

Reed: Having a kid.

Young: Settling down a little bit. It's good for me.

Reed: All right.

Young: *Oh yeah*, real good.

[*Laughter.*]

Reed: Do you have any paper to write? I have, I just wanted—do you have any favorite cities? You mentioned a while back you liked being able to fly into a place at the last moment. Any particular one you like to fly into? To work at?

Young: Uh, there's a couple of 'em, you know: Denver; Washington, DC; San Francisco; and . . . there's a few. There's a couple that've got the right kind of places to play in . . .

Reed: And you like them as cities generally?

Young: . . . that are cities that are interesting to be in. I love to go to Washington. I really get charged up when I go there. Walk up and down that green grass thing in front of the Capitol.

Reed: The [National] Mall.

Young: And that whole thing where everything's all lined up and everything. That's a pretty far out place. Just to go around there and stand around the statues.

Reed: Do you like—

Young: It's kind of weird. It's actually *very* weird, if you get really high and go and walk around there.

[*Laughter.*]

Reed: That's too good. Do you like performing as much as you like recording? Or is it equal? Or one—

Young: It's all the same to me now. I record while I perform all the time. I record live; everything I do, I record, because I feel that that's how I'm gonna get it. Because the people I'm singing for . . . I mean, I've totally given up the principal of overdubbing and everything. Since—

Reed: Did you remix and remaster your first album, do you remember that?

Young: Yeah, oh yeah.

Reed: You didn't like the way they had cross channels or something.

Young: They did the compatible stereo on my first album and blew it, man. You couldn't hear the vocal. I went crazy with those idiots. The guy who did that doesn't work at Warner Brothers anymore. [*Laughter in the room; Young chuckles.*] Those fools! My first record, they put it through this thing, man, and the vocal disappeared, man. . . .

Reed: Neil . . .

Young: What time do you got?

Reed: That's why I'm looking at it. Any final words before we split?

Young: I'd just like to say that it's, uh . . . it's been real average.

[*Laughter.*]

Reed: Has it really been? I love it. I told you it was gonna be bland. All right. Thank you.

Young: Thanks, Mitch. Outta sight, man. I think that'll be real good.

Reed: Thank you, baby.

10 DAYS WITH THE LONER

Constant Meijers | October 9, 1974 | *Muziekkrant OOR*

Young released *On the Beach* on July 19, 1974. The LP never received a proper live airing, but songs featured on the 1974 CSNY summer tour. The CSNY tour began in Seattle on July 9, with an epic forty-one-song set, and ended with a September 14 date at London's Wembley Stadium, after which this story soon takes place. The London gig was the group's last tour show until 2000.

Often more a stalled travelogue than an interview, Constant Meijers's piece offers an up-close look at Young's personal life and creative process and how the two mingled at this time.

Young's two-year marriage to Susan Acevedo ended in 1970. Around this time he began seeing actress Carrie Snodgress, best known for 1970's *Diary of a Mad Housewife*. This article finds Young trying to manage a long-distance dispute with Snodgress, in part by planning a car trip from Amsterdam to Japan in a newly purchased used Rolls Royce.

Young also coped through songwriting, as he documented the disintegration of the relationship with Snodgress, which would end in 1975. Some of the thirty-seven new songs mentioned here were scattered over various late-1970s LPs, but Young found many too personal to release. For example, "Vacancy" and "Frozen Man," both recorded months after this interview, were not released until 2020.

Meijers reviewed Young and the Santa Monica Flyers' November 5, 1973, *Tonight's the Night* show at London's Rainbow Theatre for the Dutch publication *Muziekkrant OOR*. The story of a tequila delivery that ends up as a concert review, this "new journalism" review was included, in Dutch, as part of the *Tonight's the Night* LP package. –Ed.

Monday, September 23, 1974

It's four o'clock in the afternoon and already dusk when the telephone rings: "Hello, Lesley here, we're at the Pulitzer Hotel, it's booked up, and we don't know where to go. Do you know of another good hotel in Amsterdam?" I replied, "The Memphis Hotel seems suitable to me, but it's difficult to explain on the phone how to get there. Give me a minute to meet you, and I'll take you there."

Twenty minutes later I find a whole party, divided between two cars, waiting in front of Hotel Pulitzer. Neil Young, Ranger David [*Cline—bus driver and assistant —Ed.*], Sandy Mazzeo [*friend and artist, who would go on to draw the cover of Young's seventh album,* Zuma *—Ed.*], and Joel Bernstein [*photographer and Neil Young archivist —Ed.*] are in the antique Rolls-Royce, parked on the pavement. In the Mercedes, parked behind the Rolls, are Graham Nash, his girlfriend Cally, and his secretary Lesley. The Memphis Hotel has ample vacancies to meet the requirements of the party. While Ranger David and Sandy Mazzeo unload the Rolls and take the luggage up to the various rooms, Neil tells me about his antique car, a new purchase, brought for Hfl 35,000 [*roughly $67,000 in 2020 —Ed.]* at Antique Worlds, Fulham, London. "It's a Rolls-Royce Wembley, a so-called shooting brake, built in 1934. We drove all the way from London without any serious problems."

On his way up to his room, Neil asks whether a houseboat has been found yet. "After this exhausting tour with CSNY I need a couple of weeks rest. How's the weather over here? Sunny?" "Off and on, September in Holland means the beginning of autumn, wind and rain, temperatures dropping, though sometimes the summer lasts through until the end of September."

Once in his room, Neil takes the guitars out of their cases, puts a saxophone in the corner, and puts a rubber mask over his bed, next to a drawing. A typewriter and an unbound "book" appear. It covers the adventures of the latest CSNY tour. Everybody contributed in writings and drawings. The book is called *Forward,* and like everything else that has to do with the group, it's owned by Neil.

Tuesday, September 24, 1974

It's cloudy outside, with occasional showers. Indoors the atmosphere anticipates the sun. Neil, smelling of Badedas (a brand of soap) and brushing his teeth, says he's full of new ideas and that he's looking for a studio to put them on tape. For starters, we're going for a ride. The battery of the Wembley needs charging. As we drive along we keep a look out for houseboats. We drive past the Gein and the Amstel, but the rain is restricting our view. Every time someone (Neil, David, Sandy or Joel) spots a houseboat we pull over and climb on board to see how it looks on the inside. At Baambrugge (a village), we briefly inspect the BBC Studios where the Beach Boys recorded *Holland*. Neil thinks the biggest advantage of this studio is the fact that the cows stare one right in the face when looking out of the window.

Back at the hotel, Neil retires to his room to play the guitar. "I want to improve my solo playing. Lately, I've been wanting to play lead guitar again. My voice is getting stronger, I'm able to sing much higher than I used to. The bad thing is I'm developing a cold. I need some sunshine."

During dinner Neil talks to Graham and Cally about what happened during the day. His cold seems to preoccupy him, and that seems to depress him slightly. "*Tonight's the Night* is the only project I never finished." Nash protests; "You're still working on it, man. It's only now that you're ready to finish it." Neil does not appear to be convinced. Later that night, he's cheerful about his latest plans. "I've been working on one song after the other, lately. I've got thirty-seven new songs, and I'd love to play them. Do you think it's possible? Is there a folk club or something where I could play incognito? I'm feeling great lately, thanks to CSNY. Everything went well this time. We're finished now, but I have a feeling that we'll be back together again in eighteen months' time. In the meantime, I want to put a band together to play my new songs. I always want to bring something new, like *Tonight's the Night*. I want to make a fresh start with those thirty-seven songs, like a new artist, with a new repertoire. I want to record here, too. I've sent postcards back to America saying I'll disappear for an unknown period of time."

It does not bother Neil that he's recognized and that people talk to him. As we walk back to the hotel, he even jumps for joy. "Funny I never played here, they even tell me things I've never heard before. I'm flabbergasted. . . . God, I feel so clean; I never felt so clean in my life."

Wednesday, September 25, 1974

The activities today are mostly confined to indoors. Only once do we go out, in order to try once more to find a houseboat. The long ride to the docks, the walk on the pier, and the cold visit to the boat are in vain. This is not what we're looking for, neither for Neil, nor for the owner, who, the moment he saw us, remarked that his boat would not be suitable.

Back at the hotel, Neil is again preoccupied with his cold. He wears his Arsenal football scarf and regularly orders a fresh pot of tea. Wearing white socks and sitting on the bed with his legs folded under him, he plays his latest song "Frozen Man," in which the question "Who will ever know what's inside this frozen man?" is the central theme. The lack of sunshine is now becoming a major problem.

Neil is afraid the Wembley will get too wet and asks David to find a hotel with a garage. All the hotels are booked up. The plan for a trek south is beginning to take shape. Neil suggests that they should find a route that ends in Japan. From Japan, the crossing to California can then be made by boat. Joel will buy maps. In the meantime, Neil plays songs like "Star of Bethlehem," "New Mama," "Deep Forbidden Lake" and even "Heart of Gold." "I stole the idea for 'Heart of Gold' from 'Love Is Blue'." [*Paul Mauriat's 1968 US number-one easy-listening instrumental. —Ed.*] The beautiful "Human Highway" regularly passes in revue. Neil is toying with the idea of releasing an album by that name. A photograph for the cover already exists: a fading country road, with a white line in the middle, ending in a *T* junction. Where to go? Left or right—the old dilemma?

"That my name is on the line, how can people be so unkind, o-o-o-hh . . ."

Thursday, September 26th, 1974

When I mention during breakfast that my girlfriend has run off through pure jealousy, it brings a response from Neil. It turns out that he has a specific reason to prolong his stay in Europe—an argument with Carrie. "It's time Carrie came to me for a change. I'll stay away until that happens. Those girls always get jealous when you're working on something with great intensity. Susan, who was a lot older than me, was very jealous. One morning, I got up early to work on 'Southern Man' in the studio, she threw breakfast against the door. When I opened the door to see what was going on, she threw the coffee at me. Carrie is more in control, but still, a lot of problems have to be overcome. The first few years are always happy, but then the problems come. 'Love/Art Blues' is about this, especially the second line. That's why I want to break away for a while. I'm really having big domestic problems, which until now, have popped up in about twenty songs. Hmmm, women . . . !" After breakfast, Neil wants to start up the Wembley in order to check its battery. The engine won't start, and the ANWB (Dutch motoring club) is called for help, but it's all in vain; they are unable to render assistance.

An appointment for this morning had been made with Klokgieter Repair Shop, somewhere in the Jordaan district of the city. A new spring has to be mounted; pushing seems to be the only solution. When we arrive, seventy-six-year-old Klokgieter, an old hand at fixing cars, immediately crawls under the car. Straightaway he knows what the problem is and boasts of his fifty-one years' experience. He takes out a cigar box and shows various postcards he's received from satisfied customers from all over the world. Full of pride, Klokgieter shows us a 1953 Citroën.

After Neil, Sandy, and David have rubbed the Wembley dry, we drive out to the Waterlooplein. Neil is freezing and wants to go back to the hotel. When we get there, he picks up a guitar and starts playing "Deep Forbidden Lake." Later that same day, the plans for the trek south are being discussed. Joel has put up a world map and a map of Europe and Asia on the wall of Neil's room. Together, a route is planned. Japan turns out be impossible, because of visa problems, and according to Joel, Turkey no longer receives US aid. Neil prefers to drive through Luxembourg, the Swiss Alps, and Italy, to the Mediterranean coast. From there, along the Italian and Spanish coasts, he wants to drive to North Africa. "Do you think Casablanca is a nice city?"

During dinner Neil talks about his recent extraordinary creativity. "I've got too many new songs, thirty-seven, what am I supposed to do with them? Even if I put seven on each side, I've still got twenty-three left." He starts to compile the first side of the album. "'Frozen Man,' 'Baby Mellow My Mind' [*referring to 'Mellow My Mind' —Ed.*], 'Deep Forbidden Lake'—the songs are related through their mutual atmosphere and the images I use. They all have to do with water."

In the evening we go to see *The Exorcist*. Back at the hotel, Neil tells Graham the film flopped badly. "That film reminded me of the medical treatment I had about six years ago. Because of my problems, I had to undergo a range of tests and examinations. After suffering from polio when I was six and having to learn to walk again, I've suffered from dizziness. I've had every test: the two stabs in the jugular arteries, six spinal punctions, two encephalograms, the lot. When that girl in the film had a punction, I knew exactly when she was going to scream. That spoilt the rest of the film for me, which wasn't scary at all from that point on."

After Neil enters Joel's room, where the rest of the party is gathered in expectation, at 2:30 that night, he plays an integral version of "Deep Forbidden Lake." Graham remarks, "This may sound funny, but every song is always a typical Neil Young song." Neil smiles.

Friday, September 27, 1974

Neil enters Sandy's room, Ranger David is there too. "I've had a quiet night, no nightmares. One of the maps came crashing down in the middle of the night. I tried to get it off me, but I didn't know what it was at first. On top of it all, Sam Sleaze (the rubber mask) came down. I was scared stiff! I sat up for half an hour and then went back to sleep. I'm feeling much better today; the cold is almost gone. I think I might trim my sideburns."

During breakfast at the Keyzer's, Neil says he misses Zeke. "Wouldn't it be nice if he and his mother came over?"

After breakfast, we get Neil a black scarf. In a bookshop down the road, he picks up two copies of *Rock Dreams* [*Guy Peellaert and Nik Cohn's 1973 rock 'n' roll history —Ed.*]. After that, we pay Mr. Klokgieter a visit, to see how the Wembley is coming along. Mr. Klokgieter tells us it will be ready by Monday. That's OK by Neil, because that means that the car will be parked in a garage during the weekend and will be kept dry.

Back at the hotel, we discuss whether Ibiza is a suitable winter resort. Neil's brother-in-law owns a big house there and "maybe we can cut some songs there. We could rent a mobile studio and have Elliot Mazer [*producer —Ed.*] flown in, maybe Don and Glenn [*Henley and Frey, respectively, of the Eagles —Ed.*] also, and even Carrie and Zeke. My voice is coming back. I've got the feeling that I've got to do it right now. That I should record everything I've got, and soon." Graham completely agrees; "Sure man, you can't waste it all. The songs are too good to waste. Maybe it won't make any difference to you, but it would be a shame if the people don't get to hear them." "Right," Neil nods, "These songs all have to do with water, so the best thing to do is to cut them near the sea."

Graham Nash and I drive out to the Bijlmermeer district. En route Nash tells me that "Frozen Man" is about Neil's relationship with Carrie; they've broken up. He also tells me that "Only Love Can Break Your Heart" was written for him. "I'd broken up with Joni, and Neil came to me and said he'd written a song for me, because he knew exactly how I felt. Joni is one of those people who can't make a good relationship last. When we were doing all right, she quit."

Back at the hotel, Neil and Joel are playing some Beatles songs, "Rain," "If I Fell," "Norwegian Wood," and "I Need You" are sung beautifully. When Neil picks up another guitar and starts playing some chords, I can tell by the reactions of the others that a new idea is being born. Half an hour later Graham, Cally and I have to leave, to pay Carel and Mathilde Willink a visit [*Amsterdam fashion icon and painter, respectively —Ed.*].

When I get back at De Kring at 2:30 that night I bump into Neil, Sandy, and David, all tipsy and having a great time with Sjef van Oekel and Barend Servet [*Dutch TV personalities —Ed.*]. Van Oekel, in terrible

English, begs Neil to perform on his TV show. Frank de Jonge asks for an autograph [*de Jonge is a cabaret artist —Ed.*].

Saturday, September 28, 1974

As I enter Neil's room late in the afternoon, I notice that *Rock Dreams* is opened at the Hank Williams page. It lies on the window sill. While Neil strums his guitar, the plans for Ibiza are being discussed. Mazer has been called to work out the possibilities for setting up a mobile studio. Neil says, jokingly, that he'll call everybody as soon as he's found a country where the women are different. He agrees when I remark that everything would be the same when we would get there. Neil seems satisfied with the idea for a song he's worked on the previous evening. "This new song is written in a style I haven't used for a while—the attack."

After dinner at De Keyzer's, he does some more work on the song. He uses his mouth harp; it opens new perspectives. For a change of atmosphere, Neil proposes to take a walk. Outside he thinks it's too cold, and he returns to the hotel. Back in his room he takes out the typewriter, and at 8:15 PM, he starts typing. Five minutes later, he picks up a guitar and sings the hastily typed lines. Then he puts down the guitar and types a row of *x*'s. The telephone rings; it's Elliot Roberts. A lawyer will arrive on Monday to discuss some things with Neil. When the word "Monaco" is mentioned on the other side of the line, Neil thinks that's a great idea. "I've got fourteen new songs; they're better than the old ones. I'm really into it; this old typewriter does not let me down. Listen, I've got a plan. I want you to come over, maybe Ibiza is the most suitable place. Once I get there and find a good place, I want the musicians to fly in. Levon [Helm] is all right. I know he's working on his studio right now, but maybe we could do 'Lookout Joe' with him. So if you come over, don't tell anyone where you're going. I don't want too many people around me. You should hear my new songs, man. They're really something else."

8:40 PM. Neil picks up a guitar and sings the lines he has been typing, "Who are you, where are you going to?"

8:50 PM, types, 9:00 PM, thinks and then types some more. He then reads what he has just committed to paper and stamps his foot on the floor. 9:10, he tries to sing the lines. 9:15, stops, "I'm going to use a mouth harp." Sandy: "It sounds OK from the bathroom." 9:25, Neil orders tea, toast, and ham. Two minutes later he looks for the harp. "Aah, got my old funky one." Sandy reads the lyrics: "Are you a friend, are you an enemy." "You going out tonight Neil?" "Yeah."

9:32 PM, the first version, with harp solo. Sandy says, "Call it 'Vendetta.'"

9:37 PM, Neil says it's called "Vacancy." Sandy says, "That's the same thing as 'Vendetta.'" Everybody laughs. Neil then sings "Vacancy," while Joel tries back-up vocals. Neil smiles; "Nice, good rhythm. When the whole band gets together there's a lot of mayhem. I'm really into this stuff tonight. I could play a solo at the end—we could play it with the Who!"

When Neil and Joel try to work out an arrangement, Joel asks "Are you angry with someone Neil?" "Oh, I've got my frustrations, but up until now I've been able to let them out through my music."

Sunday, September 29, 1974

Neil enters Graham's room and says he's spent an hour talking to Carrie on the phone. "How was she?" "Fine, yes she's fine. She's with friends in Santa Barbara. She was thinking about returning to the ranch. Straighten things out." "Do you think she'll be coming over?" "Maybe, at first she'll think 'going to a different place again?' but when she thinks about the Mediterranean Sea and what goes on down there, she might come to like the idea."

Lesley's gotten hold of Mazer and found out that after November 1, it rains on Ibiza; besides that, there's no electricity. So Ibiza is out. With Graham and Cally, I visit the Vinkenoogs' [*referring to the house of poet Simon Vinkenoog —Ed.*]. Karel Appel [*painter, sculptor, and poet —Ed.*] is there too. After his visit to Willink, Nash is not at all impressed.

Monday, September 30, 1974

When I arrive, late in the afternoon, I hear that Neil and Sandy have bought up half of the antique shops in the Runstraat. Neil especially likes crystal and kerosene lamps, but he is more than pleased with an old Belgian stove. "Usually I don't like shopping, but this time it was fun. Maybe I'll do some more shopping in Barcelona, and maybe I'll lay my hands on an old Bechstein [piano]."

In the evening Neil went out, he went to the cinema to see *Thunderball*; he also went to the Melkweg, but a girl recognized him there and started to make trouble, so he had to leave.

Tuesday, October 1, 1974

The Wembley is ready and we can take it with us after paying Hfl 500. Although the battery is charged, the car won't start. Neil thinks the starting motor has broken down. We start pushing the car, and on the Rozengracht it finally starts up!

Back at the hotel, we call the Rolls-Royce [Owners'] Club and order a new starting motor. That afternoon the carbon brushes need replacing. The man from the RR Club replaces them in the pouring rain. All the obstacles for a journey to the sunny south have now been removed.

Lee, the lawyer, informs Neil that he's lost about $90,000, but it doesn't seem to bother him; "The Rolls back in working order is of more importance!"

That night we go out to see the Pointer Sisters in concert. Neil likes the Sisters but he doesn't like the backing band. "The pianist played very sloppily. They'd better find some Harlem musicians, people who show their teeth and not a bored face when they look up. Thelonious Monk on piano, Roland Kirk on wind instruments, Jimmy Garrison on bass, but, well, that's not very realistic."

Afterwards, back in the bar of the hotel, Neil tells me how he likes to rip-off Stephen's riffs. "I take out one note, which he expects. 'Vacancy' is the riff I played on 'Black Queen,' which Stephen himself taught me." Everybody wants a snack, but the waiter informs us that the kitchen is closed. Ranger David, a candle in his hand, inspects the shutter, and finds out it can be opened from the kitchen side, and suggests somebody should crawl through it. The waiter doesn't mind, as long as there's no cooking or frying. He thinks ingredients for the sandwiches shouldn't be too difficult to find. Neil gets up, and with loud encouragement, climbs through the shutter; Lesley follows him. Fifteen minutes later the sandwiches arrive. The music too, is appropriate; a tape Neil made of Roland Kirk in London, followed by one Nash made of Terry Reid, whom he's producing. Suddenly Neil enters the bar through the door. The waiter has found the key to the kitchen in the manager's desk.

Wednesday, October 2, 1974

In the car, on the way to the antique shops to arrange the shipping, Neil talks about his domestic problems. "I'll go back as soon as she wants to see me. Until that happens I'll stay here. We haven't been seeing each other for a long time now. For months we've been having rows and arguments, and this time I'm not giving in. I'm not returning to the ranch unless she comes with me and dumps her shallow friends. All those girls, trying to be just like her, copying her . . ."

"Are you still planning on recording in the south of Europe?" "I don't think so. I think I'll just relax and record at home. I have a better control over the musicians I want to use, and I can always change my mind. This power struggle to get as much attention as possible—they expect you to give all your attention to them. This power struggle is terrible."

At three o'clock that afternoon, the party—not including Graham and Cally, who are flying home—leaves for the sun in the south. Honking its claxon, the Wembley disappears around the corner. The autumn sun breaks through the clouds.

Neil never got past Brussels. From there he flew back to America.

TONIGHT'S THE NIGHT: PLAY IT LOUD AND STAY IN THE OTHER ROOM!

Bud Scoppa | June 28, 1975 | *New Musical Express*

Though *Homegrown* had been recorded in the second half of 1974 and slated for release in '75, it was ultimately deemed too personal and was replaced by landmark album *Tonight's the Night*. (Though *Homegrown* would eventually surface some forty-five years later with an official release in summer 2020).

This interview took place in early June, just prior to the recording of the Crazy Horse-accompanied *Zuma*, released in November 1975. It is part of Young's reluctant, strategic, and intermittent reentry into the mediascape, at least for the next decade, at which point he becomes somewhat ubiquitous. Ostensibly intended to promote *Tonight's the Night*—and the bulk of the interview does artfully detail the creation of and his coming to terms with the LP—the interview at once shows Young's pride in the album and his desire to close a dark chapter in his life (and move on to *Zuma*). Tellingly, he frames this period as one in which he realized he could perform or act his songs, a concept that would increasingly become part of his stagecraft. –Ed.

NEIL YOUNG isn't out to win any popularity contest. Just as he reached the top of the heap three years ago with the huge-selling *Harvest*, Young divested himself of the look and the sound of superstardom and began to rework his music and image from scratch.

It wasn't out of fear that he turned away from the crowd and its expectations. Young's projects since *Harvest*—a film, three albums and several concert tours—have (whatever their aesthetic worth) been intensely, uncompromisingly personal. He hasn't stopped putting himself on the line, on the contrary, his post-*Harvest* work seems to be part of a continuing quest for some difficult truths.

Now Young has an album he cares so much about that he's willing to return, at least temporarily, to the world of media conventions to get the word out about it. Face set with the look of determined congeniality, glass of orange juice in hand, Young (who generally cares so little about "promotion" that he didn't bother to include any songs from the-then new *On the Beach* in CSNY's 74 tour repertoire) braced himself to face the press, a few at a time in manager Elliot Roberts' Sunset Strip office a fortnight before the release of *Tonight's The Night*.

His hair grown long and ratty since his CSNY appearances, still wearing the two-toned gangster style shoes that made a match with the dark secondhand suite he'd worn to the previous night's album preview party. Young didn't so much look consciously anti-style as vacantly non-style. But he was game about this pop music business nevertheless. During his single day of interviews, he'd seen not only *Rolling Stone*'s Cameron Crowe, but also radio questioners who'd come in from places like Seattle and Albuquerque for the occasion. Having, just the day before, completed a critique of *Tonight's The Night* (an album I'd found so harrowingly personal that it had kept me awake on the nights I had worked on the piece), I was eager to find out whether Young had been as unsettled during the making of it as I had been by listening to it.

In the room with me were Young, Elliot Roberts, the guy from Seattle (later replaced by the guy from Albuquerque, Crowe and Art, Young's proletarian dog). "The record business," Young sighed, in response to the invisible forces that caused him to be sitting in this smoky room on a perfectly nice day. "I don't even think I'm in it any more, I really don't. I've never done anything like this before—interviews and the party and everything. But I never had a record you could party to and interview to before."

"You feel particularly good about this record?" I asked. When he affirmed that he did, I said that *Tonight's The Night* seemed like the inevitable culmination of the path Young blazed with *Time Fades Away*, his jumpy, nearly-out-of-control live album, and the intensely introspective *On the Beach*. But why begin making these raw, personal albums just at the moment of peak popularity, in effect resisting superstardom?

"It's odd." He seems genuinely perplexed for the moment. "I don't know why, it was a subconscious move, I think *Tonight's The Night* is the most grand example of that resistance. It was actually recorded in August of '73 at S.I.R. (L.A.'s Studio Instrument Rentals), where we had the party last night. Everything on *Tonight's The Night* was recorded and mixed before *On the Beach* was started, but it was never finished or put into its complete order till later. Everybody said that *Harvest* was a trip. To me I'd happened to be in the right place at the right time to do a really mellow record that was really open, 'cause that's where my life was at the time. But that was only for a couple of months. If I'd stayed there, I don't know where I'd be right now, if I'd just stayed real mellow. I'm just not that way anymore. I think *Harvest* was probably the finest record that I've made, but that's really a restricting adjective for me. It's really fine, but that's it."

What about his live performances? "In concert, what I play all depends on what I feel. I can't do songs like 'Southern Man'. I'd rather play the Lynyrd Skynyrd song that answered it. That'd be great. The thing is I go on a different trip and I get different band together, or I group with some old friends, then they don't know how to play the stuff I did with some other group and I have to show them. That takes a lot of time and I'd rather be working on new stuff.

"So a lot of it is just laziness. I don't even know some of the old songs with the bands, you know? I'm not going to even try to do *Tonight's The Night*. If I go out this fall I probably will take this band I'm working with now. We could get into doing these songs any time, but I'd have something new in my head by then that I would be even more into. We'll do some of them. I'm working right now on recording, that's what I'm mainly interested in, because I have a lot of new songs that I haven't finished recording."

The conversation swung back to the new album. "*Tonight's The Night* didn't come out right after it was recorded because it wasn't finished. It just wasn't in the right space, it wasn't in the right order, the concept wasn't right. I had to get the color right, so it was not so down that it would make people restless. I had to keep jolting every once in a while to get people to wake up so they could be lulled again. It's a very fluid album. The higher you are, the better it is. And it really lives up to that, a lot of records don't . . . you should listen to it late at night."

"I tried that," I ventured, "and I couldn't go to sleep afterwards. It scared the hell out of me." Young was—yes—pleased. "That's great. That's the best thing you could tell me."

The title song, one of the album's most jagged and discomforting, tells the story of Bruce Berry, a friend of Young's who, the lyrics state, "died out on the mainline." Who was he, we wondered in unison.

"Bruce Berry was a roadie, he used to take care of Steve's and my guitars and amps."

"That line about his dying comes out and hits you," someone noted.

"Yeah . . . those mixes were a little unorthodox. Like it's real music. Sometimes I'd be on mike and sometimes I'd be two feet off it. Sometimes I'd be lookin' around the room and singin' back off mike . . . we'd have to bring it way back up in the mix to get it. And you can hear the echo in the room. We were all on stage at S.I.R. just playing, with the P.A. system and everything, just like a live thing. And all the background vocals are live, and the whole thing is, ah . . .

"I got tired of . . . I think what was in my mind when I made that record was I just didn't feel like a lonely figure with a guitar or whatever it is that people see me as sometimes. I didn't feel that laid back—I just didn't feel that way. So I thought I'd just forget about all that . . . wipe it out. Be as aggressive and as abrasive as I could to leave an effect, a long-term effect, that things change radically sometimes, it's good to point that out."

Roberts points out that a number of the songs on Young's recent albums have come directly from actual experience. "They're threads of life. Although Neil's portraying a character the character he's portraying saw all these things go down."

What about the chilling "Tired Eyes," with its straightforward description of a dope-dealing vendetta that ends in bloodshed? Has he seen that sort of thing?

"Yeah . . . puts the vibe right there . . . that's what I was saying, at S.I.R. when we were playing, and these two cats (Berry and Danny Whitten, the leader of Crazy Horse, who'd worked very closely with Young) who had been a close part of our unit, our force, our energy, were both gone to junk, both of them OD'd.

"And now we're playing in a place where we're getting together to make up for what is gone and try to make ourselves stronger and continue. Because we thought we had it with Danny Whitten . . . . At least I did. I thought that a combination of people that could be as effective as groups like the Rolling Stones had been . . . just for rhythm, which I'm really into. I haven't had that rhythm for a while and that's why I haven't been playing my guitar: because without that behind me I won't play. I mean, you can't get free enough. So I've had to play the rhythm myself ever since Danny died. Now I have someone who can play rhythm guitar, a good friend of mine."

Who's that, Nils Lofgren?

"No, Nils is a lead player, basically. And when I use Nils . . . like on *Tonight's The Night* I used him for piano, and I played piano on a couple of songs and he played guitar. In the songs where he plays guitar he's actually playing the way Bruce Berry played guitar. The thing is I'm talking about him and you can hear him. So Nils just fits in—he plays that hot rock and roll style guitar.

"It's just that there was a lot of spirit flyin' around when we were doin' it. It was like a tribute to those people, you know? Only the ones we chose no one had really heard of that much, but they meant a lot to us. That's why it gets spooky. 'Cause we were spooked. If you felt that I'm glad because it was there."

Young leans back on the sofa he's sitting on and laughs softly. "The first horror record, a horror record."

Young's continuing mastery of melody and texture serves his story well, although not at all in an obvious way. His musical strengths, even presented as rough sketches, provide one reason for hanging on through this grim tale in the first place. As grisly as "Tired Eyes" seems, as abrasively as it's sung, the melody is there. Done with refinement, this would be a pretty song. Young must go to extremes to keep from making pretty music.

"There's always a chance that nobody will dig it because it's too abrasive. But it's a very happy record if you're loose; if you're not loose, it's not happy 'cause you realize how tight you are when you listen to it. You really feel how different you are from being loose. It makes you feel something, it draws a line somewhere. I've seen it draw a line everywhere I've played it. Some people fall on one side, others fall to the other side. It's a surprise. People who thought that they'd never dislike anything I ever did, fall on the new side of the line. Other people who couldn't hear me, who said 'that cat is too sad . . . he sings funny,' those people listen another way now. It blew my mind when I saw what was happening. We knew it was different when we were doing it, everything live everybody playing and singing at the same time. There was no overdubbing on those nine songs that were done at S.I.R.. That's the way the old blues people used to do it. It was really real. And we did the mixes right away.

"I can remember the first time I heard it I said that's the most out-of-tune thing I've ever heard. We're going to have to cancel all four of those songs. Then the same night, after we were relaxed and mellow, and we put it on, some other people in the room started going nuts, saying that this was it, why hadn't I released it, and that I would have to worry about what to put out after this. So it's fascinating to me. It was all just an experiment. What we were doing was playing those guys on their way. We all got that high, not that high but we got as close as we could. I mean, I'm not a junkie and I won't even try it out to check out what it's like. But we'd get really high . . . drink a lot of tequila, get right out on the edge, where we were so screwed up that we could easily just fall on our faces, and not be able to handle it as musicians. But we were wide open also at that time, just wide open. So we'd just wait until the middle of the night, until the vibe hit us and just do it.

"We did four or five songs on the first side all in a row one night without any break. We did 'Tonight's The Night,' 'World on a String,' 'Mellow my Mind,' 'Speakin' Out,' and 'Tired Eyes' without any break between 'em. Then Elliot put it in a different sequence. Because he was doing this *Tonight's The Night* Broadway show . . . there was a script written and everything. We'd listen to the record of these songs, and that's how we got it finished. He picked out the other songs, 'Lookout

Joe,' 'Come on Baby, Let's go Downtown,' and 'Borrowed Tune' and we put them in with the original nine songs."

The version of "Downtown" on Young's new record (a studio version is on *Crazy Horse*, a fine record that showcases Whitten's music) was recorded at a 1970 Young and Crazy Horse concert at the Fillmore East. The night of the recording, the band, Young, Whitten, bass player Billy Talbot, drummer Ralph Molina, and Jack Nitzsche on electric piano played altogether brilliant, crashing rock and roll; for my money, the concert presented Young at his absolute peak of his powers, exerting a dynamism that his records approach only in their most inspired passages. An entire album-full of tracks from those concerts, if they approach "Downtown" in sound quality, would be an automatic classic. Young loves the sound of the track, especially in the context of the album. "It's so high and so fast," he says.

Tonight's The Night contains all the dark, tense, melancholy we've come to expect from Young's music but there's one important difference: Whereas most of his serious songs have evoked their shadowy moods through indirection, recurring metaphors of flying and dancing, for example and the mysterious Indian of "Broken Arrow," these songs work through explicit narrative details. Young has become a storyteller, an actor.

"I was able to step outside myself to do this record, to become a performer of the songs rather than the writer. That's the main difference, every song was performed. I wrote the songs describing the situations and then I became an extension of those situations and I performed them. It's like being an actor and writing the script for myself as opposed to a personal expression. There's obviously a lot of personal expression in there, but it comes in a different form, which makes it seem much more explicit and much more direct. All these people there all in there. That's why there's so much talking on the record. It's all the things I hear people saying.

"I've been listening to this album for about two years and I'm not tired of it, it's a good friend of mine. In some respects I feel like it has more life than anything I've ever done. It's not the kind of life that jumps up and down and makes everybody smile. It's another kind of life, there's a feeling in it that's really strong". "I don't think *Tonight's The Night* is a friendly album. It's real, that's all. Either you'll want to hear or you won't. A lot of records don't even make you think that much. Then after that it will take you somewhere if you want to listen to it. I'm really proud of it. It's there for me. You've got to listen to it at night, when it was done. Put on the Doobie Brothers in the morning. They can handle it at 11am. But not this album. It's custom made for night time. 'Lookout Joe' and 'Borrowed Tune' were written during my *Time Fades Away* tour.

"I never hit 'Lookout Joe' the way I wanted to. It was recorded at my ranch during rehearsals for the *Time Fades Away* tour just after Danny Whitten OD'd. He'd been working on the song with us and after he died we stopped for a while. When we started playing again, that was the first thing we cut and I wrote 'Don't be Denied' that day. So 'Lookout Joe' is one of the oldest songs on the album. If you take out 'Lookout Joe,' 'Downtown,' and 'Borrowed Tune,' all the others left just build in intensity so much that you can't take them all. Each one I liked so much I wanted them all on there. I made all kinds of lists to get them in the right order so that all the songs would set the other ones up mentally, for people.

"You mean, you see 'Lookout Joe' as a relief from intensity?" I asked. "I find it one of the most intense songs on the album. It is easier to listen to than 'Mellow my Mind,' though". Young nodded "If you get a hundred yards away from 'Mellow my Mind,'" he said in seeming seriousness, "it sounds incredible, better than anything sounds at a hundred yards. It's supposed to be part of the environment. Play it loud," he quipped. "but stay in the other room." "I wanted to get the album so it could be played while people were . . . see, it's not to sit and listen to every song, eventually, people are gonna do that and that'll be cool.

"But the thing the album is made for is to be able to put it on once you know the songs, or even if you don't know the songs and have the moods of it, that it takes you through subliminally, enable you to stop talking with your friends for a few minutes, start talking again and not feel uptight, enable you to flow. So that as it plays over and over it constantly changes and you don't get uptight, you know? I mean a lot of the sequencing was made for that reason, as well as trying to get it so that if you sit there and scrutinize it, it tells a story that really makes sense."

By this time, Young was thoroughly caught up in what he was talking about. His shyness was gone, and the dark reticence I'd heard so much about was nowhere to be found, except for a defensive sounding answer to a question about why he'd stormed off stage in the middle of a Carnegie Hall solo concert. "It was intermission," he'd said brusquely. "I just took it a little early." Otherwise he was congenial enough to answer even the most stock questions with a concern that approached expansiveness. Wondering about his seeming ability to resist getting caught up in his own heroic legend. I commented "It seems as if you've gone against your superstardom musically. You've done a parallel move during the same period in terms of the way you come off visually and image wise. Where's the teen idol.?" Young laughed. "We gotta tear down all that, it's gone now" he said his voice a sneer. "Now we can do whatever, its open again, there's no illusions that someone can say what I'm going to do before I get there. That's how I've got to feel. Whether it's true or not, I don't want to feel like people expect me to be a certain way. If that's the way it is, then I quit. I can't do it. I have to be able to feel like I can do whatever I want and it's not going to disappoint me to do it."

Was that the problem with CSNY?

"I thought there wasn't any problem at all. Last time we went out, and every time we've gone out, it's been great." "But haven't you had problems putting an album together?" "We just didn't make an album. And it's not even that it didn't happen, we just didn't do it. If we don't do something people put together all these trips about, you know. Stills and Young are fighting so they can't do this. That's all a bunch of bullshit. The only people who could put it together is the four of us, and were all in great shape. Were just not doing it right now."

"But everybody's expecting it," it was pointed out "and if it doesn't happen, then they all figure there must be some problem." "That's because they can't possibly envision why four guys would not do it and not make all that bread."

You mean you don't want to be a supergroup? "We already are a supergroup, so whether we want to be one or not, it's all after the fact. In the end, it's just another name, you know, in a list. And that's cool . . ." A minute later his feathers unruffled. Young commented on the swollen shape of big money rock 'n' roll: "The ticket prices are big and the whole thing is big. I mean, it's bigger than a football game now, it's all different. I started playing for 25 people at a time and I was getting off. Now it's just so mammoth that you've gotta get by that all over again to get off. Money doesn't . . . the biggest thing that effects it is the amount of people. That's where it is, how big the music is. Money's just a side effect of that. It's really different, though, that part of it's really blown my mind. It's such a high to get personal with 60,000 people."

"You might even be willing to do that for nothing." The man from Seattle said. "He just did," Roberts pointed out. "But my next tour," Young continued, "is going to be small halls . . so people can see what it is. And if less of 'em see it, that doesn't make no difference. When we did *Tonight's The Night* in Holland we really scared a lot of people. There was never a chance for the audience to do anything because I never stopped talking. I would play and before they had a chance to applaud, I would become the M.C. I would just talk away to these people, tying songs together with these raps that I would make up as I went along. It was a whole other period. I got to act. I had a part in the show instead of it being me, the pressure was off me a little bit. It didn't look like anything the people had ever seen. We did like a show . . . I wore this sleazy white jacket and big shades and then I'd go back and change into my funky Pendleton jeans and my acoustic guitar.

"I don't know what this new tour will be like, I'll be doing a lot of stuff that I'm recording now. A lot of long instrumental guitar things . . . progresso supremo? It's about the Incas and the Aztecs. It takes on another personality, It's like being in another civilization. It's a lost sort of form, sort of a soul-form that switches from history scene to history scene trying to find itself, man in a maze. I've got it all written and all the songs are learned. Tomorrow we start cutting them. We're ready to go. We're gonna just do it in the morning. Early in the morning when the sun's out. Sunny days . . . just . . . play. It'll probably take about a week or two, then I'll be done with that. But I been practicing for about six weeks. I feel great about it. It's Molina, Talbot and Poncho Sampedro: two guitars, bass and drums. It's fun for me because I'm playing all the guitar, and I haven't played guitar in a long time . . . so I've been practicing, I'm havin' a great time, I can fly all over the place now." Someone asked if Lofgren had inspired Young to "fly all over the place". "Oh yeah, he's great. Oh, Nils is an incredible musician. He's a great color player, he's so sensitive to lyrics." "How come he hasn't caught on commercially?" "He's too good." Young replied with finality. Everyone laughed, but he looked rather pensive suddenly. "I don't know . . . Nils is great . . . he's got a lot of time . . . so does everybody else . . . . His music will be around a long time."

"Does your earlier stuff . . . Since you've changed so much in the last two or three years, seem forced or dishonest to you now?" I asked, barging in. "No, no not at all. The earlier stuff really good to me now. I'm really happy I made these albums. *Time Fades Away* sounds nervous, but even that says where I was at, because it's a direct non-hit, a direct miss. It was like a live album of songs that no-one had ever heard before done in a totally different style from the one that came before it. But it stood for where I was at during that period. I was nervous and not quite at home in those big places."

But Young doesn't seem to be nervous any more. Having exorcised his nightmares with *Tonight's The Night*, he's now ready to go out with his new Crazy Horse and play for the people on a smaller, more intimate scale. And he can make music in the Californian sunshine again. From the sound of a rehearsal cassette I heard a few days after the interview. Young's music has come full circle: the fat sound and loping gait of this new music bears a striking resemblance to the music on the great *Everybody Knows this Is Nowhere.*

Young's first three albums—*Neil Young, Nowhere* and *After the Gold Rush*—have the irresistible power of beauty: his three most recent—*Time, Beach, Tonight* (I'm discounting the shallow and transitional *Harvest*)—have the grating power of deep anxiety. As a body of work, these albums display consistent eloquence, passion and unflinching internal courage. The man takes big chances he risks as much as any artist I can think of. Young's bravery works in support of his vision, fundamentally dark, bitter and troubled but always candidly, remarkably human. To use his own expression, Neil Young is really real.

NEIL YOUNG ON

Tonight's the Night **as a Movie**

"I'm in the music but the music is another person I'm trying to portray, I'm trying to project, an image of what could happen to someone like myself if . . . just depending on how far, which way you tip, you know. The whole thing is about, it's about dope and life and death."

—from an interview with Ben Fong-Torres,
Rolling Stone News Service, 1975

QUELQUE MOTS DE NEIL YOUNG (A FEW WORDS FROM NEIL YOUNG)

Christian Lebrun and Francis Dordor | May 1976 | *Best*

Supporting *Zuma*, Neil Young and Crazy Horse toured Japan and Europe spring 1976. For this article, Young met with interviewers after a March 23 show at the Pavillon de Paris. As often mentioned in reviews of this tour, the sonic difference between Young's opening acoustic set and the Crazy Horse portions was striking, even if the interviewers didn't appreciate the latter set at Paris's new arena.

The interview doesn't delve deeply into one particular topic, but offers Young's reflections on a range of subjects, including the American South and rednecks, the vibe playing live with Dylan, and dreams of joining the Rolling Stones. –Ed.

Holding out his bowl and spoon with childlike reserve, "No, I'll take some more soup, please," Neil Young is surrounded by four journalists (two from *Best*, two from *Rock and Folk*) as if for a domino game whose goal would be to prevent the fifth thief from being forced to pass his turn— This is the resonance of an interview, perfectly unexpected, made after the concert at the Pavilion and whose main motivation was undoubtedly this wonderful audience, one of the most receptive that we have seen in Paris. Talking about a set in a few lines would be profoundly unfair, as much for the indescribable density of the electronic part which culminated indifferently with "Down by the River," "The Losing End," or "Cortez the Killer," as for the veil of intimacy shared with 12,000 people with the acoustic songs, that delicate harmony of receptivity compensating for the aggressive and desperate misery of this rusty and malicious arena. Two hours later, his face suspect, Neil appeared in a luxury box, repairing Giscardian youth [*like 1974–1981 French President Valéry Giscard d'Estaing —Ed.*], with a paranoid shadow in the extension of his heels. He sits in front of a vegetable soup and turns his deep gaze toward us, his eyes like silver nails seem to have been thrown into his head with a hammer blow; small feminine gestures accompany his measured and patient voice . . .

Best: Did you like this first Parisian concert?

Neil Young: Oh, yeah, that was a great time. I think it was a good gig. I think it will be one of the best of this tour. I love the audience. A very sensitive room, sensitive for the acoustic part and physically present for the electric songs. Even the audience dreams of this. A perfect mix between sensitivity and physical appearance.

Best: The Rolling *Zuma* review, what was it?

NY: Uh . . . that was a joke. We played in these clubs. I have a t-shirt from this tour: "Crazy Horse. Neil Young. Northern California. 1976. Bar Tour." They were just free concerts in small venues. There were between fifty and a hundred people.

Best: Was that a mockery of Dylan's Rolling Thunder Revue?

NY: Oh, yeah! Elliot Roberts my manager told *Rolling Stone* I'd do several shows, they found out they were in clubs and they called it the Rolling *Zuma* Revue. It was very good for us, it allowed the group to come together for this tour. We did 8 or 10 clubs in 3 weeks. It was around my ranch. We drove there, Marin County, San Mateo County, old wooden bars . . . with all these people who live in the mountains and spend their money until drunk, we come up and people scream.

Rock and Folk: Can you talk about the *Zuma* concept?

NY: It was a personal choice about breaking up with a girl, about the impressions of the subconscious, in fact it is a very romantic record. But some of the songs, of course, are very cynical. "Stupid Girl" is "get lost," you see. They all come from a similar reality; I think each song adopts these reactions.

R and F: And "Through My Sails?"

NY: The whole album is based on the same feeling so I wanted to integrate it into my music. When I went through the break-up of my family, I couldn't translate the feelings but if I had waited long enough, it wouldn't have been so depressing and I could then have used this turmoil to transcribe them. This is what I wanted to do here, experience it, finish this album.

Best: But it covers up feelings of a more positive nature . . .

NY: If I had taken it out when it happened to me, it would have been more painful. So I chose to extract this experience with the support of a certain strength and not with my current weaknesses.

Best: On *Tonight's the Night*, in "Roll Another Number" in particular, you have this very chilly take on the hippies and on the Woodstock generation . . .

NY: Yes . . . on Woodstock . . . but this album is too special. That's why I didn't play any of the songs on it tonight. I had this experience, I hardly assimilated it and I translated it, but I can't play these songs on stage anymore, I won't do any more. I did it in London, people were getting mad. I will not do any more, any of the songs that touch on drugs, which can annihilate you, nor the old drug songs.

(Here Neil becomes visibly feverish, his verbal flow is more precipitous and the evocation of this tragedy seems to revive ever-fresh pains, the death of the road manager, Bruce Berry for whom Neil bears the indirect responsibility since he didn't allow Crazy Horse to reform, after several cures of detoxifications because he did not consider him able to function, made *Tonight's the Night*, a painful album of remorse that mourns a guy and his incredible human potential.)

Best: You hesitated a long time before releasing this album.

NY: Yes, because it was touching an area that could destroy me. So I thought for a long time about what consequences it might have. I'm not an artist who could remake albums as "clean" as *Harvest* or *After the Gold Rush* is, although *Zuma* is relatively clean in my opinion. For *TTN* we did not consider the technical details. We tried to recreate a mood.

Best: But you recorded *Tonight's the Night* before *On the Beach*. Yet there is an obvious tragic progression from *Time Fades Away* to *On the Beach* and to *Tonight's the Night*?

NY: *Time Fades Away* is the album I released after touring with the band that was supposed to include Crazy Horse guitarist Danny Whitten. But he died a little before we went out on the road. That's the reason I don't play any of these songs anymore. These three albums like the others reflect my life, its happy moments, its moments of depression. But after *Harvest*, I was tired of being myself, always remaking the songs on stage from this album and becoming a kind of John Denver. I couldn't stay in this state, so I wanted to destroy this idea that I had of myself.

R and F: What is your reaction to Lynyrd Skynyrd's attack on their song "Sweet Home Alabama?"

NY: Oh, that's ok, I was glad to hear that. It's like a folk song, that's good. I say one thing, they say another. And both are very good. They are very funky, I like the band (Neil's tone seems more conciliatory than anything else). I think we have almost the same point of view. They're like a distorted image of a "redneck." We're two sides of the same coin and that's what they've done here. It was not a personal attack. I represent something. I represent the hippy position for whom the redneck is bad. And they represent the rednecks for a moment and then take the other side. That's the whole story.

Best: Do you think they (Lynyrd) represent a real change in southern mentality. Aren't there long-haired rednecks?

NY: There will always be rednecks of one kind or another anyway. I think the hippy and the redneck are very close to each other. The hippy and the farmer are both natural elements.

Best: Listening to your songs ("Southern Man," "Alabama") you have the impression that you are dealing more with a young person from the south than a young Canadian, in the way you feel so forcefully this kind of rupture in this southern mentality. What are the origins of this contact with the south?

NY: My grandfather was a southerner. He always referred to blacks as "[*n*-word]" when I spoke to him. And it didn't bother me because he was my grandfather. An old guy with red hair. It was at the beginning, then I met the people down there. The images burst into my mind. I read the newspapers, the people protesting, the oppression. I understood then. The most important thing in this song "Southern Man" is not so much the rednecks, the most important is the reason that I sing it for, it's a white woman sleeping with a black man. This is what infuriates white people, this is the sore spot, the human aspect.

Best: Your political commitment to McGovern, that was quite surprising coming from you.

NY: I think so, too. I went back and listened to this song again and I felt who I was really in there and that I was spreading some energy around. I'm glad I did, because this represents a typical case of mistaken judgment, but a very human error because at the time all of us needed to believe and place our hopes in someone.

(The song Neil talks about is called "War Song" recorded with Graham Nash—it only appears on a 45, difficult to find today. We can also consider *After The Gold Rush* as an album dedicated to a total democratization of the United States. Even though it came out two years after the Nixon McGovern fight for the presidency, it represented the urgent mobilization of all-American youth.)

R and F: More and more your music seems to reflect the kind of music the Rolling Stones play. You say it in "Borrowed Tune" and "Stupid Girl" sounds like a typical Jagger-Richards song.

NY: I love the Stones. When they lost Brian Jones, I dreamed of being a Rolling Stone. I think they're the best rock 'n' roll band out there today. I think Keith Richard [*referring to Keith Richards; Richards was often called "Keith Richard" during the '60s and '70s —Ed.*] is a great guitarist, a great drummer, a great bass player, and someone will be the new Stone, the band is still excellent. Brian Jones, it was something else.

R and F: That's why you could have replaced him.

NY: That's right.

Best: Did you feel closer to him?

NY: No more than the others, it's the group that I love.

Best: You played with Bob Dylan in San Francisco last year . . .

NY: Yes, it was good. He didn't have to carry the full weight of the show with me by his side. But I am no longer sure about this. Because with Dylan, on stage, you immediately feel that you are just part of the whole thing and not the whole thing.

Best: On what instrument do you mostly compose?

NY: With different instruments. I don't think the instrument has any influence on the way you compose. What's important or who has used it before, or when. Like the time a friend handed me a guitar and said, "try this guitar," I picked up that guitar and spontaneously started playing music that I had never played before, singing words I'd never sung before. I then realized that it just came naturally. I have since stopped trying to compose, I don't try anymore, I'm waiting. The circumstances are different, but the song eventually emerges.

Best: There is an album that you recorded shortly after *On the Beach* that never saw the light of day.

NY: *Homegown* . . . yes, it's in the shed . . . maybe someday.

Best: There were a few unreleased songs tonight. . . .

NY: They're all from my new album, there's "Too Far Gone," "Like a Hurricane," "My Country Home," "It's Gonna Take a Lot of Love."

R and F: What will be the title of this new album.

NY: *Sedan Delivery*, but it's not final . . . it's a more positive and romantic album.

Best: What about the one with Stephen Stills?

NY: I have already recorded 6 or 7 songs with him.

R and F: Do you play as New Buffalo Springfield?

NY: No, that was a joke.

Best: What memories do you have of the Crosby, Stills, Nash & Young tour, two years on?

NY: Oh . . . a nice tour . . . I was alone in my corner most of the time. But maybe it was too heavy what was going on. The music was good, the people were up to the task. I would like to do it again one more time, I think we will do it again someday, maybe this summer. I feel like it'll be a good time.

Best: Have you decided on anything specific for this?

NY: No, these are just ideas.

(Again, Neil adopts a conciliatory tone.)

Best: Do you believe in your astrological sign? You are Scorpio and . . .

NY: I think I've been on earth before, and I think I will be on earth again, or somewhere else. My life is my last time recorded.

It was then that his manager interrupted our discussion by pointing out that it would be time to leave Neil. In conclusion Neil with a knowing smile, and by looking at each one of us: "If I haven't given more interviews, it is that I had nothing to say and I still have nothing to say. If you listen to this tape, you will only know about it by listening to my music. . . ."

NEIL YOUNG ON

His 1977 Santa Cruz Pickup Band, the Ducks

"We're in a place right now where we' re pure . . . it's like being born again. We're young and we need the safety of a small town to grow in. We're self-contained right now, but maybe when we get bigger, we may move on . . . the possibilities are there. But right now, The Ducks are just developing, and I'm just one of The Ducks."

–from an interview with Dan Coyro, *Good Times*, July 21, 1977

NEIL YOUNG ON

Disco

"I'm into good disco. Donna Summer, that's good stuff. "Hot Stuff." That's good. That's good music. Some of that other crap is just post-hippie elevator music though; I hate that stuff."

–from an interview with Mary Turner,
Warner Bros. Music Show, 1979

NEIL YOUNG: WHEN DOES A DINOSAUR CUT OFF ITS TAIL?

Richard Cook | October 9, 1982 | *New Musical Express*

When last we left our hero . . .

In early 1976 Young recorded the *Long May You Run* LP with Stephen Stills, the result of an aborted attempt at a new CSNY record. The Stills-Young Band's *Long May You Run* was released in September 1976, two months after Young left the tour, signing a farewell note to Stills with the admonition "eat a peach."

After releasing the eclectic *American Stars 'n Bars* in May 1977, October revealed the 3-LP *Decade*, a mixture of greatest hits and unreleased gems that would serve as a blueprint for the CD-box-set trend of the mid-1980s and Young's own *Archives* endeavor.

May 1978 witnessed the 10-date solo One Stop World Tour at The Boarding House in San Francisco, while Crazy Horse joined Young on September 16 for the *Rust Never Sleeps* tour. The brutally loud shows ended on October 24, three days after the mellow *Comes a Time* was released. The *Rust Never Sleeps* album's acoustic songs were captured at the spring shows, while the electric numbers were recorded on the fall tour and overdubbed for the June 1979 LP. Two songs, "Sail Away" and "Pocahontas," were studio recordings.

The 1978 *Rust Never Sleeps* tour also provided tracks for the November 1979 double-LP *Live Rust*, and the October 22 San Francisco Cow Palace show was released to theaters as *Rust Never Sleeps*.

For all this, the most important events these years were Neil's 1977 marriage to Pegi Morton and the 1978 birth of their son, Ben. Ben was born with cerebral palsy. The couple would spend the next few years working with therapists and other parents to understand and manage Ben's disabilities.

While caring for his son, Neil only performed live twice from 1979 to 1981 but still managed to release music. *Hawks & Doves* came out October 29, 1980, just days ahead of the US presidential election. While the first side features not-uncommon mid-1970s fare, the flip side begins a "common-man" swerve from the left side of "the ditch" over the center line and to the right, just as Ronald Reagan was taking office.

The uneven Crazy Horse album *re·ac·tor* followed a year later. With that, Young would leave Reprise Records after more than a dozen years. The separation was due, in part, to the catch-22 frustrations of Young not being able to fully promote his work because of his dedication to Ben and the label's reluctance to promote the LP without Neil's full involvement. Young's insistence that the label release "Southern Pacific" as a red triangular single didn't help, nor did old friend David Geffen making him a monetary offer he couldn't refuse.

In a touchstone career move, Young pivoted to synthesizer-based electronic music on his first Geffen Records release, *Trans*. Young telegraphed this new musical direction in fall European shows with the new Trans Band.

This interview was released during that tour, prior to the December 28 release of *Trans*. Among the interviews collected here, it's a bit heavier in the word-craft of the encounter instead of the simplicity of the interview, with Cook questioning Young's transition to electronic music and the possible loss of his readily identifiable lyrics about a "mythical America." In other words, Cook begins to wonder if Neil Young is still making Neil Young records. –Ed.

Out of all the absurd figures created and cherished by rock 'n' roll, there is none quite like Neil Young.

He may one day turn out to be The Last Rock Star. A few years ago he made a record, *Rust Never Sleeps*, that catalogued a phase of rock stretching from its folk roots to its disheveled, feedbacked afterlife—a kind of hello/goodbye gesture which has since settled into a respectful slot in a long career of work.

It is still there, its power intact though ironically asleep; and with a characteristic shrug Young has ambled on, leafing through his American sketchbook and pursuing a personal course fueled and maintained by a loyalty rare among the fandoms of the megastar. He's a lucky man.

The ambivalence of Young's position is so odd it's some small miracle that he's kept his footing. On one level he's behaved and performed with a disregard for public, press and business that might have had all three turning on him; on another he's written a torrent of bankable music, cut a great welter of records and mischievously filtered out actions and projects that suggest an operator so artful it's like every risk and eccentricity has been checked over and honed down first. For every *Rust Never Sleeps* there's a placid and pastoral *Comes a Time*; every time Young tempts the abyss he steps back from the brink again. He's a smart man.

Even with the safety net, Young has pulled stunts no other American rock veteran would dare consider. For him to have made a record as scruffily violent and personal as last year's *re·ac·tor*, after a dozen or more years in the rarified top bracket of dollar rock, is exactly the sort of liberty the American gods have forgotten to take with their careers; for him to persist in playing with a forearm bar band like Crazy Horse instead of the customary pedigree stable of session bores only freezes further the aghast expressions of his contemporaries.

At this distance it might seem like nothing more than an old Canuck busker refusing to act his age and settle into a sleepy middle life of pretty hums and regular reunions. Then something appealing and amusing sticks about the way Young has not so much fought corporate pressure as strolled along a different path, unaware that he's not supposed to go that way.

Neil Young grew into an old rebel because he forgot to watch where the rest of the parade went.

Of course, the parched bones and raw wires in Young's rock 'n' roll are tempered by a sentimental streak close to a mile wide. Even as that inimitably frazzled guitar cuts lesions in the song you can hear the romantic heartbeat pumping through—a childlike faith in the healing graces of love. His interest in the flowering of the new wave could only ever be confined to its outward spirit: Young has no interest in fatalism or despair. He loves his rock 'n' roll.

So, I guess Mr. Young has both kept and eaten his cake. Having clothed his folkie's frame in altogether tougher garb he can travel when and where he pleases. He's found his old audience has mostly stayed the course and he still plays "Cinnamon Girl" and "Old Man" for them; he's institutionalized his modest rebel music while retaining enough of the spitfire delivery to keep it breathing; and now he's looking for something new again.

At 37, Young doesn't want to stay still.

"HOW ARE things at the *New Musical Express?*" he asks me. "I don't read that much unless I'm actually doing something. I like to see a little feedback because it's hard to tell what you did when you're gone."

Does he read his record reviews?

"Depends what I'm doing. I do if I'm not too busy."

He gives me an interrogative grin. It seems like he's worked a long time on that expression: in a face little marked by age a grin will spread out, the eyes widening, the brow wrinkling up, a gentle merriment always dozing somewhere in the recesses. The rascally beam of the *Comes a Time* cover seems so uncontrived, simple, amiable in person. I look for the wiseacre in the eyes but it doesn't seem to be there. Just a big, shambling, guitar strumming Canadian.

Young's return to England at a mid-point on an enormous European tour is his first visit in six years. If any of the faithful have grown tired in the long wait it doesn't show at the Birmingham gig, his first over here.

A walkway extension of the stage enables the leader to move toward the audience like Larry Parks in *The Jolson Story,* except the way he stomps down it is more like Frankenstein's monster. With the homesteader's formal dress, old pug's haircut and set jawline the resemblance doesn't exactly end there. And always somewhere nearby is the eternally diminutive Nils Lofgren.

Lofgren's presence in this particular rock 'n' roll circus is finally no big deal. I listened quite carefully but could hardly hear his guitar with Young's being amped up so loud. His usual gymnastic leaps and trailing scarves looked at odds with a diligent blue-collar band like Crazy Horse. We began to forget he was there.

The motorway unrolls outside our window. It's not very easy to get to Neil Young. After several rendezvous earlier in the continent fell through we are face to face in his touring coach, something akin to a luxury cruiser with wheels.

Mr. Young is pleased to talk. Like on how happy he is to be here.

"IT'S THE truth! I'm really happy to be playing anywhere. I haven't toured in so long and this is what I was raised to do, what I trained to do in my whole life. The thing is it just got so big . . .

"Not to use your gifts in the right way is so abusive. I see a lot of people who are my contemporaries—who *were* my contemporaries in the '60s and '70s—who, uh, just haven't tried to continue what they were doing in the first place. They've tried to recreate what they already did thinking that's what success is—do it again and they'll like it again. What they really did first was to do something *new* that people liked—so they should try and do something new again."

The sort of healthy outlook which might be expected from Young's modern half. But I feel it a duty to remind him of what he's just been playing—acoustic bleatings like "I Am A Child" and frowsy old rockers of the "Cinnamon Girl" ilk, aged entries from his balmiest days. The temptation to rely on proven familiars is disappointing.

"I don't believe in doing my old songs in a new way. I'd rather do new songs. The new stuff that I want to do has to be introduced chronologically. But I like shock value, too. To see the expressions on faces."

The sense of communal rite is still inescapable. How does he feel when he hears cheers of remembrance on the last line of a pale little tragedy like "The Needle And The Damage Done?"

"I *know*, it blows my mind," he murmurs, oblivious, "I don't know what they're doing! I guess they just get off on it. They're reacting to seeing me doing it rather than to what I'm actually saying. Sometimes it gets to that point."

Then he could rectify it by not doing that song.

"I suppose I could—I probably will, eventually. But that song means something to me. There's so many old songs that I won't do because I don't feel anything for them. 'Southern Man''s on the edge for me—when we started the tour I could do it but now it's a little forced. When it starts feeling like that I don't wanna do it."

Why is there so little material from his last few records, the hardest and most detailed music he's ever made? Nothing at all off *re·ac·tor* or *Hawks & Doves*, one off *Rust Never Sleeps* . . .

"The band isn't right for them," is the bemusing reply. "I had these people I wanted to play with and then I tried to figure out the best songs they could do. It might seem obvious to you but to me it's like, 20 albums of material and it's all there." What does he think when he looks back at that huge body of work? "It's really hard to get a grip on it," he says, shaking his head. "I can take one song at a time, one period at a time, but the whole picture—it's big. Like Panavision."

"There's a lot of songs I haven't performed, ever. That are only on records. I only did them once, period. That was like, use take one for the record and that's it! I never sang them again. They have to jump out at me. I don't go through the album covers and decide which one I'll do."

HE MIGHT have changed direction in the past, but Young's newest offerings are a complete departure, arguably the most telling acknowledgement so far of the drift of electronic pop from a member of the senior rock hierarchy. The coming album *Trans* is Young grasping at the edges of liberating technology.

Amid some of his most ingenuous sounding anthems ("Little Thing Called Love," "If You Got Love"), a frankly bizarre respray on "Mr. Soul" and a new raddled epic in "Like An Inca" are five excursions into alien territory—the clean soar of synth-pop allied to the ugly sores of Young's scorched rock music. Voices are vocoded into abstraction, guitars dogfight with sequencers . . . it's a strange sound.

What motivated this interest?

"Well, I spend most of my time trying to remain open to new things. They reflect the fact that I've got so interested in electronics and machines. I've always loved machines. I feel that with all the new digital and computerized equipment I can get my hands on now, I can do things I could never do before!" His eyes widen still further, like a hayseed agape at a new tractor.

"I know this is just the beginning for me. I've been Neil Young for years and I could stay where I am and be a period piece but as I look around everything's so *organized.* Everything's running on digital time. The new music with its kind of perfection is reassuring for me—you know the beat's going to be there all the time and it's never going to break down. That's fascinating and I think it's still soulful. The *manipulation* of machines can be very soulful.

"The song 'Transformer Man' is one I wrote for my son with all this and to me that's probably the best song I've written in the last ten years. It's based on the freedom to be able to assume different voices and characters.

"I'm in a very primitive stage of development with all this stuff, but the things I can do . . . like I could take your voice singing a note, compute that into a keyboard and have four octaves from you singing that note. Or I could vocode it and sing with your voice. Or anybody's voice. Bing Crosby's off one of his old records.

"You can still be creative—it's still my melodies, my enunciation, my feeling. It just lifts a restriction—why should I have to sing with my own voice in 1982, when I can stretch out in different directions?" Young almost evanesces with enthusiasm for his machines, and seeing that involvement from such a figure does give fresh heart in its way.

But there's also a threat of loss: Neil Young is one of the handful to actually raise a response from the puckered old flesh of folk based rock 'n' roll. The thread that runs through Young's last half dozen records winds through a reinvented rural America, detail brushed in across scores of songs with the casual eye of films like *Two-Lane Blacktop* or *Rafferty And The Cold Dust Twins,* a giant landscape not so much reduced as fragmented inside the microcosm of a lyric. If he turns to the machine printouts of Moderne Man, won't that dust bowl vision blow away for good?

"I think that might be other people's view more than mine. I feel I need to do something that first turns me on—that's why I'm taking this course. It won't *replace* my voice and acoustic guitar.

"I don't know if I can be classed as a contemporary songwriter. I'm like a dinosaur with a large tail—I'm so big I have to keep eating all the time. I look around, there's not many dinosaurs left, just a lot of smaller animals moving very fast. And it's their vibrant energy that I need to stay alive. Sometimes I think I might have to cut off my tail because I can't afford to keep feeding myself."

Mr. Young is amused at the metaphor. How does he keep a perspective on himself as an icon in his kingdom?

"I put the perspective on rock 'n' roll because that's what I owe it to. For my spirit it's a healing force and I give everything I have when I play it. If I didn't do that I'd just be a museum, ancient history up close. Maybe I am that anyway."

THE DISREGARD for expectation hasn't been confined to a purely musical setting. The devious implants in Young's writing have wrought an overview on mythical America that reads out like a windblown panorama of tumbleweeds and the assorted debris of small-town living.

Recurrent echoes of the Civil War, the pioneer waggoneers and the blueblood heroes of idealized North American legend litter Young's later work as frequently as his loner's yearnings for a lover's satisfaction. Faded emblems and yellowing narratives haunt the precincts of "The Old Homestead," "Powderfinger," and "Captain Kennedy" like ghostly ancestors in ancient prints. In updating those spirits with the colors of the rock 'n' roll song, Young has forged anew a rusted link with a popular mythology.

"Those songs are like a landscape. I don't think with those songs—I get myself to a certain place, open up and they just come to me. I wrote 'Homestead' all in one shot, never looking at the previous line until it was finished. They might be polished a little but they first come *through* me—I never think, Oh, I'll write a song with three birds, a guy and a horse in it.

"North America's my home, I've been all over it. I don't write down all the things I see, I just watch and watch until something comes out. Really I don't have a personal view on America as a whole. They're just disparate ideas that come together,"

What's the worst thing about America today?

"Nobody's thought of a replacement for gasoline yet. Yankee ingenuity—it's on the ropes." Neil permits himself a wry chuckle. "The Yankees'd like to be able to come up with the big answer. Everyone would. I think it's less discouraging there now than it was three or four years ago. People are becoming proud to be a part of it again, on the grandest scale. I think there's a lot of creative force there—a lot of loudmouthed bullshit too—but it's like all countries, America is different all over."

What is his favorite place to be in America?

"I like to be in the forest. Near my ranch, in California. It's like a natural cathedral, you can walk in and come out cleansed. America's still so geographically immense and beautiful. Europe has been manicured over centuries but America is a huge expanse of God's work."

Is he of a religious persuasion?

"Not so much toward one story. There's a lot of stories—Jesus, Krishna, Buddha—same story, different imagery. I mean, you could have a religion on the atom. I believe in the universe, in sizes and relationships. It's too big for me—just too big! It goes on forever. Jesus Christ couldn't have walked all that distance."

One thing Neil Young hasn't looked into is the support of the No Nukes movement. When a lot of those 'contemporaries' of his have bolstered appearances with a bunch of benefits, Young has stayed adamantly clear of agitprop. He likes nuclear power.

"We don't have it down, and we don't know what to do with the waste. But how are we going to get to other planets? We need nuclear power to discover what's out there and discover another power source. A coal burning rocket won't get there. I'd like to go to another planet. I'd go now if I could!" Shouldn't we concentrate on saving this beleaguered planet first?

"We should do both. We'll need an alternative if we don't save this one. It's a responsible thing to do—there's more and more people here, more waste, more threat of war . . ."

Young waves a hand toward the limitless sky, out through the window of the bus. For a moment the stars seem to beckon . . . I blink hard. If he's so concerned about these Vital Issues, what sort of contribution to any debate does he feel compelled to make?

"My contribution?" He growls the words like a wily old Congressman. "It's ethereal, I guess. I put out all the time and if anyone wants to take me to space I'm ready to go. I'd like to take my family too. We have to go somewhere else eventually."

DOWN TO EARTH—let's talk movies. After *Journey Through The Past,* a project long abandoned to celluloid limbo, Young returned to filmmaking with the graceless if entertaining concert record of *Rust Never Sleeps.*

"It didn't take much money," he admits, "Film isn't something that comes naturally to me. I tried to paint but I can't do that. I know I'm not a great film-maker but I have a lot of fun trying."

"The concept was like a day dream. You know the way dreams jumble up things that you've seen that day, maybe with people you knew five or ten years ago at some place you think, you sort of know? That's how *Rust Never Sleeps* came out. It put the music in a different perspective."

What did he think of Dennis Hopper's *Out Of The Blue,* a bleakly realized extension of Young's 'Better To Burn Out' proverb?

"I thought it was brilliant but I wouldn't recommend it for an evening's entertainment. It's so fucking repulsive. Doesn't it make your stomach turn, seeing what those people are doing to each other?"

What's his kind of film?

"I liked *E.T. Star Wars,* I love *Star Wars.* It's like a bible for kids—the force! What message could be better for kids than, if I believe I can do it, I can do it!"

Young has completed a new film, *Human Highway,* now in search of a distributor.

"It's about a, um, gas station at an intersection of the country—power plant next door—city in the background—people living there, sort of in the future, a little in the past. A little Laurel and Hardy.

"Music in films is so limiting—everybody knows the picture and the music goes together. Film music is locked into the film. Music by itself is fuckin' *huge,* it can be anything. Movies are so straightforward. Film is a little more vulnerable—it's easier to take a shot at it than it is with music."

The Business is prepared to put up with Young's shenanigans—nixing whole albums just prior to release, playing the willful child when it comes to the routine of rock world procedures—because when it comes down to it he is the most mild and passive of outsiders. He never looks for trouble. We talk over the trends in American music, the disappointing new pretenders to the FM thrones and the smug refusal of the US mainstream to open up its ears.

"What keeps music alive is the small things which aren't even noticed on a grand scale. The new thing always has to start little."

But what about—and I start on Asia, Robert Plant, the new orthodoxy and more before Young says, "You're asking the same questions I'm asking. That's why it's difficult for me to answer! I feel the same discontent and I know that in a lot of ways I'm just like those people. That makes me even madder. That's why I should cut my tail off."

He has a good stock of dinosaur anecdotes too.

"I remember when I was living at Zuma I told Carole King, you gotta come down and listen to my new album (*Zuma*). It's the cleanest album you've ever heard. She came down and listened and (falsetto), this isn't a stoodio album! What are you *talking* about! and James Taylor on 'Heart Of Gold'—C'mon, Neil, why don't you make a *real record!*"

Would he, this last American rock star, like to make The Last Rock Record?

"No, I hope nobody does. I think there'll be rock 'n' roll on other planets. May be there is now."

And he looks again at the sky. London territory is in view—Cricklewood, Kilburn. He finishes another anecdote with a familiar line, *"Back in those old folkie days,"* a personal history diffidently rifled through every time he takes a stage.

"When I was in school I was called into the principal's office—I was always getting into trouble—and he asked me what I wanted to do when I left. I said I wanted to be a musician and play in bars and clubs. He said, OK, but what do you want to do *then?* Like I had to stop sometime. I've never forgotten that. It's like I've always been kicking against it—like I have to carry on . . ."

NEIL YOUNG ON

The Brevity of *Everybody's Rockin'*

"Song were a lot shorter then, only 2 minutes or so. I had 5 or 6 songs a side, that's only 10-12 minutes. Actually I only did 5 songs on each side–I left 'That's All Right' off the album."

–from an interview with Bry Carter, *Broken Arrow*, November 1983

NEIL YOUNG ON

Perfect as the Enemy of Good

"Everything now is pretty constricted. I notice a lot of the concerts I see that either on television, or live, or whatever, that there's no technical problems at all. Everybody seems to be perfect. Everybody stands together and they perform and they're just real good. It doesn't relate to where I come from with music."

–from Sydney Press Conference, March 1985

NEIL YOUNG ON

His Song Characters Clashing

"There are different personalities in me, and they're always at battle with each other, wrestling with each other for a place on the album, even though the characters in the songs range from some love-struck, heartbroken dude to a guy who got blown away on a cocaine deal. You know how people say about my stuff, 'I can't listen to that, Fuck! I liked the last one, but this one sucks?' that's what the characters in my head say about each other."

–from an interview with Stuart Matranga, *Rockbill*, September 1985

NEIL YOUNG ON

Being American

"I consider myself to be an American, although I'm not legally. I've made my living in the American capitalist system, and I owe almost everything I am today to the American system. I'm very patriotic."

–from an interview by Richard Harrington,
Washington Post, September 13, 1985

NEIL YOUNG: LEGEND OF A LONER

Adam Sweeting | September 7 and September 14, 1985 | *Melody Maker*

Dropping the troubled *Trans* band, Young toured the United States and Canada solo for the first two months of 1983, mixing his acoustic "museum pieces" with new electronic material. Then came another musical about-face: July 1 saw the debut of the Shocking Pinks, Young's rockabilly band, as the group embarked on a 39-date, three-month tour. *Everybody's Rockin'* was released July 27; it was Young's lowest charting US LP since his self-titled debut, which had failed to chart.

Sometime in 1983, Young submitted the country album *Old Ways* to Geffen. From electronic to country to rockabilly, the label had had enough. On December 1, 1983, Geffen Records sued Neil Young for making "unrepresentative" and "uncharacteristic" music—basically, for not sounding like Neil Young.

After a failed attempt at recording with Crazy Horse, then a few Santa Monica dates with the band in early 1984, Young adopted country full-time. From June through the end of October, Neil and his new band, the International Harvesters, played dates in clubs, theaters, stadiums, and rodeo arenas, alongside country legends such as Willie Nelson and Waylon Jennings. Young would release no LP of new music in 1984, the first such occurrence since 1971.

In February 1985, Young headed to Australia and New Zealand for the first time in his career, playing 16 concerts over the course of a month. Among the longest performances of his career, the shows opened with a country set backed by the International Harvesters (with Billy Talbot and Ralph Molina), continued with an acoustic interlude, and closed with a blistering Crazy Horse set.

By this time Young was nearing the end of his legal battles with Geffen label head David Geffen; the lawsuits would be withdrawn on April 1, 1985. However, through the August 1985 release of *Old Ways* and into the September 1985 end of the third International Harvesters tour, Young continually and purposefully didn't sound like "Neil Young."

The return from Australia found Young performing a five-song solo set and a three-tune reunion with CSN at Live Aid in Philadelphia, on July 13. The August release of *Old Ways* coincided with the third and final tour with the International Harvesters. The last tour date was the September 22 performance in Champaign, Illinois, at the first Farm Aid, a now annual event to benefit American farmers. Farm Aid 2 on July 4, 1986 saw the last appearance of the International Harvesters.

Prosaically, this interview is notable for its in-depth look at *Old Ways* songs, the ins-and-outs of the tour, and an extended discussion of *On the Beach*'s "Revolution Blues."

Less prosaically, two areas of discussion are especially notable: Reagan and AIDS. As interviewer Sweeting intones: "Redneck? Let's hope not."

While there is a rightward movement in Young's politics starting about 1980, the vociferous support of Reagan is less surprising from a left/right perspective than it is coming from someone considered a member of the counterculture: Neil Young was now supporting The Man. With the knowledge that Young would become more empathetic over time, this support for Reagan makes more sense as you hear his reason: he thinks it's the best decision for America and "people with families," a group that now includes Young among its members. But it seems clear that his support is driven by fear. And fear fuels Young's homophobic rant, which is shocking every time I read it.

Writing this the week that the first COVID-19 vaccines have been administered to Americans–a week of staggering death and great hope–and considering Young's support of progressive causes during the global pandemic, from Black Lives Matter to consumer protection to dumping Trump, it is still difficult to reckon Neil Young September 1985 with Neil Young December 2020. –Ed.

THE BUS paused for breath at a traffic light, wheezing a little. After all, it had been on the road for 10 years. It had reached a place called Troy in upstate New York, the original one-horse town. Old men in trucker's caps sat on benches in the deserted streets, watching it.

On the roof, the top halves of a couple of old Studebakers had been welded into place like twin observation turrets, silently surveying the passing scenery. One of them had a windsurfer board strapped on top of it. The sides of the bus were covered with weather-beaten wooden ribbing. As it accelerated away from the lights in a growl of exhaust smoke, bystanders could see the legend "BUFFALO SPRINGFIELD" across its rear. The vehicle could have been wandering the plains forever.

Inside the bus, a hound called Elvis sat in the front seat, keeping an eye on the road. Fittings, shelves, seats and sideboards were all made from hand-carved wood, right through from the kitchen area at the front, via the central lounge section to the bedroom in the rear.

The vehicle's owner patted the dog, who rolled his eyes mournfully upward.

"I played here once with the Buffalo Springfield," he recalled in a voice which managed to be both dark and nasal at the same time. "I remember we didn't get our money. The guy drew a gun on us, told us to get the fuck out. Those were the good old days."

Nearly 20 years later, Neil Young had returned with his latest ensemble, a squad of veteran Nashville musicians called The International Harvesters. His new country album, *Old Ways*, is, as its author sees it, the third in a sequence of records which began with the best-selling *Harvest* in 1972, continued with the winsome *Comes A Time* in 1978, and after assorted diversions has brought him back to the road in 1985.

Old Ways is a skillfully crafted piece of work, full of perfectly assured melodies and impeccable performances from familiar Young sidemen like steel guitarist Ben Keith and Drummer Karl Himmel. More significantly, the record captures the state of mind of a man who's shot the rapids of rock 'n' roll, lost some good friends along the way, willfully turned his back on the charts and pop stardom, and who has managed to become an adult in a field where the odds are stacked against it. Neil Young has survived, and he's grown too. And changed.

"I think in some ways—only in some ways, but in some ways—rock 'n' roll has let me down," he said. "It really doesn't leave you a way to grow old gracefully and continue to work."

Why's that? Because you're supposed to die before you get old?

"Yeah, right. If you're gonna rock you better burn out, cos that's the way they wanna see you. They wanna see you right on the edge where you're glowing, right on the living edge, which is where young people are. They're discovering themselves, and rock 'n' roll is young people's music. I think that's a reality, and I still love rock 'n' roll and I love to play the songs in my set that are sort of rock 'n' roll, but I don't see a future for me there."

Young paused, his lank black hair flopping forward, and rubbed his chin which was covered in a heavy overnight stubble. "I see country music, I see people who take care of their own. You got 75-year-old guys on the road. That's what I was put here to do, y'know, so I wanna make sure I surround myself with people who are gonna take care of me. Cos I'm in it for the long run.

"Willie Nelson's 54 years old and he's a happy man, doing what he loves to do. I can't think of one rock 'n' roller like that. So what am I gonna do?"

Old Ways features guest appearances from country luminaries Waylon Jennings and Willie Nelson, both of whom will be playing some support dates with Young on his current tour. A lot of the performances find Young and his International Harvesters playing to family audiences at state fairs, huge day-long gatherings of people, animals, carnival sideshows, food and drink, where everyone turns up for the entertainment in the evening. It's miles away from the rock 'n' roll crowds who've flocked over the years to see Young play with Buffalo Springfield, Crosby, Stills & Nash or his perennial backing band, Crazy Horse.

Young is still best known among non-partisan observers as the laid-back whiner who had a hit single with "Heart of Gold" in 1972. His early-Seventies albums *After the Gold Rush* and *Harvest* provided a melancholy soundtrack for any number of mentally unbalanced young people to ponder suicide to. His work with Buffalo Springfield in the Sixties brought him into fierce creative proximity with Stephen Stills, and among a bunch of fine songs recorded by the group, it's still Young's dreamlike mock-symphonies "Expecting To Fly" and "Broken Arrow" which remain the most haunting and inexplicable.

Young joined Crosby, Stills & Nash as additional instrumentalist and dark horse. His stint with them barely lasted a year, but it got him some prime exposure on their album *Déjà Vu* and set Young up perfectly for his subsequent solo career. The association also proved to be something of an albatross, but as the years passed and Young's own albums pursued a grim and tortuous path, it became clear that while CSNY had given him a priceless commercial boost, it had scarcely hinted at the depth and range of his talent.

Records like *Tonight's The Night*, *On The Beach*, and *Time Fades Away* were to prove emphatically that Young could hardly have been less like the hippy peacenik the media fondly imagined him to be.

Crosby, Stills & Nash are still playing together and grossing wads of dollars, but Young won't have anything to do with them until David Crosby kicks his cocaine habit. The topic brings out a hard puritanical streak in him, probably because he's seen several friends die from drug abuse.

"David says that he loves to play music with Crosby, Stills, Nash & Young more than anything in the world. I told them when they could prove that to me that that's really what he wanted to do with his life and give up drugs, that I would go out with them. I told them that three years ago, and it hasn't happened yet.

"The way I look at it, either he's going to OD and die or we're going to play together sometime. It's pretty simple. But until one of those things happens, until he cleans up, I'm not gonna do it. Live Aid was an exception to the rule which I made up on the spot. They all know how I feel.

"I will not go out with CSNY, have everyone scrutinize the band, how big it is and how much it meant, and see this guy that's so fucked up on drugs, and who's not really so fucked up that he can't come back because we've all seen him when he's been clean recently, where he's very sharp just like he always was.

"But he seems to feel like he wants to do that, or he would stop doing it. So, y'know, until he has more respect for life and his effects on the young people . . . why should some young person who loves CSNY's old records from listening to their parents play them, some young kid 12 years old, why should he see CSNY on TV and know that this guy's a cocaine addict, been freebasing for fuckin' years and years and years, and he looks like a vegetable but they're still on TV and they're still making it and they're still big stars? I don't wanna show anybody that. That's something non-one should see."

On the recent Live Aid broadcast, Young and his band were seen delivering a song called "Nothing Is Perfect." It's not included on *Old Ways* and is a strikingly forthright declaration of Young's current absorption with family life and an almost gung-ho enthusiasm for Ronald Reagan's America. Young in the main steered clear of the loudmouth leftish politics of Crosby, Stills & Nash, but wrote the scorching "Ohio" after National Guardsmen shot four students at Kent State University. It's something of a shock to find him supporting Reagan's arms build-up. The Loner has turned Republican.

"In the Carter years, everybody was walking around with their tails between their legs talking with their head down, y'know, thinking America's been so bad, we've done all these things wrong. But, especially militarily, we had a lot of disasters and a lot of things that never should have happened and that maybe were mistakes in the first place, although it's hard to say.

"People were being killed everywhere before we went over to try to help, and we went over and tried to help them and we fucked up. But y'know, you can't always feel sorry for everything that you did. Obviously I wish no-one had to die in any war, but war is, ah, is a dirty game.

"It seems like the Soviets, it doesn't bother them that much to walk into Afghanistan and kill people left and right and take the fucking country and do all that shit. You can't just let them keep on fucking doing that without saying enough's enough. So to do that, to have the strength to do that, you have to be strong.

"Ten years ago the US was starting to really drag ass, way behind the Soviets in build-up. All that's happened lately is more or less to catch up, just to be equal, reach equality in arms. At best it's a bad situation, but I think it would be worse to be weak when the stronger nation is the aggressor against freedom.

"So I stand behind Reagan when it comes to build-up, to stand, be able to play hardball with other countries that are aggressive toward free countries. I don't think there's anything wrong with that."

But would you have thought that way in 1967?

"No, no I wouldn't have thought that in 1967. But I'm an older man now, I have a family. I see other people with families. There's no immediate threat to American families, but there is an immediate threat to other families in free countries, y'know, a lot of the countries on the borders of the Iron Curtain. To stand there and say it could never happen is wrong, because it's happened. We just don't want it to happen anymore—at least, I don't."

It seems utterly insane when you think of the billions of pounds or dollars that have been spent since 1945 on weapons that have never been used, surely?

"It is crazy, it's fucking nuts," growled Young. "At least in our countries we have the fucking freedom to stand up and say it's crazy. And that's what we're fighting for, to be able to disagree. Openly. And it's our right, and we have to do everything we can to preserve it.

"So I don't put down anybody who says we should stop building weapons and everything. I disagree with them, practically. Idealistically I agree with them. It's like walking both sides of the fence, but I think there's too much to be responsible for as men and as people, that you have to take care of your own.

"So that's why I have more of a sympathy for Reagan than other people would have—a lot of other people in my walk of life."

But that sounds dangerously like an "every man for himself" philosophy? Correct me if I'm wrong . . .

"Sort of, but . . . I think it's more like every man for his brother than it is every man for himself. That's how I look at it. I think it's real important to be strong."

YOUNG'S attitude has not been formed overnight. Looking back, it's easy to spot traces of it on his 1980 album *Hawks & Doves*, a patchy phase in Young's continuing evolution. "Union Man" was a jokey item apparently supporting the Musician's Union proposition that "live music is better," Young celebrating the idea of communal togetherness with an exhausting slab of hoedown. In "Comin' Apart At Every Nail," he avowed that "this country sure looks good to me" even while it was falling to bits in some respects. The concluding "Hawks & Doves," a powerful slice of country raunch, examined cycles of history, both in terms of America's past and as they applied to Young's own career. He declared himself "willing to stay and pay."

In 1981 Young released *re·ac·tor*, an even scrappier piece of work. Thematic continuity could still be discerned occasionally, however, as in "Motor City," where he patriotically lamented the demise of the American car industry as the Japanese invaded ("there's already too many Datsuns in this town," don't mention the war . . .). Then there was the hard driving "Southern Pacific," a paean to the disappearance of the old railroads and the men who worked on them. Young's current live show contains a powerful reworking of the piece, and it sits comfortably alongside his hymns to home, family and an America dusting off its battered pride. Redneck? Let's hope not.

On tour, Young travels alone. Dave, his driver and minder, will motor from the gig and park for the night at a rest area or truck-stop. Young won't see the band until soundcheck the next day, though he's in radio contact with them.

On board the bus, Young played the perfect host, breaking out the Budweisers and demonstrating his fruit-juice machine. "Natural fruit juice is great, better'n any drug," he explained. "Gives you a natural sugar rush." By way of a preamble, he also vented some spleen about the mauling doled out to him by the British music press on his last British visit, when he played heavy metal at Wembley Arena. He seemed especially incensed by some impertinent scribe who'd alluded to pedal steel guitarist Ben Keith's blow-dried hair. Reading between the lines, it appears the tour was a shambles on a musical and organizational level. Today, Young seems balanced, positive and very clear about his objectives.

"I think it's time to be positive," he said, looking across the table with eyes that could bore through steel. Tour manager Glenn Palmer says he always knows from a single glance if Young is unhappy about something. If he is, he beats a retreat and comes back later.

"I think if all the hippies and everything from the Sixties, if they're still complaining about every little fucking thing, if they're not happy about anything, it's their own fucking fault. Cos they're the ones who should have changed it. Time has gone by now and what we have is what we've done so far, and if they're still putting down everything that they've done then I really don't feel compassion for that." I thought I heard the sound of distant cheering.

"We should be proud of the things we have been able to do, and the positive aspects of who we are in the world. It's our own creativity, ingenuity, whatever you wanna call it. I don't think all that's dead in America, I think it's still there. I feel that the Sixties was a decade of idealism, and the Eighties is more of realism."

On the road, Young has time to think and write. By the time the *Maker* caught up with him, he'd already written a new song called "This Old House" and worked it into the set. It's about the enduring strength of family and a sense of identity in the face of hard times and repo men from the bank. "This old house of mine is built on dreams," Young concludes.

His writing has always flirted with cliché, and paradoxically he's often at his best in that area, working the edge between insight and platitude. Consequently, he's always been ready for the country, where homespun philosophy is the order of the day—but only if it's been earned by hard experience. But, crucially, Young's work has been distinguished over the years by a mystical dimension beyond the experience of most artists. There's a feverish, luminous undertow to his best songs. It's difficult to analyze, perhaps because his most powerful images are more visual than verbal.

I asked him about the new song "Misfits." It's the odd-man-out on *Old Ways*, a strange collage of science fiction and apparently disconnected scenes, "all related" (according to the *LA Times*) "only by a modern isolation as profound as any ever experienced on the open range."

Young scratched his head, turned to look ahead through the windscreen, then pivoted back again. "There are a lot of science fiction overtones, time travel overtones, in 'Misfits.' People at different places geographically, it could all have been happening at exactly the same time. All of the scenes in that song could have been happening simultaneously, and yet they're also separate. It's an interesting thing . . .

"I dunno, it only took me a few minutes to write it. I picked up my electric guitar one night in the studio, I was by myself and I turned it up real loud and started playing, and I wrote it just that night. Just got into it. Jotted it down on a piece of paper.

"I try not to think about the songs that I write, I just try to write them. And I try not to edit them, because I think editing is a form of, ah . . . I know there's a source where music comes through you and words come through you, and editing is really, uh, something you do to something that you've thought about. If you think about it and you try to put it down, then you can edit it. If you're not thinking about it, you just open up and let it come through you, then editing it is . . . you're really taking a lot of, what's the word, ah, a lotta liberties by editing."

But if it's yours, aren't you allowed to edit it?

"Well that's the thing, I'm not sure that everything I write is mine. That's the difference. I think some of the things I write are mine, but I think some of it just comes through me. My mind is working behind the scenes and puts these things together without me consciously thinking of it, and then when the time is right it all comes out. That's more like, y'know, creation in the true sense of the word than it is a contrivance.

"So it doesn't really need to be edited so long as you get it out right, get it out clean y'know, without second-guessing yourself every line thinking 'what are people gonna think of me if I write this?' That's something I try to stay away from. I try not to worry about what people are gonna think about it till after I've recorded it and it's too late to change it. Then I'll start worrying about it. But then it's too late for me to fuck it up, so . . ."

Do you have to be in a certain mood to write?

"Yeah, it just kinda comes and goes. Sometimes I write first thing in the mornings. There's no rules. A lotta times I write driving vehicles, or moving in vehicles, with no instruments, and I'll write the whole song and remember it all and know exactly what the music is before I even pick up an instrument. The whole thing, it just falls into place."

Do you ever dry up?

"Yeah. That happens. I just wait. I don't try to think of something cool to write. Because sometimes I won't have a record out for a long time, and then I'll have two or three out really fast. The time between *Everybody's Rockin'* and *Old Ways* was a longer period of time than Buffalo Springfield or CSNY was together. I still wrote a lotta songs in that period, I wrote two and a half or three albums' worth of material, so really I have a lot of stuff in the can that's been recorded, and a few songs that haven't been recorded."

THE Neil Young roadshow seems to cut across several generations. The shows I saw in Rochester and Troy were both in arenas in front of some 8,000 people, a lot of them college students. "I just accepted this is what I'm doing now, I'm not 25, I'm not jumping around just doing rock 'n' roll, this is me, so I shouldn't try to be something I'm not. And once I accepted that in myself everything was all right. But it is hard sometimes to see a young crowd and to go out there and remember that I played in front of crowds that age when I was that age, and what I was like, and not try to be that way."

Doesn't it feel strange, singing songs like "Once An Angel" and talking about your family to a bunch of kids?

"If they can get something from that then fine, and last night they seemed to," said Young the day after the Rochester show. "Even though they're young, most of 'em are only a couple of years away from being married or having a meaningful relationship, and a lot of them are married. There's a lot more older people at the back that aren't running up to the front, so it's there for all of them. A lot of them come because to them it's history—they're seeing things they've only heard about."

The sets contain material from every phase of Young's career, though he's whittled down the demented electric side of his music. His main chance to stretch out on guitar is in "Down By The River," where he attacks his familiar black Gibson as Joe Allen modifies the long-familiar bassline slightly. Rufus Thibodeaux, the Cajun fiddler from Louisiana who's built like Mount Rushmore, perches himself immovably stage left, jigging massively in time to Young's twisted soloing—though it's noticeable that Young's playing is more organized and better sculptured than it might have been in a show with Crazy Horse. Young's even written a punchy new song about his band, called "Grey Riders."

The sets open with an old song, "Country Home." There are several tunes from *Old Ways*, plus "Looking For A Love," "Helpless," and a beautifully loping "Comes A Time" as reference points. The best reception of the night, though, is not for "Heart Of Gold" but for the haunted "Old Man," with the evergreen "Sugar Mountain" running it a close second.

"I do 'Sugar Mountain' really for the people more than I do it for myself," Young explained. "I think I owe it to them, cos it seems to really make them feel happy, so that's why I do that. They pay a lotta money to come and see me and I lay a lotta things on 'em that they've never heard before, and I think I owe it to them to do things they can really identify with. It's such a friendly song, and the older I get and the older my audience gets the more relevant it becomes, especially since they've been singing it for 20 years. It really means a lot to them, so I like to give 'em the chance to enjoy that moment."

He paused for a moment, then the familiar wolfish grin spread across his face. "I had it on the B side of almost every single that I had out for 10 years."

No doubt this careful consideration of the audience's wishes stems from the balance Young has managed to strike in both his personal and professional lives. His wife isn't on the road with him this time as she usually is—she's back at the California ranch looking after the kids, a brother and sister. Young has another son, who suffers from cerebral palsy. This has profoundly influenced his outlook on life.

"I've always felt that God made my son the way he is because he was trying to show me something, so I try to do as much positive as I can for people like that, and for families of kids who are handicapped. I have a lot of compassion for those people and a lot of understanding for them that I didn't have before, and I think it's made me a better person.

"And I think since I have the power to influence so many people, it was only natural that I should be shown so many extremes of life, so I could reflect it somehow. Nothing is perfect y'know, that's it."

PART 2

LOOKING back 10 years or more, Young can now put his well-documented bleak period into a longer perspective. After *Harvest* had clocked up sales running into millions, Young's fans were horrified first by the release of the double album *Journey Through The Past*, a bitty and meaningless "soundtrack" for Young's rarely seen film of the same name.

After the album came out, the film company refused to release the movie, to Young's continuing disgust.

Next came the nerve-shredding live album *Time Fades Away*, a dingy and macabre affair notably devoid of the pure melodies beloved of his soft-rockin' afficionados. Young, feeling boxed in by commercial success, had steered away from it. The chart performance of "Heart Of Gold" had brought him a lot of things he found he didn't want.

"I guess at that point I'd attained a lot of fame and everything that you dream about when you're a teenager. I was still only 23 or 24, and I realized I had a long way to go and this wasn't going to be the most satisfying thing, just sittin' around basking in the glory of having a hit record. It's really a very shallow experience, it's actually a very *empty* experience.

"It's nothing concrete except ego-gratification, which is an extremely unnerving kind of feeling. So I think subconsciously I set out to destroy that and rip it down, before it surrounded me. I could feel a wall building up around me."

To add insult to injury, his next studio recording was the harrowing *Tonight's The Night*, though with a perversity that was becoming typical of him the latter wasn't released until after the subsequently cut *On The Beach*. Both albums stand up strongly to this day. Both use the rock format as a means of redemption and rejuvenation, the very act of recording (no overdubs) serving as therapy.

"*Tonight's The Night* and *On The Beach* were pretty free records," Young pondered, lighting another unfiltered Pall Mall. "I was pretty down I guess at the time, but I just did what I wanted to do, at that time. I think if everybody looks back at their own lives they'll realize that they went through something like that. There's periods of depression, periods of elation, optimism and skepticism, the whole thing is . . . it just keeps coming in waves.

"You go down to the beach and watch the same thing, just imagine every wave is a different set of emotions coming in. Just keep coming. As long as you don't ignore it, it'll still be there. If you start shutting yourself off and not letting yourself live through the things that are coming through you, I think that's when people start getting old really fast, that's when they really age.

"Cos they decide that they're happy to be what they were at a certain time in their lives when they were the happiest, and they say, 'that's where I'm gonna be for the rest of my life'. From that minute on they're dead, y'know, just walking around. I try to avoid that."

One of the key tracks from *On The Beach* was "Revolution Blues," a predatory rocker in which Young adopts the persona of a trigger-happy psychotic, eager to slaughter Laurel Canyon's pampered superstar residents. Reflecting on the song prods Young into some unsettling areas.

"That was based on my experiences with Charlie Manson. I met him a couple of time, and er . . . very interesting person. Obviously he was quite keyed up."

Gulp. Before or . . . after the Sharon Tate killings?

"Before. About six months before. He's quite a writer and a singer, really unique—very unique, and he wanted very badly to get a recording contract. I was at (Beach Boy) Dennis Wilson's house when I met Charlie. Coupla times.

"The thing about Charlie Manson was you'd never hear the same song twice. It was one of the interesting things about him. He had a very mysterious power about him which I'm hesitant to even fuckin' *think* about, it's so strong and it was so dark, so I really don't like to talk about it very much. I don't even know why I brought it up."

Young stopped talking for a moment. Thought we'd lost him, but he continued.

"There is a saying that if you don't look the devil in the eye you're all right, but once you've looked him in the eye you'll never forget him, and there'll always be more devil in you than there was before.

"And it's hard to say, you know. The devil is not a cartoon character, like God is on one side of the page and he's on the other. The devil lives in every one and God lives in everyone. There no book that tells you when the devil said to God 'fuck you' and God said (makes raspberry noise). All those books that are written are just one person's opinion.

"I can't follow that, but I can see these things in other people. You can see it and feel it. But Manson would sing a song and just make it up as he went along, for three or four minutes, and he never would repeat one word, and it all made perfect sense and it shook you up to listen to it. It was so good that it scared you."

A couple of years later, then, Young wrote "Revolution Blues"—"well I'm a barrel of laughs with my carbine on, I keep them hopping till my ammunition's gone" . . . So how did the superstar community take it, Neil?

"Well, see, I wasn't touring at the time, so I didn't really feel the reaction of *On The Beach*. Then when I went out on the road I didn't do any of it, so . . ." He did, however, perform the song on the Crosby, Stills, Nash & Young reunion tour, to the discomfiture of the others.

"David Crosby especially was very uncomfortable, because it was so much the darker side. They all wanted to put out the light, y'know, make people feel good and happy and everything, and that song was like a wart or something on the perfect beast."

WHEN it came to the release of *Tonight's The Night*, Young again incurred the wrath and disbelief of people who thought they knew him fairly well. The album had been recorded with a Crazy Horse reconstituted after the death of songwriter and guitarist Danny Whitten, a close friend of Young's who'd given him early encouragement in his career.

Whitten had been due to go out on tour with Young, but was too heavily dependent on heroin to cope. Young sent him home. The same night, Whitten died of an overdose. *Time Fades Away* documented the subsequent tour, while *Tonight's The Night* was made in memory of Whitten and Bruce Berry, a CSNY roadie who also died from heroin.

Young remembered the day he'd taken *Tonight* into the offices of Reprise, his record company at the time.

"It was pretty rocky," he grinned. "I would describe that as a rocky day. They couldn't believe how sloppy and rough it was, they couldn't believe that I really wanted to put it out.

"I said 'that's it, that's the way it's going out.' It's a very important record, I think, in my general field of things. It still stands up. The original *Tonight's The Night* was much heavier than the one that hit the stands. The original one had only nine songs on it. It was the same takes, but the songs that were missing were 'Lookout Joe' and 'Borrowed Tune', a couple of songs that I added. They fit lyrically but they softened the blow a little bit.

"What happened was the original had only nine songs but it had a lot of talking, a lot of mumbling and talking between the group and me, more disorganized and fucked-up sounding than the songs, but they were intros to the songs. Not counts but little discussions, three- and four-word conversations between songs, and it left it with a very spooky feeling. It was like you didn't know if these guys were still gonna be alive in the morning, the way they were talking. More like a wake than anything else."

Why did you take it off, then?

"It was too strong," said Young slowly. "It was really too strong. I never even played it for the record company like that. We made our own decision not to do that. If they thought *Tonight's The Night* was too much the way it came out—which they did, a lot of people—they're lucky they didn't hear the other one."

It was here that Young hit the lowest patch, spiritually, of his career, probably of his life. His impatience nowadays with the hippy generation, and his endorsement of a right-wing President, believed by many to be a dangerous lunatic, can probably be traced back to the traumas around the time of *Tonight's The Night*. Until then, the ride had been more or less free.

Was it, I queried, a case of Whitten's death being not only a personal tragedy, but a metaphor for a generation and a way of life? Or death?

"It just seemed like it really stood for a lot of what was going on," Young answered. "It was like the freedom of the Sixties and free love and drugs and everything . . . it was the price tag. This is your bill. Friends, young guys dying, kids that didn't even know what they were doing, didn't know what they were fucking around with. It hit me pretty hard, a lot of those things, so at that time. I did sort of exorcise myself."

Did you feel guilty that perhaps you and people in your position had encouraged that?

"Somewhat, yeah, I think so. That's part of the responsibility of freedom. Freedom to do what you want with not much experience to realize the consequences. I didn't feel very guilty, but I felt a little guilty."

IT'S fitting that Young's latest re-emergence in public with yet another shift in musical direction should coincide with a wave of new groups who acknowledge a debt to his past work. Green On Red's Dan Stuart freely admits that their *Gas Food Lodging* LP was heavily influenced by Young's epic *Zuma* collection ("if you're gonna steal, steal from the best," as Stuart puts it). Jason & The Scorchers play "Are You Ready For The Country," The Beat Farmers turn in a welt-raising treatment of "Powderfinger," and Pete Wylie's just cut a version of "The Needle And The Damage Done" as an anti-heroin gesture. And Dream Syndicate's Steve Wynn will reminisce about Young and Crazy Horse any time you like.

With half the material for a follow-up album to *Old Ways* already in the can, Young is in the middle of a renaissance of sorts. Not even the AIDS terror can dent his confidence.

"It is scary. You go to a supermarket and you see a faggot behind the fuckin' cash register, you don't want him to handle your potatoes. It's true! It's paranoid but that's the way it is—even though it's not just gay people, they're taking the rap. There's a lotta religious people, of course, who feel that this is God's work. God's saying, y'know, no more buttfucking or we're gonna getcha." Young cackled dementedly.

"I don't know what it is. It's natural, that's one thing about it. It's a living organism or virus, whatever it is. I hope they find something to stop it. It's worse than the Killer Bees."

Young obviously isn't making a play for the Gay vote. They probably don't hold with that sort of thing in the country. But his conception of the entire universe is, to say the least, unorthodox.

"I'm not into organized religion. I'm into believing in a higher source of creation, realizing that we're all just part of nature and we're all animals. We're very highly evolved and we should be very responsible for what we've learned.

"I even go as far as to think that in the plan of things, the natural plan of things, that the rockets and the satellites, spaceships, that we're creating now are really . . . we're pollinating, as a universe, and it's part of the universe. Earth is a flower and it's pollinating.

"It's starting to send out things, and now we're evolving, they're getting bigger and they're able to go further. And they have to, because we need to spread out now in the universe. I think in 100 years we'll be living on other planets."

On a more earthly plane, Young's excited about the prospect of playing a benefit for the people of Cheyenne, Wyoming, whose houses and land have been devastated by a freak sequence of natural disasters. Young's band and equipment will be airlifted in for the show, by National Guard C130 transport aircraft and by private jets loaned for the occasion by some giant corporations.

"There's something different about it," Young mused, "having the government help us get there so we can help the farmers. The National Guard's gonna help us load and unload, get in and outta the place, help us set up the stage. It's interesting."

But it's something else, above and beyond his this-land-is-your-land preoccupations, that gives Neil Young his lingering aura of menace and strange purpose. You can feel it when you talk to him, and it permeates all his best music. He sees it something like this.

"I've got a few demons, but I manage to coexist with them. The demons are there all the time y'know, that's what makes you crazy, that's what makes me play my guitar the way I play it sometimes. Depends on the balance, how strong the demons are that night, how strong the good is.

"There's always a battle between good and evil in every second in your life, I think. In every judgment you make both sides are represented in your mind. You may hide the bad side, but it's there."

NEIL YOUNG ON

The "Payola Blues"

"It's no secret, and it's part of the mechanism of things. That's how Mr. Big stays Mr. Big. That's why the little guy with the independent label has got to have something GREAT to break through to where the people will say, 'I want to hear that record! I don't care whether they pay you.'"

–from an interview with Bill Flanagan,
Written in My Soul: Rock's Great Songwriters Talk About Creating Their Music, 1986

NEIL YOUNG ON

His Folk Fans During the Rock Numbers

"I can always tell when I'm blowing away some people in the audience: They are standing there and their hair getting gray by the moment and their eyes are slanting back and they are covering their faces and hiding under their chairs when we play."

—from an interview with Dave Fanning, RTE FM 2 (Ireland), June 5, 1987

NEIL YOUNG ON

Drugs

"I'm one of the lucky ones who was able to do that and able to stop. But it wasn't that easy to stop that lifestyle. I had to spend some time. The monster kept coming back every once in a while."

—from an interview with James Henke, *Rolling Stone*, June 2, 1988

BLUE NOTES FOR A RESTLESS LONER

Dave Zimmer | April 22, 1988 | *BAM*

Moving on from country in 1986, Young completed the failed Crazy Horse project *Landing on Water* with studio musicians and insidious 1980s production. Released July 21, it commits the sin of not being so much bad as being dull.

In September, Young hit the road with Crazy Horse for a two-month US tour, Live in a Rusted Out Garage. On stage, the *Landing on Water* songs found some redemption. As with *Rust Never Sleeps*, tour recordings formed the basis for the Crazy Horse-backed *Life*, released June 30, 1987. *Life* was Young's last LP of original material released on Geffen Records.

In support of *Life*, Young and Crazy Horse set out on a late summer 1987 American tour, the fifth consecutive year Young cashed in on the lucrative shed-tour market. He followed this up in November with a 20-date Northern California club tour with the Bluenotes, a new grouping of the usual suspects plus a horn section. The Bluenotes would regroup in April 1988 for another club tour, during which the band's *This Note's for You* was released, marking Young's return to Reprise Records.

Neil talks at length here about the Bluenotes project and its continuity with his earlier work, multiple bandmates and fellow musicians (from Suzanne Vega to Michael Jackson), and the potential for more film work behind and in front of the camera. –Ed.

The Robert De Niro of rock 'n' roll, Neil Young has continually transformed himself throughout his career and inhabited musical characters in much the same manner that De Niro became a brooding taxi driver, menacing Mafioso, and raging prize fighter.

So when Young turned up on Northern California stages last fall in the middle of a ten-piece band dubbed the Bluenotes, he adopted the persona of a bluesman, lurking behind dark glasses and fingering his black Les Paul guitar. Enough people must have felt the sincerity in Young's latest creative turn, because at the recent Bay Area Music Awards the Bluenotes were voted Outstanding Blues/Ethnic Group. And this month, the reactivated Reprise Records released *This Note's For You*, a striking collection of Young-authored blues. Rock's most intriguing chameleon is obviously deep into his new set of colors.

But history tells us Young has never stayed in one place for long. In fact, outside of the Buffalo Springfield records and the *Rust Never Sleeps* and *Live Rust* albums with Crazy Horse, he has never released consecutive LPs that cover common musical ground. It's hard to believe, sometimes, that one individual could ricochet so forcefully between garage rock, gentle folk, roots rock, country roll, new wave, techno-computer music, Nashville country and now the blues. But then how many musicians have created such an enormous volume of work that probably only half (a conservative estimate) has been released to the public?

Living on a secluded ranch in the Santa Cruz Mountains above Redwood City since the early '70s, the Canadian-born Young has always relished his privacy and granted few interviews. He's usually been content to let his music speak for itself, and once referred to journalists as "unnecessary middlemen" between him and his audience. But after returning from lunch one day late last month, I found a message in my box: "Neil Young wants to do an interview tomorrow."

Now every music journalist has at least one artist that occupies a special place a bit apart from the rest, and for me, that artist has always been Neil Young. So you can imagine how I felt when I got picked up at San Francisco International Airport by one of Young's neighbors and was driven deep into the Santa Cruz Mountains. A "closed" sign hung in the front window of the restaurant where we were scheduled to meet. It was a little after two o'clock. "I better give Neil a call," said the neighbor. A couple of minutes later he returned with the news: "Neil still wants to meet here at 3:00. So let's go back to that place up the road and have a couple of beers."

Just a few minutes past 3:00, a vintage, late '50s Cadillac swung wide across the gravel parking lot in front of this deserted restaurant and came to a gradual stop. Neil Young was at the wheel. After extending a hand in greeting, he invited me to climb in. "I bought this yesterday for 800 bucks," he said, admiring the Caddy's rectangular steering wheel and gaudy dashboard. When Young didn't restart the engine, instead settling back into the car's cushy upholstery, it became clear that this was where we were going to talk. And it proved to be a great place to have a long, uninterrupted conversation.

I'm sure you know that some people will look at this Bluenotes project as Neil Young, the rock 'n' roller, just experimenting with the blues, rather than think of you as someone like John Lee Hooker, who's never played anything but the blues.

Right. John Lee Hooker and people like that are . . . blues is their life. And who's to say blues is not going to be my life? But who's to say it is? Music is my life. I just do what I like to do. And I've been searchin' around for a long time, trying everything I can to make me feel good or to try to keep me from getting bored. That's why a lot of times I do different things. And sometimes I do it in styles that people can't understand or they don't want to understand. They don't want to see me like that. But that's the people's hang-up. That's not mine. My thing is: I'm creating a life's work. And the Bluenotes feel really right to me. It's easier for me to sing this music than any other music I've ever sung. It may be I should have been doing this all my life. (Laughs)

Was there something specific that sparked this turn to the blues?

Well, I like music that really makes you feel. And this kind of music . . . it's not rock 'n' roll where you have to come up with a hook and you play the hook over and over again, and you got to have the big beat and you got to have the impressive sound and the cool moves and all that shit. I might try to do that once or twice, in my own way, but I don't want to just do that.

Since I started off playing rock 'n' roll, people tend to think I should continue to play rock 'n' roll, but if they look at my music . . . I've played all kinds of music, all the time, since the very beginning. The changes in style have just become more radical in the last decade. That's all. But they've always been there. From *Everybody Knows This Is Nowhere* (recorded with Crazy Horse in 1969) to *Harvest* (recorded with the Stray Gators in 1971), there's a huge jump there. They're two totally different things. People could make a career out of either one of those things, like Creedence made a career out of their style, all the way. And they did it great. I could have kept doing *Everybody Knows This Is Nowhere* for 10 or 15 years. It would have been cool. Or *Harvest*. I could have been John Denver the Second (smiles). But I couldn't have, really, 'cause I'd have gotten bored. This kind of music—the blues—it doesn't bore me.

You know, I'm 42 years old and what I love about country music, I also love about the blues. That is, an old man can play the blues and an old man can sing country music; but an old man can't really get into rock 'n' roll on the down and dirty, immediate level that it's supposed to be done at. It becomes more of a re-enactment or more of a museum display, rather than the real thing. Blues enables you to still be real and sing about things that are real to you and so does country music.

Which is something you got to the heart of on *Old Ways* in 1985. Then you played some shows with Waylon Jennings.

Yeah. I had a great time doing that. And my original country album, I suppose, was *Harvest*, which if it had been done now . . . If I did (the song) "Harvest" now and "Old Man" and "Heart of Gold" and those things, they would be almost pure country by today's standards. There's also "Comes A Time." I don't know where to draw the line. (Young pauses a minute to pour a bottle of Perrier into a glass filled with ice and cracks, "Sounds like a beer commercial.")

Listening to the song "This Note's For You," I guess the chances of you really doing a beer commercial are pretty slim.

Well, all I'm talking about is me. I'm just talkin' about how I feel and how the Bluenotes are. And that is, we're playing for the people. We're not playing for corporate sponsorship. If we have a huge hit, the next time you see us we're not going to be selling beer, you know? We're just playing for the people that want to listen to us, singing about things that are real to us, not for products.

When did you first try and make this move into the blues?

Back in 1982, I got into an R&B thing for a while, but I couldn't record it, because I was playing with Crazy Horse. That's when I first started to try and do it. I went to the Power Station in New York and recorded with baritone (sax), alto (sax) and trumpet, and Crazy Horse. But the tracks weren't together. The guys in the Horse, I don't know what it was. They hadn't played together in a long time or something, but it wasn't happening. We were banging our heads against the wall. So we aborted the whole thing. And then I lost interest in the songs, because if I try to deliver a song and it doesn't happen, it may be years before I'll try it again. So I had these songs around, but there was no way I could do them. No band I was in could play this material. So the Bluenotes, when we got together, made it possible for me to do all of these old songs. I said, "Now I can do these. They all fit now."

How did you round up the Bluenotes personnel?

(Crazy Horse bassist) Billy Talbot introduced me to four guys from the East LA Horns. Then for baritone sax I got Larry Cragg, who's been my guitar repair, tech and tuning guy for fifteen years. And Ben Keith, who played steel guitar on *Harvest* and has been with me since 1970, plays alto (sax).

I needed a keyboard player and Pancho (Crazy Horse rhythm guitarist Frank Sampedro) had broken his hand. He couldn't play guitar, so he sat in on keyboards. I just love Pancho's musical touch. He plays good keyboards. So I said, "Shit, let's just go out and play." But after the Bluenotes and Crazy Horse got together for a while, it turned out this kind of music was not really suited to them. So they bowed out, but still jam with us once in a while. (Crazy Horse drummer) Ralph (Molina) plays on "One Thing" on the album and Pancho just stayed on keyboards when we got a couple of new guys.

I tried out a lot of different people for bass and drums. For a while we had (bassist) Bruce Palmer and (drummer) Dewey Martin from the Buffalo Springfield. Then I found (drummer) Chad Cromwell. He played with Joe Walsh for a long time and just finished doing an album with Albert King before coming to the Bluenotes. And Ricky "the bass player" Rosas I met at Farm Aid III. I thought he was an excellent bass player and also felt a sense of brotherhood with him. He moved in a way that moved me. There was something about the way he was together with his bass. So that's the Bluenotes as they are now.

Regarding the Bluenotes material, how many of the songs are new and how many of them are old songs that you've just rearranged?

"Sunny Inside" came from 1982. All of the other songs on the album are new. But when the Bluenotes first started out, we had a repertoire of about fourteen songs. About nine or ten of them were older songs that I'd written in the blues vein, some of them dating all the way back to high school. I used to listen to Jimmy Reed then and wrote a lot of songs that sounded like Jimmy Reed when I was at this impressionable age. I used to play them in my high school band. But I forgot 'em. Then one day all the lyrics to 'em came in the mail from the bass player who used to play in my high school band with me. They came with a note that said, "Do you remember any of these songs?" And when I read them, I remembered them. This was about the time the Bluenotes were getting together with Crazy Horse. We did all of these songs around the Bay Area. They were very funky. But the truth is, as great as the (Bay Area) gigs were, if you listen to the tapes, which I did over and over again, because I recorded every show, the rhythm section is so shaky. I kept feeling it come and go. I don't know why and it was funky live and everything, but on record it just wouldn't do it for me. So I decided to do all of it again, at SIR (Studio Instrument Rentals) in Los Angeles, with all new songs I wrote for the new bass player and drummer and the new feel that we were starting to get.

The first song on the Bluenotes album, "Ten Men Workin'," seems to embody this feeling.

Yeah. That's a cool thing, "Ten Men Workin'." I had this groove going through my head and I was playing it on my guitar, which is actually my wife's guitar, which she's had since she was just a little teenybopper, I guess. She took it everywhere with her. And it really feels like her, so I wrote every song on this album, except one, on that guitar. (Young gestures towards the backseat where the guitar is lying.) It's an old Gibson, like a J-45 or something. It just feels so good. I'd be walking around the house playing. (pause) And I had this groove going, didn't have any lyrics, but I don't try and make up words. I figure something'll happen and I'll start singin' the words. Until then, I don't have any words. I never just try and think of something clever.

So the way "Ten Men Workin'" came to me was . . . one morning I was gettin' ready to go into where we recorded the Bluenotes record, on Melrose Avenue across from the Hollywood Cemetery. One of the guys, the engineer of my boat, had a Men At Work T-shirt on. I just kept lookin' at that T-shirt and started thinkin', "Yeah, that's me. I'm workin' and we're workin'." It's like we were building something. We had this job to do. It's like it was our mission to make people feel good and to make 'em dance.

But the Bluenotes is not a real job, the Bluenotes is a way of life and everybody's into it. Everybody in the band is there. They're all part of it.

So I really hope people like this music, because I really enjoy it and it gives me a home in my music where I think I'm going to be able to live for a while, instead of going from door to door all the time.

You've changed styles so frequently, though, and have made use of a lot of different vocal qualities . . .

Well, on these songs here, a lot of them are in the same range. But it's not so much the song as it is the personality of the singer. When I do an album or a project, and it may be several albums long, there's a thing that happens. There's an identity that comes to me that I assume, and it's deep. The content of the songs, and the attitude of the singing all sort of comes to me at once. And that's why the voices are different. When I was in school, I always used to change all of a sudden. This is when I was just in junior high school, and I'd wear the same kind of clothes and everything for like half a year. Then one day I'd be wearing all different clothes and I'd never wear those other clothes again. I'd do a whole different thing. So I don't know what it is. But there's something I don't like about being obviously who I am. For some reason I don't feel safe like that. So I'd rather be . . . I don't know . . . I don't feel disguised, because it's still me and I'm singing. There's just me there.

But on one song, "Stupid Girl" from *Zuma* (released in 1975), it's like there's two of you when you combine two distinctively different voices: one's low, the other's real high . . .

(Laughs) Yeah, that's pretty wild. You notice how that one starts off at one speed and ends up at a whole 'nother speed? You see, you can't do that with the Bluenotes. It doesn't work. I don't know why. But with that song . . . I recorded it with Crazy Horse at 4 o'clock in the morning. We were all messed up and did the track, all the vocals and everything, all in one shot. But when I listened to it with just the low vocal, I said, "That sounds too dark." So I added the high one. I was probably just zonked out of my mind when I did the whole thing. But at that time, all I wanted to do was keep moving, keep going.

I made three albums that year (1975). I had a wonderful record company, Reprise Records, that backed me up, no matter what I did. They never questioned me. They never said, "Neil, you can't do this. You can't do that." They never said, "We'll never release it." The only thing they ever said was, "Are you sure you want to release this? This could be the end of your career." They didn't say, "There's not a hit on this record." They never once would say, "Neil, there's no hit records on this. We can't put it out." I never ran into that at Reprise at all, so I'm so happy to be back. It's so great to be back where I belong, basically. They had a big party for me and even had a big sign up that said, "Welcome back." Then I played this record for them which I'd worked really hard on.

I did this record on my own, in between record companies. And like I said, I recorded a whole thing with the first band and then I thought, "This is a great idea and it's almost right. But it's not going to be what I take into Reprise, where they're going to give me all this support and everything." Of course, at the last record company (Geffen), the idea of me playing with a blues band was so stupid to them they didn't want to have anything to do with it, so I was paying for this myself from the start. As a matter of fact, we didn't even ask them, I was so sure they would hate the idea.

But I just kept going and these new songs I was writing just started coming so fast. Every day I'd wake up and write one. We'd record all afternoon at SIR, starting at around 3:00 or 4:00. Then about 7:00 or 8:00 we'd go out and eat, all together. After we'd come back, usually the first thing we'd play would be killer, a one-take thing.

You've always been known for this "first take is the best take" philosophy.

First-take situations are still my favorite things. I never try to drive a song into the ground by doing it over and over again. We don't overdub like a lot of other bands. So it's important to get the buzz. You've got to get the performance. So what happens is, if you don't get it in two or three takes, you stop. Then when you start up again, it's a fresh thing.

I still go for that essence of recording the moment. You know when it's comin'. You can feel it in the room. And quite often this will be a period of time rather than a single take. Let's say we start playing at 7:00, the moment might happen from 7:10 to 7:15. We might have really nailed it at the end of take one and the beginning of take two. So you edit them together and then you have the moment in time where you really captured the feeling of the song. Even though you didn't play it all in a line, it's all from the same period of time. And if I felt something then, people should feel the same way I did or feel something themselves every time they hear that record for the rest of time.

Throughout your career, you've always followed your own course and made musical shifts without warning. Not being in a permanent band situation, you didn't have to ask someone else if they were into a particular shift, you just did it.

Right. And if the people didn't fit, I just got different people. But I've been lucky enough to have people play with me, a *few* people, like Pancho and Ben Keith, who can play many different kinds of music with me.

Now if you look back, this blues thing is really not that new at all for me. Listen to "Tonight's The Night." If the Bluenotes do "Tonight's The Night," it'll be over. I don't know if I will do that song, but if I ever felt like it, it would be a really great thing. There's a heavy blues influence playing on that whole (*Tonight's the Night*) record. *Everybody's Rockin'* had a lot of blues in it, too.

And your guitar playing, particularly your electric lead work, has always had a bit of a blues edge to it.

Yeah. I like to play with a little blues edge on my guitar all the time. But now it's just that. There's nothing else there. You know my favorite guitar players have always been blues players. I think Hendrix was a blues player. He just had an unbelievably unique sound. Of course, it was psychedelic as well, 'cause he was so high, but based in the blues, for sure. Hendrix has always been one of my favorites, and B.B. King, Lonnie Mack, Hound Dog Taylor, Jimmy Reed. Actually it was Jimmy Reed's harmonica playing that was really super good.

There are a lot of blues singers I like . . . Bobby Blue Bland, Howlin' Wolf. I mean, what a great voice and great rhythms and great things happening. Mike Bloomfield, Paul Butterfield . . . There are just so many great people I've heard and known and been around in my life. It's just rubbed off on me, and I guess now it's just coming out.

It's not like I'm trying to sound like a blues guitar player. I'm just playing my guitar and singing songs about life. And I've never heard anything that moves me like this. It's just there. And the guys I'm playing with now . . . I feel like I'm surrounded by the best.

Taking a look at all of the musicians you've played with over your career, what is it about them that attracts you? Is there a common quality shared by players like the guys in Crazy Horse and Ben Keith?

Well, there's a quality of realness to Ben. Whatever he plays, he sounds like he's really doing it. Whereas, some other musicians that I might play with, as great as they may be, are only emulating what they're doing. It may not be a natural thing to them, to go from one kind of music to another. So it doesn't sound sincere. It sounds like a school boy playing what he heard on the radio, not understanding where it's coming from, but knowing how to play the notes.

So I try to get the best out of the people I know and not let them do things that I think they can't do well. Then I take the responsibility for telling them and live with the fact that they may feel rejected. That's part of my job.

And in many cases, I come back to people. Crazy Horse may play again. Just because I'm not playing with them now doesn't mean that Crazy Horse is not great. I think Crazy Horse is a great garage-type rock 'n' roll band. There's always some kinds of music that I can never play better than I can with Crazy Horse. It's just . . . is my head into doing it? Right now it isn't. I did it for two years and it was great. We had a fantastic time and then it started to feel like a job. We did one tour, then another tour. We pushed it. There wasn't anything more we could do.

But I like to keep playing and my energy's getting stronger instead of weaker. I'm physically much stronger than I've ever been before in my life. And I'm much straighter than I've ever been. It's the other way around with 90 percent of the guys that I know. They're drinking too much or their families are fucked up 'cause they can't handle whatever their abuses are. And they're not practicing and they're not serious. They only play when I call 'em. Those people lose out in the long run. Because I play all the time. And I work out all the time. I keep physically fit. Not because I want to be Superman or anything. But I found that, as I started getting older, parts of my body really started going on me and it was interrupting my music. It was hurting. My hands were hurting. My arm was throbbing. Stuff like that. So I had to overcome all of that and get myself together. I'm sure some of my physical problems were residuals from early polio that I had when I was a kid. So by working out I overcame the need for chiropractors and all that shit. You just build up until you're so strong that you stay strong, all the time. That's helped my music immensely. It's also made it tough on the people I work with, because I'm a maniac. When I start working out, I think everybody should do it. Which is really a bad thing. Anybody who's been to AA can tell you that. You're not supposed to preach when you find something good. But I didn't go to AA. I don't have a drinking problem, so I preach: Physical fitness is life itself. I push that down everybody's throat, that you should be on top of it. Be great or be gone, you know? If you're going to overdub being great later, you've lost my interest. Anybody who says they're going to overdub their part later, I say, "Well, what are you doing here now? Why don't you just go home and come back later? I mean, what's the deal? Why don't you just phone it in?" Because I'm not into that. I want to do it now. I want people to come and work with me and BANG! be there.

I don't know if this is a project you want to talk about now, but I understand you've been doing some recording with Crosby, Stills & Nash.

(Pause) Well, I'm doing the Crosby, Stills, Nash & Young album. And we're about halfway finished with the recording process. Five songs are basically done. They just need to be mixed. We started off with Stills and I recording together for two weeks. Then David and Graham came up, and we've worked now for two weeks with them. And, during that period, we've got five complete records, which is a good thing.

Sounds like it's more productive than previous CSNY recording attempts.

Yeah. It's very productive and it's been very good. I think that the music really sounds magnificent. I think that the harmonies and everything are as electric as . . . they're more electric than they ever were before. There's more happening . . .

Now that David's in good shape . . .

Saying David is in good shape is pushing it. David's not strung out. He's not addicted to drugs and is very alive. Emotionally, he's living life to the fullest. He's going through every little thing that happens, and feeling everything, to great extremes, after having not felt anything for ten years. So, he's very much alive and I really love him for being strong enough to do what he's done. But the job's not over yet.

Looking at CSNY as an entity now, how is it different from when you were with the band in '69 and '70.

The difference now is . . . it's more CSNY than it ever was. I was just sort of an add-on before. Now I'm the driving force in the band. And basically, that says it. But I don't think we've reached our true potential yet.

Several years ago, you commented that CSN had become like the Beach Boys, that the band was just stuck in a groove and wasn't progressing.

Well, that's true. But now they've got new songs. Graham is writing some great songs, David has some great ones, and Stephen also has some great songs. The energy is . . . in the studio it's really great. Live? I don't know what it would be like. If CSNY was to go on the road today, it would be an inconsistent high. It wouldn't be a consistently great thing every night. So I'm hoping that, given time, it will reach a place where everyone can fully give everything that they have, that the band will reach its potential and truly live up to what people expect of us. That'll be when I go on the road with them.

This CSNY potential you speak of, wasn't that reached the first time around back in 1969?

On stage, but not on records. Except maybe on "Ohio" and maybe "Almost Cut My Hair" and a few things like that, where I felt like I was truly part of the band. But of all of the *Deja Vu* stuff, I only played on four songs. I wasn't even on "Teach Your Children." I wasn't even on, what's the other one? "Carry On." There are several songs that I wasn't on, where I wasn't even there. So *Deja Vu* was like CSN with me added on, me singing a couple of my songs with them singing with me. But that's not CSNY.

There's never really been a CSNY studio album. What we're doing now is more a CSNY studio album than anything that has ever happened. And I really believe that it's a great record. I don't know how long it's going to take to finish, but we're dedicated to finishing it.

CSNY is a different thing from CSN. CSN will probably be on the road this summer. And I'll be out with the Bluenotes. But I'm dedicated to doing this (CSNY) record, then some day in the future doing a tour with CSNY when it is capable of being strong and consistently aware and on top of it. That'll take work.

I know you want to avoid having CSNY go out just as a nostalgia act.

Well, it always will be that. There's no way around it. But if nostalgia is what people want, there's a healthy nostalgia and an unhealthy nostalgia. The worst kind of nostalgia is when musicians stand up there and are a shadow of their former selves. And all of the people that loved them so much start to think that they are only a shadow of their former selves. And the whole audience goes home with this feeling like their life is over, as if they're just sort of marking time until they die, like those guys they just saw on stage. I don't want to do that to people. I mean, people believe in CSNY. When they see CSNY, even if it is a nostalgia trip, I want them to believe that their life is worth living, and that the rest of their life is going to be better than the first part. I want people to feel an energy from the band that makes you feel great and makes you feel like these guys really believe and are strong and are alive and value their lives and their bodies and the way they are and everything. Not that we're capable of actually transferring energy, but people will see the good things in themselves and get strength from themselves out of seeing how strong we are and how sharp we are, and how we are still creating, and how everybody is still a hundred percent and everything is there. But if we were to go out now and it wasn't happening and the audience could see, "Hey, the sparks aren't flying tonight. The guys look a little sleepy. I wonder what they did this afternoon to be like this tonight? Wow, did you see that?" I don't want any part of that kind of show and I will not be part of it.

I remember being in the crowd at the Oakland Coliseum in 1974. When CSNY played "Don't Be Denied" and "Pushed It Over the End," there was definitely some kind of energy there. You could feel it.

There were good moments on that tour. There really were. That was before Crosby was fucked up and everybody else in the band was very strong. I mean, the band wasn't really a hundred percent clean, but they were still young enough so that whatever they may have been doing wrong wasn't screwing them up so much that the initial feeling was gone. You see, when you reach a certain age, you have to stop doing abusive things to yourself or you really are only a shadow of your former self, just turning pages in a book, hoping that there won't be any new words on them. But at some point the body gives out and can't continue at the same level unless you step back and rebuild and stop doing all the things that hurt you, so that you can continue to create and rise higher, not just tread water. That's my whole thing now. I'm really dedicated to that awareness of living.

I know you've also been diverting some of this energy into the film world. Last year, you were in Alan Rudolph's *Made In Heaven*, now you're in *'68*. And then there were your own films, *Journey Through the Past*, *Rust Never Sleeps*, and *Human Highway*. How do you view this part of your career now?

It's an interesting avenue. I've been approached to be in some other films, and there are a couple of parts that I would like to do that are not the parts that I was approached to do. I made my feelings known, as to what I want to do and we'll see how things go. I'm at a point now where I don't want to be typecast as a certain type of guy—like the guy I was in *'68*. A lot of people wanted me to be that guy again in other movies, 'cause I guess I was effective. But that's just one guy. There are many other people that I want to be and project.

That philosophical truck driver you played in *Made In Heaven* seemed like a pretty unusual character, one that people might not have expected you to play.

(Smiles) Oh yeah, that was quite a guy, that guy. He was on. Yeah, I liked him a lot. I wished he'd been in the movie more. He had a lot on his mind, that guy. (Laughs) I enjoyed doing that part a lot. And Alan Rudolph is a great director. He's truly a great director. I hope I get to work with him again. You know the studio really screwed that movie up. That movie could have been an incredible work of art and they took it away from him (Rudolph) and re-cut it into what it came out as, which was a shadow of its original form. If you saw *Trouble In Mind*, a great Rudolph film, and imagined that the same energy that was in that could have been in *Made In Heaven*, you would see what I'm talking about.

Still, in its released state, the film has moments, particularly the way your song "We've Never Danced" is used. How did it feel to have Martha Davis singing that?

Well, I was originally supposed do it. But once again my old record company (Geffen) was standing in the way of that happening. It's just another one of those things. There's really no sense in dwelling on it.

All right. But as for some of your other music in the film. "I Am A Child" was the perfect soundtrack for this childhood sequence.

Well that's Alan Rudolph. And Tim Hutton, to a great extent, wanted certain songs. Tim's very sensitive to that kind of thing. I hope I get a chance to do more things with those people.

Do you have any desire to do soundtracks or write specific songs for films?

I don't like doing that. That's not my thing. I don't like the soundtrack business. I think it's a bunch o' shit. They get some song and somebody walks by a store and you hear the song come out of the store. They just dub the damn thing in there to sell a soundtrack album! So you know, I don't want my songs in there. I don't want my songs used like that and then put on an album with a bunch of schlock that I don't even like. I don't dig it. What would I be doing it for? Money? That must be the only reason I'd do it for. Hopefully, I won't ever need to do that.

Regarding a couple of your own films: why have *Journey Through the Past* and *Human Highway* never been released on video cassette?

Well, I think that they both will be released on videocassette this year.

Switching gears a bit here, how does it make you feel when a whole crop of new bands come along who were obviously influenced by your early work, particularly in the Buffalo Springfield?

Well, I don't listen that much, so I'm not aware of it. OK? And even back then, when the Buffalo Springfield was happening, I didn't listen very much. We listened to the Beatles, then ultimately ended up listening to the Rolling Stones instead. The Rolling Stones . . . they have put out a great body of work. They are, by far, the most interesting, to me, of any of the contemporary rock 'n' roll bands that came along. At first we were flashed by The Beatles. I thought they were dynamite and I still think so. But the more perspective I get on the whole thing, the Stones were really the ones that blew my mind.

Stills once told me you guys tried to get a Stones-like sound happening. But it was never quite there on record.

No, it never was. But it was there live. Some of those shows . . .

Like the ones at the Whisky in '67?

(Smiles) Yeah, they were great . . . We were happening.

You were saying earlier about how, in order to really play at that kind of down and dirty level of rock 'n' roll, you need to be young . . .

Age has nothing to do with years. I mean, there are guys that are younger than I am who can hardly walk who should be able to beat me. So rather than age, it's the kind of life that people live and how much real energy is there, when it comes right down to it. An hour and a half into the show, is the guy faking it? Is he running out of breath? Or is able to rise and get even stronger at that point? That's the difference. And it all comes down to what kind of a life you live. You can't have it both ways. So it is possible to play rock 'n' roll indefinitely, as long as you care for yourself. But the energy and the desire also has to be there, otherwise you're just kidding yourself and cheating the people who listen to you.

What kind of music do you listen to these days?

Let's see, what do I listen to now? (Pause) You know I hear all this music on the radio when I go to the gym, and they're playing these radio stations. God, I can't believe the stuff (laughs). It's contemporary music, but I think it's very . . . (Pause) I love Bruce Spring-streen . . . Springsteen! (Laughs) I'll get his name right one of these days. I'm sure I'll pick up on it. But one of my favorite songs is "Dancing In the Dark." I think that's just a great, great record. I think the energy is unbelievable. It's hard to believe that he is what . . . 37 or 38 years old? You listen to that record and there's not one ounce of fatigue in that record.

It's just a beautiful feeling, a beautiful record. And I like that girl, she had a record out last year. I think she's from New York. She sang on the Grammys.

Suzanne Vega?

Yeah, her. I think she's good. I think she's made some nice records. And I like the sincerity that comes across, although she was terrible on the Grammys (pause) but I'm not a Grammy kinda guy. I thought Michael Jackson was the best thing on the Grammys. He was fantastic! He was arms and legs above the whole . . . I mean, he is what everybody else was trying to emulate at that thing. He is it. OK? Michael Jackson is pizzazz and on fire. My only thing is . . . how long can a guy burn that brightly before he explodes? I mean this guy is really out there. And he is an incredibly creative force in the world of music and dancing and everything. The guy's a genius. They can say what they want about him, but he's burning a line across the sky forever, that guy. There's never gonna be another Michael Jackson.

I watched the Grammys. I wanted to see what was going on and everything. But to me . . . it's like watching a foreign country or something. It's a different thing. It's not what my music's about. (Pause) It's not me. People ask me, "Do you ever think you'll ever win a Grammy or a lifetime achievement Grammy or something?" (Laughs) I don't know. It was an honor to win a Bammy, even though I wasn't there to pick it up and nobody from the band was there, because we never thought we'd win. We thought it was nice that they mentioned us, but that's not why we're playing music. It's not in our program.

But back to this Grammys thing . . . It's like the best song this year ("Somewhere Out There") . . . I never even heard it. So how could it be the best song? I mean, what the hell are they talkin' about? What is this? Hollywood? Is it the movies? What are we doing? Is it the Oscars? I can't believe that. And you know the thing that really gets me is that people take it so seriously. It's like, it makes me want to say, "No, I'm not in the music business." I'm in the (quietly) song business. I'm in the business of (quieter still) giving away notes. I don't know. (Laughs) It's funny, I can never really articulate my feelings on that subject.

Well, I'm sure it's not something you think about much living way up here. And I'm curious, why did you decide to settle in Northern California?

(Pause) I like where I live because it's away from everything, yet it's still close enough so I can fly around the country and do what I have to do and what I want to do. The air is clean . . . relatively clean . . . not as clean as it used to be. And I love the natural things, the redwood trees and everything. As far as being a citizen of San Francisco, I'm no more a citizen of San Francisco than I am a citizen of LA or New York. But as far as being out in the country and liking where I live and where I'm bringing up my family and everything, it's great.

Being so remote does have its drawbacks, though. I'm sure that my little girl might not be so shy if it wasn't for the fact we live way out in the country. We were noticing today at the Easter egg hunt she was too shy to go out and hunt for eggs with the other kids. She just stood there. My wife said, "Well, we live so far away from everybody, she doesn't see enough kids." I told her, "Well I was always shy. I never would do things like that. I never took part in anything. If there was some group thing, I always just sort of stood and watched." So I see my little girl doing that and I don't know if it's because of me or because we live out in the country. But I love it out here. I have to stay away. There's something inside me that makes me not want to get involved, that makes me want to stay removed from everything, except for the people that I really love and that are very close to me—my family and close friends.

The distraction of other people's work and having other people being around and coming in and commenting on what's going on and hanging on is not . . . I like to walk out of the studio and look at the sky, count the stars, then go home. I don't want to walk out of the studio, then hear Tears For Wham down the hall, you know? I don't want to hear it. I'd rather go out and look at the moon.

I've heard that whenever there's a full moon, you like to record.

(Smiles) That's when the best stuff happens, as far as I'm concerned. Not always. Every rule is made to be broken, but when I record . . . I'm always conscious of the moon. If I start a project, if I can, I'll start it about three days before the full moon, then let it go until a day or two afterwards. Then there's always a bottoming out period that happens right after that. So if I'm going to record for four or five days with some people, I'm going to put it together during that time of the month every time. Because I feel something's happening.

And to tell you the truth, when I walk outside I like to see the moon. It's gotten to be a friend of mine over the years, so I like to see all of it. Of course, I'm not saying everybody should shut down and forget it unless the moon's full, but I'm going for moments in time, captured on record. So for me, these things are important.

What else is important to you now?

My family's important. Instead of the social part of things, I've chosen to spend the time with my family and now I'm trying more and more to work at home. The Bluenotes record was recorded in Los Angeles, but it was done in ten-day spurts. I'd be gone ten days, then come back. I don't like to be gone a lot, but if I stay home all the time, I'll never be creative. There's no way I can be creative just holed up in my studio. Then it's just like being holed up in the city. You have to keep moving and keep moving around. But I try to balance it out and keep as much of my family in there as I can and still not lose the creative edge that I'm trying to keep.

NEIL YOUNG ON

His Mutton Chops

"I don't know—hey, I don't know. Elvis, maybe. When I was a kid, I don't know exactly how old, I collected the Elvis cards that came in the Elvis chewing gum packages. It cost five cents and for those five cents, you had the chewing gum and five Elvis cards with a photo of Elvis on one side and 'questions to Elvis,' asked by fans, on the other. Elvis answered two lines below, see. Like, for example, (silly American boy voice): 'Eh, say, Elvis, why are you wearing pork chops?' And Elvis on the same card would reply (big Elvis voice): 'Well, kid, I wear 'em cause I like 'em. I wear them because I find them classy, yeah.' And I'm afraid I wear them for that reason too. Like Elvis. Hey, I don't know."

—from an interview with Laurent Chalumeau, *Rock & Folk*, September 1988

NEIL YOUNG ON

The Age of His Audience

"Couldn't give a flying one. I'm not George Michael. I'm an old jerk. I am beyond that. Teens can listen to my records if they want. Why not? It's sincere music, it's tried and true music, it's music that transcends age groups. But if they consider that at their age it is more fun to listen to George Michael, fine."

—from an interview with Laurent Chalumeau, *Rock & Folk*, September 1988

PRESS CONFERENCE

December 9, 1989 | Amsterdam

Late summer 1988 saw a Bluenotes shed tour of North America, followed by a brief tour as Ten Men Workin' after Harold Melvin threatened legal action over the Bluenotes name. Unfortunately, no legal action halted the November 1 release of CSNY's *American Dream*, the nadir of Young's recording career.

After some early 1989 shows backed by old friends Frank Sampedro and Ben Keith with relative newcomers drummer Chad Cromwell and bassist Rick Rosas, Young spent summer 1989 on an extensive acoustic tour of the United States prior to the October 2 release of *Freedom*. His first US Gold album since 1979's *Rust Never Sleeps*, the album marked his return to critical and commercial acclaim, a celebrity-worthy plateau he would remain on through his mid-'90s work with Pearl Jam.

Freedom's release was sandwiched between the real-life "freedom" events of June 4's Tiananmen Square Massacre and the November 9 fall of the Berlin Wall. While predictably refusing to explain the album and its themes, an understanding of what "freedom" means for Young develops in his responses to questions that reference his children and earlier support for American conservativism.

Also notable in this press conference, which took place in Amsterdam during a five-country, seven-date European acoustic tour, is Neil's reluctance to think of himself as "working in a library," although he is both nonchalant and quite concerned with accurate descriptions of his past work. To this end he offers a detailed chronology of the *Old Ways* LP(s), disputes a reporter's assertion about the debut of "Like a Hurricane," and lays out his plans for a career-spanning collection that would arrive "next year," the 180-track *Two and a Half Decades*. . . . –Ed.

Elliot Roberts: We'll see you all in thirty-five minutes to the second.

Neil Young: OK, Elliot.

Reporter: None of us has done this before in such a big crowd. We always do one-to-one interviews.

Young: Oh, yeah. I'm sorry that I don't have all the time.

Reporter: It's supposed to be informal anyways, so I guess—

Young: I guess it's OK.

Reporter: Uh-huh. Well, we're very glad to have you here for concerts anyway. Are you doing solo shows by your own choice?

Young: Oh, yeah.

Reporter: Uh-huh. But I understand you are bringing some musicians.

Young: I got a couple of friends with me that I play with. They come out and do a few songs.

Reporter: And it's mainly acoustical?

Young: Yeah.

Reporter: Why do you choose to do an acoustical tour when you just released an electric-orientated album?

Young: Well, I don't know. [*Laughter.*] It was just what I felt like doing. Solo I can do anything I want. I haven't played solo and I feel like if I play solo I get closer to myself, closer to the guitar and the singing, and I haven't done that in a while. You have to do that every once in a while to get back to what makes it all happen. So I'm doing this for myself. I did it all summer and this is the last of it and it's been getting better from the beginning. When I started it, it wasn't, it was in the middle of the summer somewhere, in New York somewhere, so, when I started, it was OK, but I wasn't good. So I just kept working at it. To stay in touch with myself.

Reporter: Did you actually start out as an acoustic folk singer?

Young: Ah, hmmm. Well, it always went back and forth. I think, first time I sang in public, I was with a band.

Reporter: Yeah.

Young: Now I sang with a band, and then I started singing by myself and then I went back to the band. And ever since then, it's just—

Reporter: What do you prefer?

Young: It's all the same. It is.

Reporter: But, for instance, what happened to the Bluenotes? It started out as an idea for a film and then you formed a band to perform in the film.

Young: Um-hmm. And then the money for the film never came through. I thought it was gonna come through but it didn't. So we didn't do it.

Reporter: When you finished the Bluenotes record, you said that from now on you would stick to that kind of music and you said—

Young: You ain't gonna believe that, are you? [*Laughter.*]

Reporter: But you said the same thing after the *Old Ways* album.

Young: And the same thing after the—

Reporter: Why do you say that and then afterwards change your mind?

Young: Well, I didn't expect anyone to believe me. [*Laughter.*] But, I don't know. I get into each thing I do to the point where nothing else matters. I guess I'm an extremist. So I get into it and then I get out of it. And when it's finished, it's finished.

Reporter: But why do you always switch from one extreme to another extreme?

Young: That's not really true. I haven't really done that.

Reporter: Well, after you made—

Young: The Bluenotes record is not extreme, too extreme, it's one kind of music, but it's just focused on one kind of music. That kind of music is in *Freedom*. It's there. The feeling is there from the Bluenotes. On "Crime in the City" you can feel it. It's evolved. But it's not in its pure form. But nothing is really in its pure form on *Freedom* except for the very simple guitar things. It's a blend of different kinds of music.

Reporter: But in the early ’80s, you switched from one style to another. First you did a rockabilly then a synthesizer album and—

Young: I know.

Reporter: That’s hard to figure out for an audience, I guess.

Young: That’s OK.

Reporter: Yeah, I agree.

Young: That’s OK. ’Cause at the end of the ’90s, then, I’ll look at that period of time and it will make perfect sense. But right now it’s just starting to make a little bit of sense. But, while it was happening, I know, people thought I was crazy, but I don’t care. I was having fun. I was doing what I wanted to do. I don’t try to do the right thing.

Reporter: But you also said about those records that they weren’t really Neil Young records. What did you mean by that?

Young: Well, the difference is this record, *Freedom*, and go back to *Rust Never Sleeps*—there’s a period between those two things. That, where everything is a step away. Where you don’t—there’s a wall there. Nothing comes out. To a certain point everything’s fine and then you get to the door, the door is closed. So, that’s the way it was. So I’m still here.

Reporter: If you say you had fun doing things, does that apply, too, for your reunion with Crosby, Stills & Nash?

Young: That was, that was fun, yeah. But it was not as good as I hoped it would’ve been. Although we tried very hard to do a good job, to do a good record, but maybe we were trying too hard or something. I don’t know.

Reporter: But you always said, I think, that you never wanted a reunion unless everybody had shaped up and was clean. So, I suppose that . . .

Young: Crosby’s fine.

Reporter: Yeah, well, we’ve all read the book.

Young: Yeah, I read the book, too.

Reporter: You once said that you could take three of your albums and put them together and like, *Harvest*, *Comes a Time*, and *Old Ways*—

Young: *Old Ways*, uh-hmm.

Reporter: *Time Fades Away*, *Tonight's the Night*, and *On the Beach*. Would it be possible to link *Everybody Knows This Is Nowhere* and *Rust*, and the latest album, *Freedom*, together?

Young: *Freedom*?

Reporter: Made in '69, '79, '89.

Young: I don't know. I don't know.

Reporter: [*Inaudible.*]

Young: I guess you could. Crazy Horse isn't on this one. But that type of expression is there.

Reporter: Seems like you tend to work up a decade of material and then make a statement record and then start going elsewhere again.

Young: Oh, yeah, well, sometimes, I guess it looks like that, but it's not really—

Reporter: Don't plan things out.

Young: If I planned things out like that I'd be working in a library trying to keep track. No, I'm not in control. I just do what I want to do. It's just like anybody.

Reporter: I know one song from the album, "Too Far Gone," from way back. Are there more songs, older songs?

Young: "Ways of Love." "Ways of Love" is an old song.

Reporter: Yeah. So you do have a library of stuff you can take.

Young: Yes. I'm putting it out next year. I think it's *Two and a Half Decades*. And there's a list of songs for the record that I'm working on. There's 180 songs and there's 60 unreleased songs and 15 more unreleased versions of released songs. So there's a lot of unreleased material. There's three complete albums unreleased. That are in there. And an unreleased EP, and so I'm organizing this. It's gonna be a multiple-CD package, and the CDs won't all be full. CDs—some of them will be short, some of them will be long. But everything's separated into chronological time so that, it's a different way of seeing my music, with a lot of things that you didn't see before because I didn't put them out.

Reporter: Yeah, talking about *Human Highway* and *Homegrown*, albums like that.

Young: *Homegrown, Homegrown*—what's the other one?

Reporter: *Human Highway*?

Young: *Old Ways. Old Ways I.* 'Cause there was *Old Ways I* and then there was *Old Ways II.*

Reporter: Right.

Young: And then there's all of the songs done between there. So there's twenty-four unreleased tracks right there, done for *Old Ways I* and then *Old Ways II*, then I record, somehow I had twenty-some odd tracks left from that.

Reporter: Is there a difference between those two *Old Ways* albums?

Young: Oh, yeah.

Reporter: In style?

Reporter: I should hope so.

Young: No, it's different. All three. There's actually three different things going on. One of them was very funky, kind of, a very funky one, recorded at Gilley's, Gilley's Club in Texas, in the barn where they have the rodeo and you record up on top, above the chute where the animals come out. And they ride around and lasso them. Up on top of that there's a place where usually the announcer is and dignitaries, people, and big guys with hats on. So, we played up there, set up up there, and we recorded up there, and we got three or four songs that night that were very good from that show, and then many other sessions around that time were very funky. Much harder sounding than *Old Ways. Old Ways*, that came out like a Nashville studio album and neither of the other ones were like that. The first one was more like *Harvest.* It was clean and it was all the same thing. Nine songs all done in the same period of time, three days with the same singers, but only three or four of those songs showed up in different versions on the *Old Ways* that came out. So, it's different.

The one I liked the best was the first one, but they wouldn't put that out. They sued me when I gave them that. [*Laughter.*] So, then I made the funky one, which I paid for myself, because, no record company, and I keep all those tapes for myself and those are the roughest ones, the funkiest sound, the best. Then there's the worst, which was the last one that I did. Which is still very good, I think. But it's, unfortunately, since I was sued for doing this music, I wouldn't stop doing this music. If they hadn't sued me I would have been able to move on, but they put me in a corner telling what to do so I just stayed right there and did it over and over again until they stopped suing me. Then when they stopped, I immediately changed to something else. So you might say the last part is, I may have been there a little too long or something. But it did go through an evolution to get to this studio kind of thing with the studio players and the Nashville sound and it started off completely different and then got really funky and then what happened on the record.

Reporter: Would you say that you're in rock 'n' roll for your own entertainment?

Young: Oh, yeah. Why else would I be here? I couldn't do it this long if it wasn't just for—

Reporter: Do you have a title for the collection you're releasing? Won't be *Twenty-Five Years or So*?

Young: No. *Tricade.* [*Laughter.*] *Tricade 2.5.*

Reporter: Yeah, *Sea of Madness.*

Young: Yeah, that's another one. I already had that on the list. That's right. People keep mentioning songs and I—

Reporter: "Soldier"?

Young: I thought of . . . No, that's on, because that's on *Decade. Decade* comes out again, this time with different songs. Most of the same songs, but added songs. There's one song called "Bad Fog of Loneliness" from the same session of *Harvest*—"Heart of Gold" and "Old Man" and "Bad Fog of Loneliness"—so three cut that day. They all had the same sound, so I picked the two and left the other one off not because it wasn't as good, but 'cause it has everybody, Linda and James singing on it and everything, but it would be too much of the same thing for that album so I had to take one off. So now I'll put that out. That's how I'm doing it.

Reporter: Do you still have periods when you don't want to touch an electric guitar?

Young: Well, yeah.

Reporter: Why is that?

Young: I don't know. [*Laughter.*]

Reporter: Neil, what's your opinion of not having you wanted this year as a soloist on the tour, at the Werchter festival in Belgium.

Young: What happened?

Reporter: Well, you went solo and then the organizers said leave him off the bill. That's what happened, I guess.

Young: Oh, right. Oh, well.

Reporter: And you were expected since you . . .

Young: He made a huge mistake. [*Laughter.*] I think I'm more aggressive solo than I am with a band. With a band I'm in it, but the solo thing, I'm right out there.

Reporter: It will be an acoustic version of "Like a Hurricane"?

Young: No, I don't try to do things that I can't do, that I can't re-create. I don't try to do that. I'll do other things that I can do better with acoustic.

Reporter: But it takes long for you to release "Like a Hurricane" on official record, so bootleg—

Young: "Like a Hurricane"? Yeah, I released it, didn't I?

Reporter: Yeah, you did, but there were bootlegs three years ahead of *American Stars 'n Bars*, which have the song on it already. It was there for three years until you released it.

Young: Oh, I remember, ah, "Like a Hurricane"?

Reporter: Uh-huh.

Young: I don't think so. No, I don't think so. I don't agree with that. I think you're wrong on that. 'Cause I know what I did. I did *Zuma* before *Stars 'n Bars*. After *Zuma*—I did *Tonight's the Night*, *Zuma*, and *Stars 'n Bars* in one year. And after I did *Zuma*, the record company wanted me to put out *Decade*, which I had been working on, and I got *Decade* finished and I handed it in. On *Decade* I had "Hurricane" for the first time, but I didn't want it to come out on that record; I wanted it with a record that had, that felt like it, that it fit into, not a compilation. So I asked the record company to wait till I made one more record and then put out *Decade*. So I recorded "Like a Hurricane" after *Zuma* and all of the songs that I recorded, if I can remember what's on it. "Will to Love" is on there? And there's a whole side that was cut in my house, on the ranch with Linda Ronstadt and Nicolette Larson. And the other side has got four songs on it and I can't remember what the other three are but they're, there's "Like a Hurricane." So I know those are all from the same seven months. So, you could never have heard "Like a Hurricane" before then because I know when I did that.

Reporter: No, it said in American reviews that while you were on the *Zuma* tour you played it.

Young: Ah, yeah, while I was on the *Zuma* tour?

Reporter: Yeah, you played that song.

Young: Oh, maybe, OK, well *Zuma* came out after *American Stars 'n Bars*?

Reporter: No. [*Laughter.*]

Young: No? Well, now you know that I don't either. [*Laughter.*] Write it all down and send it to me.

Reporter: What about Crazy Horse's working unit? Are they still with you?

Young: They're working. Actually they're gonna come over here, I think.

Reporter: I know, I know.

Young: Pancho's here with me. Billy and Ralph are playing with, they have two other guys playing with them now, which I think is good because now they're playing instead of not playing.

Reporter: Otherwise they would be hanging around waiting for you to take—

Young: Well, probably not. But maybe. But, at any event, I'm just really happy that they're playing. Because you have to keep playing and then when we play together sometimes, then they'll be—you know I play all the time, so if they don't play all the time it gets harder and harder for us to play. So that's very sad.

Reporter: You have been known to support Reagan and conservative causes which a lot of fans have thought you were going a right-winger. And then I think in *Rolling Stone* interview you said you weren't very fond of Bush's perspective. It was before the election. Um, I wonder—

Young: What was that? That I was, that I wasn't—

Reporter: In favor of George Bush being elected. That was before he was elected.

Young: Ah, right.

Reporter: I was wondering why you apparently changed political views or—

Young: Ah, because that's only an apparent thing. I don't have a view. I have an opinion that changes because every day is a different day. I don't have—I'm not a liberal or a conservative. I'm not like that. With Reagan, some things he did were terrible, some things he did were great. Most people tend to take a president and say, you hate, ah, he does one thing that you really don't like, like he builds up massive amounts of warheads or something. So you write him off completely, which I think is completely stupid and I think is very narrow minded. I mean, anyone can have an opinion and be right. You don't want warheads on earth. I agree with that. But, that is a decision that he made to do that and I disagree with that, as many of us disagree with it. On the other hand, there are other things that he did that I agreed with. And because I had the ability to say what I feel, people only write part of it, because it's news that I would agree with Reagan. So they say, "Neil Young supports Reagan." So, fuck 'em. I don't care what they do. I—every day is different. Sometimes I like George Bush, sometimes I don't like George Bush.

Reporter: But, like, in the beginning of your career, I think you were expressing a lot of feelings for your fans which were kind of idealistic, I think.

Young: Right.

Reporter: And what happened to your idealism personally? Like, what would it mean today?

Young: Well, it's still there, but it's just a deeper thing.

Reporter: Referring to title *Freedom.*

Young: Well, idealism, like "Hangin' on a Limb," or, there's different kinds of idealism. Also, in the '60s, I was in my twenties. A teenager's coming into his twenties. It's much more idealistic than a forty-year-old. Wouldn't you agree?

Reporter: Of course, of course.

Reporter: Maybe your ideals change.

Young: Doesn't life experiences dull the naive side of things? So I'm only reflecting how I feel, based on what I know, based on having children, being concerned about the welfare of the children, wondering about, realizing that all children are all our children. You don't think about that when you're twenty years old. So you can be idealistic to a point and then, then when it gets right down to your children being affected you have to start being realistic and balance these two things. Youth is idealism and it's tempered through your life to this other thing that's, how strong your idealism is in the beginning and it gets weaker and weaker as you go on but it fights against realism and that's your life.

Reporter: But what, for instance, would your definition of freedom be?

Young: Oh, that's why I made the record. [*Laughter.*]

Reporter: Yeah, right.

Young: I can't say that. It took me sixty minutes to say it on the record. It's a long record and I had to edit it down a lot to get it sixty minutes. It's the longest record I've ever made and I still haven't said everything that I've wanted to say. I can't say. What freedom is to me, is the ability to make a mistake and try to correct it.

Reporter: You write a lot of personal things, things about your personal life. One thing I kind of miss is things about your children. You don't dedicate a song to them? I guess if I would be able to write songs, I would dedicate some to my children.

Young: Um-huh. I have several songs that I've written for my kids.

Reporter: "Transformer Man"?

Young: Some of them are out. "Transformer Man" is for my son, Ben. As most of *Trans* is for my son. Then there's other songs that I've written for members of my family, which are going to come out on this next record because I never released them.

Reporter: Why not?

Young: I just didn't feel like it. I had to, they're good, but they just didn't fit. That's what I was doing.

Reporter: The fact that you have two handicapped children, how, what was the effect on your musical point of view? Did that change your attitude toward the audience, or in communicating in general?

Young: I think it was, there was a lot of hurt when my, my second child was born and I came to understand what the situation was. At that point I think I might—you know how when something happens that's a heavy thing to you, you tend to either completely accept it, or deny it, or deal with it in a way by ignoring how much it bothers you. Part of me stopped to protect my feelings. You don't want to go around crying all the time or complaining or being sad all the time about things, so at some point you get, you govern that part of yourself so that you can go on with life and communicate with people. So you close the door. Only problem is, when you close that door, there's a lot of other things, all the feelings, behind that door, closed. Not just that one, but anything that deep, gone. You can't open the door or everything comes out. That's it.

Reporter: It took quite a while to cope with that.

Young: Yeah, I think it took, it's taken eleven years and—

Reporter: Why didn't you, um, sorry.

Young: No, go ahead.

Reporter: Why didn't you grow old like most of your colleagues of the '60s? I mean—

Young: I am just old. [*Laughter.*]

Reporter: What he means is you're on a creative peak right now, whereas the Who are still doing old stuff.

Young: Well, I don't know about them. But I loved them with Keith. There's no Who now.

Reporter: But that's a question that's keeping you busy, I think, how to, if you get older and still be creative. I think you once said it in an interview.

Young: Well, yeah. Well, that would be the idea. Another fifteen or twenty years of records. That's what I think should happen if everything goes well. I'd like to do that. I don't know who's gonna buy the records, but I think the record companies keep letting me do it because this company, they like me, they like to have my complete body of work.

Reporter: You once said that the difference between a rhythm-and-blues and country-and-western on one hand and on the other hand rock 'n' roll is that you can play country and blues at an older age without losing your dignity, while when you're performing rock 'n' roll there's a great chance that you lose that dignity as a musician.

Young: Yeah. I think I was wrong. [*Laughter.*] That was the way I felt then.

Reporter: So you agree with Keith Richard. Keith Richard said it's up to people like you to prove that you can grow old and rock out.

Young: I think so, yeah. I agree with him on that. If that's what he said, I definitely agree with that. I think you should just do whatever you wanna do. If you feel like you can do it, then do it.

Reporter: Do you still get inspiration from anger like you used to with "Ohio" and "Southern Man"?

Young: I was thinking "Don't Cry" is pretty angry. Yeah, I get inspired.

Reporter: Do you think an artist has a responsibility to tell people about his views on the world?

Young: No.

Reporter: So why do you?

Young: Just, it's irresponsible of me. [*Laughter.*] No, I don't know. I just do it. I don't think you have to. It's just what I do. It's just me. What I do doesn't have to have anything to do with what artists should do or shouldn't do 'cause I don't think there's any rules. I think the only rules being followed that, there seem to be rules, but it depends, if you wanna be commercially successful, there's rules. And, everybody—you know what the rules are. So many people follow them it's obvious.

Reporter: I'd like to ask you something about your electric guitar playing: When you're playing a solo, how do you perceive a solo? Do you work up to a point to see what happens? Do you think about—

Young: I think it's just—I'm just seeing what happens. It's a chemical reaction. It's not like a calculated thing.

Reporter: Just go up to a point where a solo comes in and then you just let it go.

Young: Just, like an explosion. You put the elements together and "bksssh!" [*Laughter.*] But you don't calculate out, that this is this and pretty soon you get really big and [*hits table*] and twice as big [*hits table*], twice as big—that's calculating. That's how they make computer records.

Reporter: But how can you explode night after night without getting hurt?

Young: That's what, that's what makes you the change kinds of music and the way you play.

Reporter: That's why you're acoustical now.

Young: A sense of survival. Survival. It's a musical survival. I don't want to go out and just try to explode the loudest sound in the world every night.

Reporter: Came close.

Reporter: But you like noise.

Young: Huh?

Reporter: You like noise.

Young: Oh, very much. I live in the middle of noise. Chaotic.

Reporter: Would you like to, if you started now, to do a heavy metal band?

Young: As I look back, the *El Dorado* EP was recorded about twelve months ago, to the day, as we sit here. This is about the time of year last year when I recorded all those songs, which were, five or six of those were very hard. Then we recorded just about a month and a half ago another song that was done, was done in the same studio and the same kind of song. And I really enjoy that. So I'm still doing that and I think that after playing with my acoustic guitar for so long, you build up, you get really good because you hear everything—every mistake, every little nuisance is all there is—you don't hear anything else. So you get very good, but it's not very loud. But you hold off, you don't make it loud, you just stay the way it is, keep doing as much as you can. It's like the chemicals and then you take the electric guitar. It's like the guy who goes out and he swings the heavy bat.

[*The tape cuts here.*]

Young: I think it's good. I like it. I like *The Bridge* album. I'm happy that made it and that some of the money from it's gonna go to the school and that's nice. And I like the songs and the versions.

Reporter: Do you have a favorite?

Young: "Lotta Love" is my favorite one. It's nuts. It's a crazy one.

Reporter: I wouldn't expect that.

[*Laughter.*]

Reporter: So you go for the crazy ones.

Young: Yeah, yeah. I think they all, they sound, that's what impressed me the most, that there's a certain crazy thing that happened. That they picked up in my music that's there and I can see that's what they like about my music, is this ability to get hung up or something. There's some kinkiness to it that they, quirkiness or something.

Reporter: Would you like to have *Bernard Shakey* do a cover on *The Bridge* album?

Young: I don't know.

Reporter: He makes films, doesn't he?

Young: He's a filmmaker. You don't know what he sounds like.

Reporter: It would be interesting.

Young: Those same guys asked me if I wanted to do a song on a tribute to the Grateful Dead album. And I would be playing on this song, one of their songs.

Reporter: I wouldn't know any of their songs.

Young: Well those songs. It's not a song, it's a feeli—it's a whole thing. They'll play for seven hours and it doesn't matter what song it is. [*Laughter.*] It's a thing. It has its place in music.

Reporter: Have you heard any of the Dutch bands who played cover versions of your songs and sent it to the radio stations?

Young: No, Elliot just brought me the tape.

Reporter: OK.

Young: And I never listen to anything, especially while I'm touring. I don't listen much. I find it fascinating that they're doing it and I would like to hear it by accident, but to sit down, and sit down and listen, it takes too much of—there's only so much musical space in life. I like to use mine to my best advantage.

Reporter: *Freedom*, it's got, *Freedom* is being kind of a concept album. Do you agree with that?

Young: It came out that way, but I think it just evolved into what it was. I realized that I wanted, my goals evolved as I was making it, but I didn't have a concept when I started. All the concept was was just to use songs that were mostly new songs that reflected how I felt about what was happening now and that were not in any particular style, that used a lot of different ways of saying things.

Reporter: So it's the words that fit, combine the songs, more than the music?

Young: Well, yeah, but the music also. The music is all different kinds of my music. So that gives it more depth when you listen to it. All the other ones are just focused, the last decade, focused on one thing, another thing, except for *Trans*, which is two things.

Reporter: It seems as if you're more looking to the world around you than to yourself.

Young: Yeah, yeah. Some of it. But there's personal, songs about personal freedom, though, "Hangin' on a Limb," "Ways of Love," "Someday," "Wrecking Ball." So it's not all.

Reporter: Nope, but, for instance, the theme of poverty that's in at least three songs, I think.

Young: Yeah, well that's part of life in the big city, which is what I'm, that's part of freedom.

Reporter: Do you get to see a lot of that, poverty in the big city?

Young: Yeah, you just have to go to the big city and take a look.

Reporter: Not here.

Reporter: Well, it's not like here in Holland.

Young: No, it isn't. And that's good. I don't know how long all these things are gonna last because now the economy here is based on the separation of Europe.

Reporter: Um-huh. And the Americans coming in.

Young: The Americans are here because of the separation of Europe.

Reporter: Is there already a "Sixty to Zero, Part II"?

Young: It was all recorded at once. It was eighteen minutes long and then I edited it down to twelve verses, so the other seven verses are still there. I don't know what I'm gonna do with those.

Reporter: Why don't you play them live?

Young: It doesn't feel right. It's too long on one thing. It's meant to be stand alone and by itself, not to be played with anything else, so if I play the long version in a concert, it's too overpowering. You can imagine listening to something for eighteen minutes. It disturbs the flow. It's too much of the same thing. So I do the short version.

Reporter: The song "On Broadway," was it, especially the lyrics of that song, were they positive to you?

Young: Well, it's the same lyrics that everybody sang.

Reporter: Except, for the crack part.

Young: Well, that's at the end.

Reporter: When you hear the version of the Drifters then your version, the song done by the Drifters sounds more positive than the lyrics are, in fact.

Young: Right. Well the Drifters are, they did the great version of it. I'm, my thing is based on that. You have to know that version to appreciate my version for what it is. My version is like the verse of "Rockin' in the Free World" and their version is the chorus of "Rockin' in the Free World." Theirs is a positive reflection, even though the words are the same.

Reporter: Yeah, well they were more naive times.

Young: And George Benson, I don't know what that is, that's in the middle somewhere.

Reporter: Nowhere. [*Laughter.*]

Young: So that's in the void. [*Laughter.*] That dangerous place.

Reporter: The twilight zone.

Reporter: How does it feel to have millions of people all around the world listening to your records and thinking they know all about you? While you seem not to be willing to talk so much.

Young: Well, I'm talking to anybody and I talk to everybody.

Reporter: I'm not sure.

Reporter: So what is this free world you refer to? Is that an ironic statement?

Young: It's a little bit of irony in it. But on the other hand, when you consider the Communist countries, and especially the Chinese students and their dream of freedom, of democracy, it's unrealistic.

Reporter: So would you go there to be one of the first persons to play Western rock 'n' roll?

Young: Where, China?

Reporter: China or Russia?

Young: I'd go anywhere. Anywhere they want me to go. I was supposed to go to Russia last year. They asked me. Then they kept changing their minds.

Reporter: Why?

Young: I don't know. They kept changing the date. One date, then another date and pretty soon I, even I couldn't keep up.

Woman: Excuse me, we've got only seven more minutes, so I suggest everybody asks their questions.

Reporter: My man, Dave [Kleijwegt], we haven't heard you yet.

Reporter: No, it's OK.

Reporter: You recorded the song "El Dorado" and there's a big break in it with the guitar thing. Was that on purpose, or?

Young: Oh, you mean, loud?

Reporter: Yes.

Young: Oh, yeah.

Reporter: Blew some speakers in Holland.

Young: Oh, yeah? Well that's good. Yeah, that's the only thing that digital's good for. [*Laughter.*] "Oh, this is good. Let's listen to this. Turn it up, turn it up."

Reporter: Was it your choice to put out that mini album?

Young: Yeah.

Reporter: Uh-huh. So why wasn't it released worldwide?

Young: 'Cause it was my choice to put it out limited edition.

Reporter: Right.

Young: In two countries. Five thousand copies.

Reporter: Right.

Reporter: Why?

Young: Why?

Reporter: Yes.

Young: Because it was a pure thing. And I knew it didn't have a chance of being a big hit, and so I just left it the way I wanted it, exactly, and I took away everything that took away from it, and just had it be concisely like the hard music that it is and put it out there. And made it very personally mine, writing all over it myself and did the cover myself and everything and sent it out. Just to see what would happen.

Reporter: Now we all have to buy it on import. [*Laughter.*]

Reporter: Too bad.

Young: Eventually—there's only two songs on it, there's only one song on it now that you can't get.

Reporter: Yeah.

Young: "Heavy Love" is the one that's hard to get, 'cause "Cocaine Eyes" you can get from the German "Rockin' in the Free World" single. But they did that without my permission. But, anyway, that's the kind of thing that you start when you start doing things like that. So that's OK. I put it out because it's real, it's one of my records, but I didn't want it to go through all of the bullshit that one of my records has to go through. I put it out, it's protected.

Reporter: But what kind of bullshit do you mean?

Young: Oh, these reviews and everything. They can't even, they can't—we're not trying to push this record down anybody's throat. We're trying to make a record unavailable. [*Laughter.*]

Reporter: It's the other way around.

Young: Yeah, it's the other way around. Maybe I'll put out a hundred records and sign 'em all and only release 'em in Holland.

Reporter: Please do.

Young: And that's all there'll be, just those. Everything else'll be a counterfeit.

Reporter: Please release it in Holland.

Reporter: That would be nice.

Young: I'm thinking of the next time that I do that, of doing it in Germany and Holland. Because Japan and Germany . . .

Reporter: Two big markets—[*Laughter.*]

Young: I put it out in Japan before and they had a great CD and a beautiful package. So if I do that in Germany, they'll have the production and everything and then I'll put it out in Holland, too. Suppose I could put it out in Australia and New Zealand.

Reporter: Seeing that you are playing the [Sydney] Opera House tomorrow, is it gonna be different from a rock club?

Young: No. I don't know. I mean, it should sound good.

Reporter: Yeah.

Young: Last night we played a rock club and in Hamburg. Was it last night? Yeah. And that was good. It sounded great in there.

Reporter: Are you an opera fan yourself?

Young: Yes, very much so.

Reporter: What do you listen to?

Young: Well, I don't listen to it. [*Laughter.*]

Reporter: You like it from a distance.

Young: Yeah. It's nice when you're walking by an Italian restaurant. [*Laughter.*]

Reporter: The "This Note's for You" video was first banned by MTV and later on declared video of the year. On the night of the awards, there was a camera, because you were somewhere else, I guess, and there was a camera and you just grinned and didn't make any statement.

Young: Well, they didn't have any sound. [*Laughter.*] They took the sound off, you see—

Reporter: I thought you would refuse to make a statement.

Young: Well, no. Some people thought that I would refuse the award, that that would be the cool thing to do. But I didn't think that would be the cool thing to do. I don't want to start a war with MTV. I think I already, we made our point with MTV. So I wanna be friends with MTV.

Reporter: Do you get offered any sponsorships?

Young: I don't know. Ask my manager.

Reporter: Old cars, car dealers.

Young: Old car dealer, yeah.

Reporter: Neil, Crosby, Stills & Nash reunited again. While David Crosby was here in Holland, he was very bitter about Stephen Stills. So, you are not surprised by the reunion of them?

Young: Oh, no. They're all in very good shape. Stills is in good shape. And they sound very good right now. The fact that they went over to Berlin, played over there, like, that fast, that could only happen when three people decide to do the same thing at the same time. So I think they're together in a way they haven't been together in years. They could make a great album. They could really make a great album right now. I really think they might really do that and it's something they should do themselves, that they could do a great album.

Reporter: Thank you very much for your time.

Young: Thanks.

Reporter: We look forward to tomorrow.

Young: All right.

NEIL YOUNG ON

Having an Affair

"What that song ['Wrecking Ball'] is saying is that I really don't have the freedom to have an affair. If I was going to have an affair, if I went into a bar and saw some woman in the bar and I was thinking, well, you know . . . my wife's miles and miles away, could just do this, you know. But I really can't do that."

–from an interview with Richard Skinner,
BBC Radio *Saturday Sequence*, December 10, 1989

NEIL YOUNG: AN EXCLUSIVE NYAS INTERVIEW

Alan Jenkins | August 1990 | *Broken Arrow*

The first part of 1990 was publicly quiet for Neil Young as he recorded his next Crazy Horse LP, *Ragged Glory*, in April, and played a handful of charity shows through the end of the summer. The album, for many the crowning glory of Young's career, was released September 9, 1990. The work not only cemented Young's critical reputation after a decade adrift, but the untamed energy reached a generation who otherwise had no need for an old hippie with an acoustic guitar.

Broken Arrow was the magazine of the Neil Young Appreciation Society (NYAS). It was an indispensable resource for fans, gathering all manner of Neil Young information from around the globe. The magazine was published more-or-less quarterly from August 1981 until June 2014, when what editor Scott Sandie termed the "Facebook effect" rendered the publication redundant.

Although they had better luck with band and entourage members, NYAS writers managed only a handful of brief interviews with Young over this time, with Young often participating less than enthusiastically.

This interview is included not because it offers any headline-worthy insights into Neil Young as an artist, but because it provides contrast to the big-picture interviews and feature-pieces that, by commercial necessity, tend to cover a lot of the same thematic ground. It's not broad, but more in-the-moment and specific. The questions, and responses, cover the seemingly trivial aspects of Young and his work that matter to his hardcore fans.

And Frank Sampedro's along for comic relief. –Ed.

I was very fortunate recently when Frank Sampedro offered to help me secure a short interview with Neil Young. The outcome has been transcribed here, and Poncho's comments are also included. Some of the questions didn't draw much of a response, but at least the answers cleared up one or two things.

Back in the late '70s Jack [Nitzsche] was interviewed by Who Put The Bomp. He talked extensively about his career and spoke in detail about Neil Young playing on some sessions with The Cascades, including their cover of "Flying on the Ground is Wrong."

I've been told that you played on The Cascades version of "Flying on the Ground is Wrong," and that one track on Love's Forever Changes ("The Daily Planet") is your production. Are there any other collaborations we don't know about, or any at all that you recall?

I don't remember any of those.

You didn't play on "Flying on the Ground is Wrong?"

No.

I've also been told you did some uncredited work on Graham Nash's Songs for Beginners album?

I was credited, but under a different name.

Can you give any information on two Buffalo Springfield tracks called "Whatever Happened to Saturday" and "Slowly Burning" (I'm not too sure if I've got the titles correct)?

"Whatever Happened to Saturday Night." It's an unfinished Buffalo Springfield master, sung by Richie and written by me, produced by me. It was done at Sunset Sound and I have the master here at the ranch. It's one of those things I'm going to finish and mix for the archives.

(Frank) We could play that. Sounds like a good title, "Whatever Happened to Saturday Night."

Well, you know it is a good title, but you know . . . I just heard "Whatever Happened to Saturday Night," I heard it about four weeks ago.

And "Slowly Burning?"

"Slowly Burning" is an unfinished song. It's a Buffalo Springfield track, but only in as much as "Expecting to Fly" is a Buffalo Springfield track. "Expecting to Fly" is basically a Jack [Nitzsche] / Neil Young track. "Slowly Burning" and "Whisky at Boot Hill" are two other tracks that were recorded at the same sessions as the "Expecting to Fly" track. "Slowly Burning" actually has words and it's similar in some ways, some parts of it are similar to "Long Walk Home," but not the chorus. So "Long Walk Home" is slightly based on that track.

(Frank) That wasn't released either, huh?

"Slowly Burning" has never come out, it's just an instrumental track and none of the Springfield play on it. It was done when I was out of the group, like "Expecting to Fly" was done when I wasn't in the group.

Will they be on the Buffalo Springfield boxed set of CDs? Can you give NYAS members any news of this project?

They might be. The Buffalo Springfield boxed set of CDs is a project that I don't currently authorize. Because it's a bunch of people I don't know, that have gone into the archives and have listened to some of our tapes. I've met the guy, talked to him on the phone, but it's not us. When I have time to do it right, it's waited 25 years, when I have the time to do it right, after I've finished my own archives, I'll be able to contribute songs and time to that project. Well, it should be done by Buffalo Springfield.

So you don't know when the Buffalo Springfield CD set is going to be released?

They started working on it and I believe they've stopped working on it, but I'm not sure. Elliot Roberts told me they'd stopped working on it. But that may be something they told us just to get us off their backs!

Talking of boxed sets, can you also pass on any news about your 25th Anniversary boxed set? I've heard rumors of 5, 7, and 12 CD package. What can we expect to hear in the collection?

You're going to hear a lot of stuff you've never heard before.

(Frank) That's for sure.

Will we finally get to hear "Ordinary People" and the full version of "Sixty to Zero?"

It's not finished yet so I can't tell, but there are a lot of CDs. There will be books, there'll be a book that comes with it. There's also a complete archives video and a book that goes with that, too. It should come out on digital CD in original analog mastered set. They (Reprise Records) say they want to make records, too, but they don't know how big it is. Probably if there is a record it will have to be condensed.

How many songs do you have in it at the moment?

It's still wide open, there's just countless things. There are more unreleased tracks on the list right now than released things.

"Crime in the City" is subtitled "Sixty to Zero Part 1" on Freedom, *but it sounds more like Part Two—why is this?*

Really, as far as the records go "Sixty to Zero" hasn't even been heard yet, so this is all that's been heard and this would have to be part one. You can call it part two if you want. I call it part one because nobody's heard part two, and I don't even know what part two is going to be. We can edit it together or we could put out the original version from the Bluenotes. Part One, "Crime in the City" is edited, completely edited all the way through. Pieces were taken from here and there.

Early last year there were reports that Human Highway *and* Journey Through the Past *would be released on video.* Rust Never Sleeps *has been deleted on video for some time and is extremely rare. Will any of these films ever be made available?*

Ever is a long time. I have a deal with a company in New York and they may release them some time, but I don't know when it's going to happen.

Can you remember any details of the 1975 and 1976 bar tours (December 1975 and October 1976)?

(Frank) Can you remember any details, Neil (laughing)?

It's a little hazy. We had my white truck.

(Frank) Yeah.

Probably by the time you read this we'll have already done another one.

(Frank) Looks like there might be one coming up, Alan.

What is the title of the song performed at Cotati in December 1975—"When I play my guitar so well / That my life don't have no plans / One thing I'm sure of is I'm a man."

(Frank) That's my song. It's called "I'm a Man." It's the answer to Helen Reddy's "I Am Woman" (both Frank and Neil are laughing intensely). It was. That's why I wrote that.

It had to be answered.

There was talk some time ago that most of the tracks on Landing on Water *were also done as videos, is this correct?*

There was a plan to do them like that but I couldn't get the funding so I did four. And the one that hasn't come out, has never been seen is "Pressure."

Of all the videos Tim Pope has worked on he cites "Touch the Night" as the best, because it looked so real, having been shot in four hours and it looked so different on MTV—more like a newsreel. What are your opinions and which is your favorite so far?

They are all the same to me.

How did you come to work with Englishman Julian Temple?

(Frank) I didn't know he was English!

Just good luck. Was "This Note's For You" the first one we did with him?

(Frank) I think so.

Yeah, right, I remember now. We tried several people. We "This Notes For You," then that other one, "Hey Hey." The reason we used Julian Temple is because he came up with the best idea for the video. We tried several different people, we tried several different ideas before Julian's idea came along. I like working with him a lot so I kept on working with him.

I have seen '68 and Made in Heaven. *Just released in Europe (although it won't be out in Europe for some time) is* Love at Large. *Have you any plans for further cameos appearances in feature film?*

No.

What happened to Dennis Hopper's Backtrack *film? I believe you had a part in that film also?*

My part was so bad they shipped in the whole movie (laughing).

Would you know the exact venue and date of the first Bluenotes show? I believe it was at a Mexican restaurant in Montebello in L.A., probably in October 1987.

(Frank) No, no, no! The first Bluenotes gig was the Halloween party.

Yeah, and the first real Bluenotes gig was the Coconut Grove, with Mazzeo. Mazzeo the promoter, not Mazzeo the artist. They are two different people.

(Frank—laughing) Yeah, they are. Mazzeo was the worst promoter we ever had.

The worst promoter!

(Frank) We didn't make any money (still laughing).

How did you come to play on the Stealin' Horses track "Harriet Tubman?"

Put it down to the dangers of making records in Los Angeles.

You've also played on 2 successive Warren Zevon albums. It also seems that the two recent Zevon tracks you worked on were recorded at your ranch. How did this collaboration come about?

I did it for Warren, I didn't do it for Andy.

(Frank) It had nothing to do with Andy Slater. It had something to do with Niko Bolas.

Yeah.

Were you invited to the recent Nordoff Robbins Silver Clef Winners concert in Britain this summer? You seem to be one of the few winners not booked for the event!

No I wasn't. You know why? Because I bought John Lennon's suit. But they wouldn't show me the suit so I wouldn't give them the money. When am I going to see the suit!

You've been doing a lot of traveling lately but I've always been led to believe that you have a fear of flying. Have you overcome this in recent years?

I've never had a fear of flying!

What do you think about the fact that "Rockin' in the Free World" is turning into some sort of anthem in the wake of what has happened in the world over the last nine months, especially China and Eastern Europe?

No comment.

How did you come to use "On Broadway" on Freedom? *You've written new lyrics for it and besides the melody it seems to be almost unrecognizable from the original?*

Maybe you think so, but I think it's exactly the same. The lyrics are exactly the same as the original!

Well, my version of "On Broadway" is by the Crystals—perhaps they did it differently to the Drifters.

Besides the 25th Anniversary project, what else are you involved in at the moment.

It's not a 25th Anniversary project because it hasn't been named.

I just called it that as it's the title the US press seem to be using the most.

It's an archive. It's just a collection of all this stuff. It's got nothing to do with my 25th anniversary. It's already been more than 25 years anyway.

A few years ago I published a list that apparently includes all the tracks you have finished and handed in to Reprise up to 1981. There are some amazing things in there! Each track was dated but it's hard to work out what the date relates to, was it when you finished recording it, when Reprise received it, or when it was published/copyrighted?

The dates on all those Reprise things are generally in the ballpark of when it was done. They are all different dates. Some of them are the actual dates that they were recorded, some are the dates we recorded it being recorded. Other times we'd put in for sessions and stuff, we'd just make up a set of song titles, it didn't make any difference what they were or what day it was or anything. We made all that up. Those are the details that slip through the cracks.

What is "Gator Rag 1 and 2" and "Gator Stomp"?

Those are just names for jams.

Listed for 26 November 1975 is a track called "Hurricane," while "Like A Hurricane" is listed as an August 1975 track. Are they both the same songs or is "Hurricane" something different?

They're the same.

And that was it—my time was up. I supposed there were many more questions I could have asked and other questions I should have asked and didn't. Anyway it was very good of Neil Young to spare the time.

NEIL YOUNG ON

Roy Orbison

"I've always put a piece of Roy Orbison on every album I've made. His influence is on so many of my songs . . . I even had his photograph on the sleeve of *Tonight's the Night* for no reason, really. Just recognizing his presence. There's a big Orbison tribute song on *Eldorado* called 'Don't Cry.' That's totally me under the Roy Orbison . . . spell. When I wrote it and recorded it I was thinking 'Roy Orbison meets thrash metal' (laughs). Seriously."

–from an interview with Nick Kent, *Vox*, November 1990

NEIL YOUNG ON

Playing with Sonic Youth

"Yeah, a lot of my old fans hated Sonic Youth. They had no fuckin' idea what Sonic Youth was about. And yet, a lot of people who'd listened to my harder stuff were going, 'Hey, these guys are pretty good out there.' So I introduced Sonic Youth to a whole new audience and it didn't hurt them."

–from an interview with Steve Martin, *Pulse*, December 1991

NEIL YOUNG ON

Guitar Effects

"I have a digital echo that I use for a special sound. When I wanted to try it at the Guitar Center in Hollywood, the salesman was showing all the sounds that you could hear on Phil Collins and Cindy Lauper records. I asked to try it for a couple of minutes. I turned all the controls to full, except the volume, then I started to mute the chords–Whoop, whoop, whoop–like a huge popcorn machine popping."

–from an interview with *Guitare & Claviers*, April 17, 1992

NEIL YOUNG'S NEW AGE METAL

Andrew Hultkrans and Jas. Morgan | Summer 1992 | *Mondo 2000*

January 1991 saw the start of the ambitious three-month Crazy Horse Don't Spook the Horse US tour in support of *Ragged Glory*. As a nod to a somewhat younger demographic, the ear-bleedingly loud shows included noise-punk pioneers Sonic Youth. The tour produced the three-CD collection *Arc-Weld*, a collection that included Young's studio-manipulated collage-of-noise disc alongside a more traditional double-live album.

In fall 1991 Young reunited with the Stray Gators and recorded the quiet *Harvest Moon*. Hoping to mitigate hearing damage suffered on the 1991 tour, Neil set out in January on the first of three 1992 American acoustic tours. These appearances were capped by the November *Harvest Moon* release and a December appearance on *Saturday Night Live*.

This interview contains another look at *Trans*, but it's most telling for the probing of Young's continuing concerns about the (in)ability to effectively and accurately communicate and the role of technology in facilitating or hampering communication. All on the cusp of a popular technology explosion–the Internet, DVDs, cell phones–that would change how Young communicated with his audiences. –Ed.

Neil Young is the definitive axe murderer.

His backwoods psychotic glare and tremulous sneer render Jack Nicholson milquetoast by comparison. A torturer of the Les Paul (and Fender amp), Neil is a study in frenzy and distortion. A Neil Young solo is the sound of electricity suffocating.

His latest serial spree, the *Ragged Glory* tour—recorded as Armageddon faced Jihad in the Gulf—bristled with hostility at an America drunk with the urge to kick butt. Acknowledging his influence on a number of Noise and Industrial bands, Neil treated his audience to a heady dose of Sonic Youth as an aperitif, only to outgrunge them with his own set of harrowing sonic chaostrophy. The result—*Arc/Weld*—dispels any notion that Neil Young and Crazy Horse are sucking wind.

We met him in a remote juke joint amongst the Redwoods on Skyline Ridge. The *Twin Peaks* resonances were immediate—buttressed by a pair of lovely young Warner Bros. women greeting us near the fire. Jas. dazzled Simone with McLuhanese, as Young—cordoned off in the restaurant beyond—baffled some pad-and-pencil man from the *S.F. Chronicle.*

Neil goes off into insane rants occasionally, then glares at you hungrily, ready to devour your next question. Music crits always edit him down to passable respectability. We decided to leave him intact.

—Jas. & Andrew

MONDO 2000: Does high-speed technology in itself interest you? Fax machines, camcorders . . .

NEIL YOUNG: Yeah. Unfortunately, the biggest area of suffering is sound. What we have to listen to is infuriating. Technology that works for everything else is killing music. It doesn't sound like it should; digital doesn't give you the music.

M2: In theory, it should get everything—break it up in little bits, record each frequency on its own level—but you're right. It doesn't sound as warm or as rich.

NY: If you look out the window you'll see a roof or something green. Now, imagine you're looking at *sound* outside, a visualization of it. You're seeing sound from a live performance—the energy and the vibrations of the whole building. Between the different colors and the way it hits you, there are so many nuances.

If you look at it through a multi-paned window, take the dominant color in one of the squares and make the whole square that color. Take away all the variety in the square, replace it with the dominant, and do the same thing with all the squares—that's digital.

DISSIN' DAT

NY: That's why you don't get the feedback, your mind and heart are not challenged.

M2: You're missing all those grey areas.

NY: Or all the *color*. And the top part of the sound is where all the magic is—up there with the hiss and the air.

M2: Certainly in *your* music . . .

NY: But it's not there now, because of digital recording.

M2: But didn't you record *Arc Weld* digital to digital?

NY: I've done everything digital since 1982.

M2: Are you just hoping it will get better?

NY: There's no alternative. CDs are CDs. If you're going to come out in digital you might as well *record* in digital and take advantage of the control factor. But it's not therapeutic, it's not healthful, it's not rewarding, it's not challenging to the mind. It's just enough to trick you into thinking that it's music, but you're not being rewarded by listening to it. You're not getting *enhanced*.

If you listen to an old record on an old set, and it's an all-analog recording, then you can get whatever therapeutic or spiritual value that music can bring you. It comes much easier because your brain is completely occupied by the myriad of possibilities in the sound and the mix and the depth—all these little different sounds that are broken into their smallest parts. In digital you don't get any of that; you get an averaged sound. A million little sounds replaced by one color.

M2: So if I put on my album of *Everyone Knows This Is Nowhere*, and listen to it on a good stereo system, it's a richer album than *Ragged Glory*? For just that reason alone?

NY: Absolutely. Maybe not richer music, but richer tonal quality. It has the flaws inherent to analog. If you turn it up too loud your turntable will start feeding back in the speakers: you've got surface noise. But those aren't that important compared to getting the full depth of the music . . . and the *echo*. I mean, how do you take echo and make it into a big square? Echo is subtle variations. You can't average out all the subtle variations into one color and expect to get the same impression.

HOW, EXACTLY, SHIT HAPPENS

M2: I've always been interested in the tone of your guitar. It's a very rich sound. I'm wondering what you hear in it, and your approach to distortion.

NY: The guitar and the amplifier work together to feed each other. And you have to get the amplifier big enough, so you're far enough away from the guitar that you can still feed, vibrate the area. And you move the guitar around in the area, finding the angles and places where the guitar sits and responds to the sound.

And then you start building the sound coming out of the amplifier with effects after the guitar signal is entered. It has to have strayed in. And then you take the effects and you introduce them again between the guitar and the amplifier, through a different route, and you blend them together and they start feeding back.

It's a very natural thing. And to hear it live is really awesome.

M2: What do you hear onstage when you're really overriding the amps and you've got heavy feedback?

NY: You feel it in your chest.

M2: Is it a different musical place than being within a regular song?

NY: Oh yeah—when we get to that point we're entering another domain. That's the expression of the song, the essence of what we had just sung put into raw sound. It's pure, it's not refined at all. It's the real *goo*.

TRANS OUT

M2: I wanted to ask you about *Trans*. Was there a larger concept behind it than was expressed in the album?

NY: There was quite a larger thing behind it originally. In the original conception there was a video. If it was today, I'd have been able to do it, because I'd have the support of my record company. But at that time for me to ask for the money to make a video that was going to be 20 minutes long for an EP—there was no way.

Trans was about a baby that couldn't talk, couldn't communicate. The whole operation in the hospital was trying to get the baby to push a button. Everyone around the baby was talking in synthetic voices, and the baby was going to get a synthetic voice as soon as he learned how to push the button. He could then start to learn how to talk.

PUNCHING THE DIGITAL COWS

"Computer Cowboy" was a song about a guy named Syscrusher. During the day he was a cowboy. All his cows were the same; they were digital cows, square-block cows. He had a floodlight out on the pasture which he kept lit all night, so there were 24 hours of light for the cows to be eating and moving toward their final goal. The perfect cattle ranch.

But at night when he turned on the lights, he'd go into the city and start fuckin' around with the computers of these companies. He'd go inside buildings, fuck up the memory systems and the government records . . .

M2: He was a cracker . . .

NY: Yeah. And then there's "Computer Age," which has to do with the doctors in the hospital talking to one another. There are families trying to get into the hospital, getting caught in traffic and watching the lights change. Their eyes start to be like traffic lights.

"We R In Control" is sung by the airport and traffic systems. And "Transformer Man" was the nurses singing to the little kid: "Control the action/Push of a button/Trying to break through/There's so much to do/We haven't made it yet . . ." They're telling the kid that he's got to press the button or he's not going to be able to communicate. That was the beginning of my ideas of my own son being able to communicate through technology.

TONGUES OF THE COLLECTIVE UNCONSCIOUS

M2: Do you think communications technologies have a positive effect on culture?

NY: Oh yeah, because disabled people have an incredible amount to add. People who don't talk have a different perspective—they're listeners. They've accumulated a lot of information.

Some of these people are unaffected mentally, and yet they've developed very strangely. Because they can't communicate, other people assume that they can't *think*.

There are documented occurrences of people who couldn't talk breaking the silence after 30 years—through the use of a little toe on a computer, or an eyelid interface for blinking Morse code into a computer. And the doctors find that these people have *intertwined composite languages*. They have the language of their time, and then a throwback language that hasn't been spoken for centuries, like Gaelic. It's just there.

It's fascinating to find out what's on these people's minds. Their wisdom about how to deal with their own peers, and how to help us deal with them. Not to mention the artistic side and the musical side.

WHEN THE AIR IS YELLOW & RED, AND REFRIGERATORS RULE THE WORLD

M2: Your lyrics over the years have been very down-to-earth: relationship based or issue-based, but sometimes you slip in some futuristic element. Even as far back as "After The Gold Rush," the last verse, "Silver spaceships . . . flying Mother Nature's silver seed to a new home in the sun." Is that something that interested you then?

NY: It seemed a lot farther away then than now. But that's about three times in history: there's a Robin Hood scene; there's a fire scene in the present; and there's the future, where the planet's all yellow, the air is yellow and red, ships are leaving, certain people can go and certain people can't. It's like planting seeds.

M2: It was very vivid. Do you see that as something that could happen?

NY: I think it's going to happen. I don't know if it'll happen in my lifetime, but there are definitely going to be people leaving here to go somewhere else. It's a natural progression.

M2: If you could get naturespheres up into the space stations rather than the sterile scenario we have now . . .

NY: We only think it's sterile because we believe that everything has to be so *organized* for us to get there that it *must* be sterile. In actuality, it's the opposite. The kind of power that we're going to have to use to get there is chemical, it's natural.

Everything is going to be different. Nanotechnology, where machines are alive, refrigerators building new refrigerators, then *bigger* refrigerators—soon they can freeze the whole state . . . (laughter)

M2: You just have to tell it when to stop building refrigerators. Do you have any gadgets you just play with?

NY: I've got a big train set and I'm working on a computer control system for it. That's a mind-boggling keypad—it's a whole environment.

M2: How large is it?

NY: About the size of this room. It's pretty radical.

NEW AGE METAL

M2: What about *Arc*? You've hinted at this kind of atonality in live albums, but here it's completely brought out. I was wondering if you listened to a lot of free jazz.

NY: I don't listen to that much music. I just listen to the radio. Whatever's on, whatever people play in the car, whatever my wife listens to, I'll listen while I'm in the room. If nobody else is in the room, I'll turn it off.

M2: So *Arc* is purely an emotional expression. It doesn't come from any school of music that you enjoy.

NY: No. It's New Age metal. That's what I would call it, because you can listen to it really quiet. It's soothing. I should play it between sets in clubs—to cleanse the palette. It's a generic rock 'n' roll sound; it has no identity. It's the tone, the metal tone. It's like being inside a giant milkshake blender. It's another dimension. Most bands' beat defines who they are. There is no beat in *Arc*. So it doesn't take away from any other music. It's the universal mixer.

Anyone caught playing *Arc* loudly on their car stereo at a stoplight is making a *definite* statement.

M2: How did you record it?

NY: Live on stage. It's all live from the tour.

THE SPARKS WITHIN THE ARC

M2: And it's all in one line?

NY: No, there are 57 sparks. They range from 15 seconds to 3 1/2 minutes in length.

M2: Where would you insert them into the regular set?

NY: Well, those would be extracted from the songs, like the songs on *Weld*, although none of the pieces from *Weld* are used. If you listen to *Weld* and you listen to *Arc*, you can hear parts of *Arc* on *Weld* as it goes by. If you listen to them both a couple of times you can tell where all the pieces come from. They all have an order to them.

So I digitally edit them together and use as much of the same night as I can. I get a good night and then I take what I'm doing and put it all together and then go to another night. Just remove the songs and only put in the sonic stuff. And then put the nights together.

There's three of those happening and it reaches a sort of crescendo finale. Some new things come in, and then there's a little mood change, and then there's a huge ending. It's sort of like a classical piece.

M2: It's pure Neil Young music though. But you do sound nastier on *Weld*. Some of the versions of your older songs—songs that were also on *Live Rust*—sound angrier, grittier than I've ever heard.

NY: Well, it was during the Persian Gulf War. That's why, 'cause the audiences were supporting us and bringing that out. The songs weren't old or new. There was no old or new during that tour: the whole thing was like *one*.

NEIL YOUNG ON

Rap

"It's speaking to the people on the streets. It's a whole new way of communicating that's so open to saying exactly what the hell's on people's minds in a clever way, a way that you can listen to and move your body to. Similar to, like, 'Subterranean Homesick Blues.' Dylan is early rap."

–from an interview with Alan Light, *Rolling Stone*, January 21, 1993

THE MEN ON THE HARVEST MOON: YOUNG-BUCK!

Mark Rowland | April 1993 | *Musician*

Among his few 1992 electric shows, Neil Young named and participated in Bobfest, the thirtieth anniversary celebration of Bob Dylan at Madison Square Garden on October 16. Young was backed by Booker T. and the M.G.'s on four songs, including a slow-burn rave of "Just Like Tom Thumb's Blues." Two weeks later, on November 1, he would return to the stage solo at the sixth Bridge School Benefit and the next day release *Harvest Moon*, which would become one of his best-selling albums.

The success of *Harvest Moon* found Geffen records claiming their final Neil Young album, *Lucky Thirteen*, released January 6, 1993, and curated by Young. It's half LP tracks and half rarities from the Geffen era.

On *Harvest Moon* Neil Young reunited the Stray Gators, the backing band from *Harvest*. Just as he confounded post-*Harvest* tour expectations by mainly focusing on material for the next LP, *Time Fades Away*, Young didn't tour *Harvest Moon* with the full band. Instead, they backed Neil on a handful of shows, including the February 7, 1993, recording that would generate *Unplugged* in June 1993.

Joined by Warner Bros. stable-mate Peter Buck of R.E.M., this piece is notable for being less a journalist-steered interview than a chance to eavesdrop on two accomplished musicians chatting, going places one doesn't usually visit in a formal Young interview. As expected for *Musician* magazine, Young and Buck dip deep into gear talk and recording. Young also discusses the benefits and drawbacks of being in/leading a band and how he negotiated song selection for *Lucky Thirteen* and *Unplugged*, then seems to admit that he's become the "pack-rat" librarian he formerly disparaged. —Ed.

Outside the sky was dark and the rain was falling hard. But the pre-concert scene congealing toward the rear of Universal Studios stage 12 was warm and convivial. The occasion was a taping of MTV's *Unplugged* featuring Neil Young, performing by himself and with the band he put together for his gorgeous record *Harvest Moon*.

Set designers had surrounded the stage with nets festooned with autumn leaves, while nearby a small industry reunion of execs, pop stars, press types and old friends of the band commingled in happy expectation of the hour to come. In that homey celebration no one seemed to even notice as a bearded, rain-dampened middle-aged man in a black jacket and toting a battered leather carry bag—Neil Young—walked through the door, sliced through the center of the chattering crowd and disappeared behind the staging area. His eyes were set straight ahead, his mouth tight in an expression of quiet, even grim concentration. But if you did notice, you suddenly realized: Everyone was having a wonderful time because Neil was coming to work.

Among those in the audience was Peter Buck, who'd been a Neil Young fan since he was a kid learning guitar licks off the radio. Since then, Buck's band R.E.M. has managed to simultaneously embrace and transcend the do-it-yourself ethos of the underground rock revolution. Though a generation apart, you could draw plenty of parallels between Buck's and Young's accomplishments—a sound based in the deceptively-simple melodicism of folk and country, a compositional range from careening rock 'n' roll to elegant orchestrations, an understanding of guitar as a voice whose feeling makes a sham of technical virtuosity, a refusal to take their art too lightly or themselves too seriously, an aversion to razors . . . but what it ultimately comes around to is an attitude, a shared sense of musical purpose. Both elicit respect from rappers, grunge-rockers and yuppies the old-fashioned way. They earn it.

"The first Neil record I ever bought was *Time Fades Away*," Buck recalled. "Looking back, *Harvest* was a great record, but to me at the time it wasn't very interesting. Then I read this sanctimonious review of *Time Fades Away* by some obviously mellow hippie who was really taking Neil Young to task, like, 'Man, *Harvest* was great, you could twist up a doob and smoke it with your old lady and it was really groovy—and then he makes this thing! It's loud and the guitar solos are deranged and everything's out of tune! Man, his career's over unless he gets back to that mellow music.' And I thought, wow, out of tune, way too loud, deranged guitar solos—that sounds like a good thing to me. And I loved it."

For some fogies, *Harvest Moon* may indeed mark a welcome return to the sweet melodies and countrified laments of *Harvest*, Young's most popular album, after a prodigal detour of nearly 20 years. For others like Buck, the two albums bookend an astonishing body of work that can hold its own with anyone's in pop music. In either event, no one's accusing Neil of coasting. Indeed, he'd already taped an *Unplugged* show about a month earlier in New York, which he decided to scrap because it didn't meet his standards of performance.

So here he was, walking the tightrope again, warming up with heartfelt renditions of "The Old Laughing Lady" and "Mr. Soul" on guitar, then moving to the pump organ for a literally breathtaking version of "Like a Hurricane." On to the piano for an affecting "Stringman," a song he wrote decades ago and has performed maybe five times since. He tentatively struck the opening chords of "Tonight's the Night" . . . "Play 'Needle and the Damage Done'!" someone shouted from the bleachers, and you could see him hesitate. "All right," he decided, to the cheers of the crowd, who began clapping along to that familiar undulating melody before the chill from the lyrics stopped them cold. He further sabotaged expectations with two songs from *Trans*, of all things, and the new arrangements revealed them as songs of haunting, delicate beauty.

After the show, Neil and Peter were introduced and quickly developed the rapport of seasoned musicians who only need a few bars to recognize a consonant harmony. They even put their two camera-shy mugs together for a picture or two, with Neil strumming Hank Williams' old Martin guitar for spiritual support.

An hour later, after braving the canyon mudslides that inevitably occur any time it rains for more than two days in Los Angeles, they hooked up at a Mexican eatery in Hollywood that featured Naugahyde booths and a smooth-singing mariachi trio, along with Nils Lofgren, Neil's producer David Briggs, his manager Elliot Roberts and a few other unindicted co-conspirators. Over bottles of beer info was secured ("Did you tune that low E to D for 'Harvest Moon'?" Peter asked Neil. Yes, he did) while David Briggs described Young's recent feats of derring-do driving down Nichols Canyon road. Peter explained that his Southern accent doesn't appear until he's had enough to drink—"then I start saying y'all"—but he barely got that far. Relieved and tired and cracking jokes, Neil admitted after a spell that he still wasn't all that thrilled by his performance earlier that evening. "I guess I'm losing my patience as I get older," he said. He smiled and added dryly, "'Cause you know, I always had so much to begin with."

The next morning, they got together for the following conversation, after which Neil, the family man, would catch a plane home while Peter, the wanderer, would embark on a two-month sojourn through Mexico and Guatemala. Topics ranged from a gargantuan series of archival recordings Young is preparing for release this year to the public burning of Ice-T to the Rock and Roll Hall of Fame to . . . well, you'll see. Breakfast was granola and fruit, respectively. Not very rock 'n' roll, but there's a price to keeping your energy up as you get on in life. In the old days, Neil explained, "I didn't get up until two in the afternoon, so it wasn't a problem. Now I have to get up sometimes before I want to, because I have a family and there's a routine. Now, you're going off hitchhiking," he nodded to Peter. "That's great. I envy you." "Yeah," Buck agreed. "Just don't tell my mom."

MUSICIAN: *How do you happen to own Hank Williams' guitar?*

YOUNG: Well, I bought it from Tut Taylor in Nashville back in 1976. So I've had it for almost 20 years now. And I have it on the bus with me. Only recently did I start playing it. I wrote songs on it before, occasionally. But it was more of something to just have around and feel. When I carried it on my bus I might have writers that knew who Hank was who were visiting me or something, I'd send 'em back there and tell 'em they could hang out there with the guitar for a while if they wanted to. So . . .

BUCK: It's nothing like Hank Williams, but I know with guitars I've played all my life, it does absorb something from you. A guitar you've played for 10 years is way different from one you just bought off the rack.

YOUNG: That's right, and if you stop playin' 'em they're not as friendly as they were when you were playing them all the time. I guess it must be the way you play changes, but it almost seems as if the guitar is not as easy to play as it was.

BUCK: I had the black Rickenbacker that I'd used on almost every record I'd ever done, and then I gave it to our drummer Bill for a while, and he said, "Peter, it's really a very nice guitar, you should play it again." So I got it back and it was really difficult to play, I don't know why. Then after a while it really worked again. I guess if it ever gets stolen I'll just have to quit the business.

YOUNG: Yeah, it's funny, I'm attached to a couple of pieces of equipment. I think my amplifiers more than my guitars.

BUCK: Like that P.A. system from 1948 with the accordion input? When you were doing *Still Life* we were doing Warren Zevon's record and we bumped into each other; I was there when you were mixing 'Mideast Vacation.' But I'd walked in earlier and one of your guitar techs let me play your guitar through the rig and I could sort of hear the sounds—"Is that the 'Cinnamon Girl' sound?" I love amps with the accordion input. You know they're the real thing.

YOUNG: Plus, it goes to 12.

BUCK: Have you had that stuff for a real long time?

YOUNG: The Deluxe I bought at Saul Bettman's music store on Larchmont (in Los Angeles) back in the '60s. Place was full of old piggyback amps and tweedies, lot of Fender amps. I used to go in there every week after we'd do a gig with the Springfield, I'd have a few bucks and I'd go in and buy another amp. That one I bought for about 70 bucks (*Peter groans*). I also bought this old funky Gretsch there. I went back to my place in Laurel Canyon and turned the thing up all the way, and my guitar that was on the bed started going nuts. And I went holy shit, this thing's really got something. After that I just sat there, feeding back. That amp actually shows up on a couple of the Springfield records. I think on 'Everydays' there's a feedback note that goes all the way through the song. I don't know what album that's on [*Buffalo Springfield Again*].

But it goes back to the very beginning, that amp. I didn't use it with the Springfield, just on that section. But I always had it. And then with Crazy Horse, right away, that first album—

BUCK: It's great that you have that continuity. Because with albums, you're in a different studio and with different musicians. I like to use the same equipment. I've had the same amps and guitars for years. It gives you the feeling that something's permanent.

YOUNG: I'm just married to the sound, you know. I suppose if I lost all that stuff it might even be good for me. But I don't want to lose it.

BUCK: I tend to let things go in circles. I don't like to plan things out anyway.

YOUNG: Well, you're lucky you're in the same band for so long.

BUCK: It's pretty ideal. This is actually the first real band I was ever in. We always had this rule that if one of us left it wasn't gonna be the same band—you couldn't use the name. I couldn't have that "one original member left" group. I remember I read this interview with the band Krokus. They asked a guy what the name meant, and he said, "All the original members have left so we don't know what it means." Like it was something passed down from the elders that they forgot.

A friend of mine is a session musician who auditioned for one of "The Association." They had three original members in three different bands, and they just booked them all at once. So it'd be, you're the West Coast Association, you're the East Coast one . . . they'd learn their 12 songs and go out.

YOUNG: I saw the Platters once in a bar in Evergreen, Colorado. It was Buck Ram's Original Platters. He was alive but he wasn't touring with them. So it didn't matter that much when he died, apparently.

BUCK: I went to see the Drifters once when I was in college in '76, and they were all like, 22 years old. I was counting back . . . there was one old guy with them who didn't seem to know which were Drifters songs and which weren't. But it was fine. Given that it wasn't the original singers. They did the hits.

YOUNG: So what are you gonna do in Mexico, besides just travel around—you taking a guitar?

BUCK: No, I'm not taking anything.

YOUNG: That's a good idea. You can probably get one down there if you need one.

BUCK: I know this guy who plays in this bar in San Francisco called Athens by Night. He's a great bouzouki player. He's about 60 years old. He said in Chihuahua they make really great instruments. So maybe I'll look down there and pick up something interesting. I don't know, I keep seeing myself carrying a guitar in the rain. That doesn't seem like fun. I may get an instrument there, but for a couple of days I want to just see what I'm doing. I don't have a real plan.

MUSICIAN: *What are the best and—*

YOUNG: Don't talk with your mouth full! (*smiles*) That's what mom would say.

MUSICIAN: *What's the best and worst of being in a band for any length of time?*

YOUNG: The best thing about being in a band is, the longer it's together, the easier it is to fall into a groove. Obviously if you're in a band, it must *be* a groove or you wouldn't be in there. So that's the best thing.

BUCK: You can be really creative without thinking about it. Ideally, you want to get to a place in songwriting where you're not consciously writing a song; that you can just pick up an instrument and the song comes. If you can get that with four people it's really nice. You can be tuning up and playing some inconsequential riff and all of a sudden it makes sense as a piece of music. That's something we've been doing for a long time. We've been writing for 15 years. On the other hand, it's real easy to do the same thing over and over again. You've got to consciously think, oh, we've used that key too much this year . . . I think there was a period around 1989 where we decided we didn't want to sound like anything we'd done in the past. Just to get away from it.

YOUNG: Well, the negative side of being in a band is, generally a band can only do what that band is capable of doing. On a general level. And that may be a lot—but whatever it is, it's not everything. For instance, with me, on *Ragged Glory* and *Harvest Moon* I had two bands. And so the limitation is that, in a situation like last night, I can't play the right groove on some of the things, because it just doesn't fit—the whole thing doesn't go. Some people can play one thing, some people can play another, and I'm caught in the middle—I can't go from one to another in my own show! So I have to commit myself when I put a band together, which is another thing I hate to do, 'cause I don't want to put a band together, I want the band to already *be* together. But if I'm gonna play and I'm not gonna play with Crazy Horse, I've got to figure that out. First of all I don't want a bunch of guys that are great that are on the road all the time—they've had it, as far as I'm concerned. I mean, they're great for somebody else, 'cause somebody else needs them. But I don't need somebody who thinks that they know the right thing to do. I need somebody who doesn't know shit, and is just happier than hell to be there, and will try anything. That's the person I'm looking for. Ultimately it would be people who would play for nothing, who just want to be there, but who are not impressed with me at all.

So that's part of my struggle: to put together new things, something different that has already got some kind of depth to it but is completely innocent and naive and not cynical and all of those things that musicians get with more experience. 'Cause I like to play really stupid, dumb things, OK? Fuckin' obvious shit—but with a feeling of "We didn't know it was obvious. We were believing this." I like to play with people who can play simple and are not threatened by it, by other musicians thinking they can't play or something. And that eliminates 99 percent of the musicians, OK? (*laughter*) So right away we're down to one out of a hundred. And I'm trying to find maybe three of those, who have been together for a long time.

BUCK: I did this record for Kevin Kinney and hired these guys from a folk music society to play on it. They were so naive about the whole process I had to explain the concept of multitracking and overdubbing.

They were like, "You mean I can do it twice?" It was really great, they had never been in the studio and it was so much fun to work with them. None of them felt like they had to have a solo. I'd say, why don't you play something here? And they might play one note—that's what they heard.

YOUNG: I say sometimes to guys, don't play music. Play a sound. Identify this part, put a signature on it. It doesn't have to be musical. Maybe it is musical, but maybe it sounds as if you dropped the dobro. You get the thing going and you drop the other end—maybe that's the sound. Because it's the tone, in some cases, not the music that you play. So many people try to play all the time.

BUCK: Spooner (Oldham, who plays keyboards on *Harvest Moon*) played at Muscle Shoals, didn't he? I heard they nailed the mikes and amps in one place there. They found the sound they liked and then nailed everything so it couldn't be moved . . . I like that idea too: that there is a certain sound, here's the way you get it, and it's not gonna change. Kids listened to Motown, say a Supremes record, and didn't realize what world-class bass playing and drumming were going on 'cause it just fit the song so great.

MUSICIAN: *Neil, you were a Motown artist for a while.*

YOUNG: Yeah, and it was great playing there. We were the first white group that Motown had. Rick James was our lead singer and the rest of us were white. It was a pretty cool band. We used to do a lot of Rolling Stones-type stuff, and then Rick and I wrote a couple of things together. And we played in there. I remember I had an acoustic 12-string on, playing these country kind of licks, and it was cool—this was '65. The drums were nailed down. We used their drummer, he came in and played. We were singing the background parts, but after a while these three guys were standing behind us and singing all the parts—they'd learned 'em, you know? And they were going, "C'mon, let's go, let's get it moving!" and they helped us get it into the groove. It was really cool the way they did it. This is what they did for everybody. If it wasn't swingin' right away, they'd bring in more people and get it swinging, and they never did anything that didn't swing. So that was a really great experience.

Something happened with the tapes—I don't think they know where they are. There is some archivist who has seen them on a list . . . but there's not that much there really, just the memory and the experience of the way they did it.

I remember signing a contract that was like two inches thick. But I was a minor. It was all in really small print, too. I'm sure I gave everything away.

BUCK: You better be careful, (*mimics a record executive*) "You realize we've owned everything Neil Young has done since 1965?"

YOUNG: Right. Come and get me in the redwoods, boys. I'll be waitin' for ya.

BUCK: When you came out to Los Angeles and started working with Buffalo Springfield, was it done really differently? Were you cutting live at that point? Because that was only about a year later.

YOUNG: Well, my very first records that I made in Canada were live, I sang and played. When I got down to L. A. with the Buffalo Springfield it was just about the time multi-track recording was starting to come in. Four-track was available and people were starting to talk about eight-track. So most of the things that we did didn't have lead vocals on them—they told us that the way to do it was to put down the track and then sing. And that's the way the Buffalo Springfield stuff is. I don't think there's anything on those records that isn't overdubbed vocals.

With the advent of the Beatles and the Beach Boys and multi-tracked recording it took a while for me to realize that the real thing I liked to do was sing and play all at once. And that it was possible to do that. That that's the way they used to make records, and those were the records that I liked. Even back then I thought the way records were being made in the '60s was wrong. But I didn't know what was wrong with it. It just didn't sound right. I mean, the Springfield records are terrible compared to what the band sounded like. If the Springfield had recorded the way I recorded some of the things I did with Crazy Horse and other bands, where I sang the lead and we all played the song and later overdubbed some choruses with maybe a couple of effects, that would have been a great record. But we missed that whole period.

The first stuff where I sang live would be *After the Gold Rush.* Ninety percent of my first album and *Everybody Knows This Is Nowhere* I overdubbed the vocals. *After the Gold Rush* I turned it around and after that there was no more overdubbing. Until I got to *Landing On Water.* Aptly titled.

BUCK: Hearing those songs from *Trans* last night, I remember hearing you say all this stuff was of a piece, and it sounded like you were right.

YOUNG: I wanted to do a version of those songs where people could understand the words. And I felt that enough time had gone by to where that would lend a new dimension to it. Because my original purpose for *Trans* and the videos that I planned for *Trans* was a story about a sort of strangled communication, where you're dreaming and yelling out but no one can hear you, and you're talking but nothing is coming out of your mouth and you can't get it to work. That's why I sang through the machines, because it would make it so people couldn't—or wouldn't want to—hear it, or they could tell that someone was trying to say something but they couldn't tell what the hell it was. So I figured after 10 years that a couple of acoustic versions of those songs would have been cool—but they had to have the magic great groove. You can't make it work without that. The band had it in rehearsal, but they didn't have it last night.

BUCK: I saw that show in '80 where you did a lot of that *Trans* stuff and I thought it came across like a real band, almost. It was really weird.

YOUNG: Oh yeah. Is that the one where I did a solo show, and did "Computer Age" and "Mr. Soul" with the television set and all that?

BUCK: Yeah. But it was really great in a way to look around and see your fans looking really shocked. I guess *Trans* hadn't come out yet. But it was a great version of "Mr. Soul," very incendiary, kind of crazy. It made you see what the point of the technological stuff was.

YOUNG: Well, I was trying. I was out there in the woods with my analog tape recorders and vocoders and all of that stuff. Nothing ever works out the way you want it to, but I had a vision for videos and this whole thing, you know? It was my first record for Geffen, and it was the first time I ever ran into a situation where they wouldn't do what I wanted them to do. They didn't think it was a good idea, I had to convince them that I thought it was cool. Right then I knew, "Oh God, what did I do, what the hell is this?" (*laughs*) 'Cause if I'd been at Reprise I could have come in and said this is gonna be an EP, there's only six of these, but I want to do videos and tell a story with the videos . . . I had almost a comic strip, TV kind of look for all that stuff. But there's only so much you can do. I was frustrated in that period. So I'm trying to get those songs out now.

MUSICIAN: *Though you recently helped put together the* Lucky Thirteen *compilation CD of your records for Geffen.*

YOUNG: Yeah, I put that together. I have a contractual obligation and that's why that came out. It was part of my deal to get out of Geffen.

BUCK: I know there's a Shocking Pinks song on there, that minor key blues you used to do? ("Don't Take Your Love Away From Me") That's a great song. I saw you do a show in Atlanta in '84 where you did some acoustic and then some *Trans* and then some Shocking Pinks and it was almost getting kind of Bluenote-y at the end with the horns. It was like The Four Ages of Man. If you play those records back to back you don't really think they'd link, but there's a bridge.

YOUNG: With *Lucky Thirteen* you get a sense for that eight-year period. Thank God they let me do what I wanted, in that instance. I said, there's no hits here, that's why you sued me. (*laughter*) So let's not make a greatest hits, 'cause that's a joke. I picked the songs and put them together to represent a kind of encapsulation of the whole experience.

BUCK: Is that a preview of the archive stuff coming out?

YOUNG: I did take some things out of the archives to give you some kind of an idea of what's in there.

BUCK: I'm real excited about that, as a fan.

YOUNG: There's a lot of stuff in there. I think for fans it'll be fun. There's several ways of doing it, which we haven't quite decided yet.

There's a lot of options, since there's so much stuff. I tend to want to do the complete thing, just put it all out in chronological order, and then if you want to get it by mail order, it's expensive as hell but we're not trying to shove it down your throat. Then there's a commercial version where you have respect for the fact that you don't want to make 'em buy a bunch of stuff they may not want to hear but there's still depth and stuff they haven't heard. Not for fanatics. And there's the surface type of thing for whoever, you know, maybe all they have is enough money to buy one CD and have an overview. But nothing's locked in yet.

My idea is to have an unbelievable amount of CDs, each with their own package, representing the time they came from. Some of them being 35 minutes long, some of them being 70 minutes long, depending on what the content was, not just trying to cram the CD full but to make it an era. Some eras have three volumes, some might be only 35 minutes long. But you can hear what was happening and see the images and pictures from that time and take that CD with you. Then you've got 1968, or 1964. There are 11 songs from 1964 and '65.

BUCK: Is that the Squires stuff?

YOUNG: The Squires and other stuff, studio, band stuff. Really funky.

BUCK: There are some bootlegs of some of the Squires.

YOUNG: Yeah, but they don't have the stuff that we have. We've got a couple of really good ones back there—the first time I felt that I'd made a really good record, we have a tape of that. Plus there's a lot of solo performances of early stuff, real early stuff. It's interesting, if you're into it. It's fascinating purely from a librarian's point of view that we managed to keep all this stuff together. I'm such a pack rat.

BUCK: We've been doing that too. Our lawyer was real farsighted and had us recording shows 24-track when we first got our recording contract. So every tour we've done there's probably five shows recorded in 24-track live, then of course all the stuff in the studio which is on a computer, and all our video stuff which we own the rights to. We've got this little vault in Atlanta. It's kind of a daunting prospect to look at—hundreds and hundreds of hours of tapes.

YOUNG: As long as somebody has a memory of what you did. You probably know everything on there that you really care about and you know there's some gray areas where you should go into it and then maybe 80 percent of it—you know.

BUCK: When we were getting off I.R.S. we were looking for one particular song that we wanted to use for a B-side, and it was the only thing we couldn't find. And none of us could remember how to play the song! I still think that's floating around somewhere, but that's the only thing we're missing as far as I can tell. That's when we got the computer and sent this poor guy looking for a song that was either called "the new song" or "the new new song." We have about 50 "new songs" spread out over the space of 10 years.

MUSICIAN: *It must be an odd sensation to realize you can't recall your own songs.*

BUCK: There was a benefit show we did where we were going to do *Murmur* all in order and then our new record, which at the time was *Green*, all in order. And we had to go buy a copy of *Murmur* to learn it again, just like any bar band. There are a couple of chords in the bridges that I had no idea what they were. Maybe they were wrong. But it was a great, kind of humbling experience to realize you had no idea what these songs were like.

YOUNG: Well, you know it's fun to play the new ones. They're easy to play. And when it starts getting to be work to play the old ones, there's a point you get to where you don't want to do them. And I'm at a point now where the hardest thing for me to do is teach somebody one of my songs—unless I just wrote it. But if it's on record, it's like it's impossible. If you give them the record they'll try to learn it exactly like the record and it sounds like somebody playing somebody else. Then if you don't give 'em the record you're sitting and playing a song over and over again, and it drives you nuts. 'Cause I've got new songs in my head. I don't want to waste my time at this point.

BUCK: There's always that problem with the audience too. Because they think they want to hear the old stuff, but once you do that you're an oldies group.

YOUNG: Right. I've got a problem already with *Harvest Moon.* The band that plays *Harvest Moon* best was there last night. But what I'm gonna do next, there's no way for them, it'll never happen. And I don't even know what that thing is. But I know that whatever band I have next, there's probably no way that *they* can play *Harvest Moon*! So I'll go out there and won't do it. And people think that I do this on purpose, go out and not do what they want to hear, because it's some streak that I have. But the truth of the matter is, it's impossible. How can I go somewhere else and still be where I am? How can I change and not change? I can't drag this with me or it won't let me go all the way. It's like a fuckin' bungee cord. (*laughter*)

BUCK: I saw y'all and Crazy Horse in '78—oh, there I go, saying "y'all"—

YOUNG: Hey, let those y'alls come out!

BUCK: —when you did *Rust Never Sleeps*, before the record came out. And that always fascinates me, when a band challenges you with new stuff. I hate when it's just "these are the hits." 'Cause they always look bored—and I know I am.

YOUNG: I like to do it backwards. Go out and play the songs first before anybody knows what they are, then you really got to bang 'em down. And they get to either dig it or not dig it, but it's real. That makes it fun even if you don't get the big reaction.

BUCK: It's funny, because for years we would make a record and go on tour and do like three or four new songs. And every time, the next year's hit single was one of the new songs. We'd say, here's this song that really means a lot to us, and they liked the old stuff. The next year they're screaming for that one they didn't notice the time before.

YOUNG: Then somebody throws the paper at you: "The new songs don't have the edge of songs you were doing a year or two before." Like somehow you've lost something. Then you go back (to that time) and the same guy was saying, "These new songs are not as good as the ones on the last . . ."

MUSICIAN: *The songs got good in retrospect.*

BUCK: It's a lovely process. Our first record did relatively well with critics or whatever. And I still hear: "*Murmur*, best thing you've ever done." Well, you just wiped out the '80s and '90s for me, thank you very much.

YOUNG: Oh yeah. What was it some guy said to me? "Oh man, I used to listen to your stuff all the time. You were great!" (*laughs*) I said, what did you do, hit a wall or something? Ah well . . .

MUSICIAN: *Speaking of critics, what's your feeling about Ice-T being released by Warners, your label?*

YOUNG: Well, Ice is great so wherever he goes it's gonna be great. I've known him for four or five years now, since I met him in New Zealand. I think what he did with "Cop Killer" indicates that people don't understand art. They think art is obvious. If you say it literally, that's what you mean. The context you present something in and the way you present it is meaningless to these censor-types. That's where art meets the wall. That song's attitude is no more bothersome than any other song.

BUCK: I don't know the machinations. Personally, I think (Warner Brothers) should have stuck with him if that's what he wanted. If they dropped him out of cowardice, I think it's a cheap move. If he wanted to get away because of the controversy, that's something else. But I think there's probably racism in that I don't think a lot of people believe that a black guy can create a character and make a piece of art about an experience. Like, "It has to be real 'cause that's all he knows."

YOUNG: I remember when I first saw him, in some little club in New Zealand. God it was crazy. There was this brown line along the wall as people were lined up to go to the bathroom. Ice was playing and these lights were going on and off—and then I realized, the line was a line of shit. Somebody had taken a piece of shit and dragged it along the wall. (*laughter*) Now this was way before Ice had his corporate problems. But it may have been kind of a premonition.

MUSICIAN: *When you perform, how much does the audience or the mood of the place determine what you play?*

BUCK: What we owe the audience is the best we can give them. It's not necessarily the hit songs. Some nights I'll put in all five of our semi-hit singles. But you know, that's cheating! What we need to do is what we feel real strongly about. Nothing against the hits. But what I feel I have to do for the audience is show up on time and play to the best of my abilities. It's not necessarily the songs they want to hear.

I do a set list every night but over the course of our last tour I'd say we did about 100 songs, and we do about 25 a night. Only once in our entire career have we gone from the first song to the last according to the set list. The road crew had that one framed for about a month.

MUSICIAN: *Were your solo selections last night predetermined or improvised on the spot?*

YOUNG: Well, for the camera guys I made an acoustic set list. And I stuck to it, mostly. When I started playing out acoustic again a year ago January, I had a set list. I had 15 songs and 11 of them were new, and I didn't even know the songs that well. But after I proved to myself that I could do that, it didn't hold the same kind of challenge. Then it didn't matter anymore, so I started chucking the list and doing it the way I did a long time ago, where it didn't matter if they were old or new songs. That's generally the way I do it. Which is probably the way I appeared last night, even though in reality I sat down and thought about it. 'Cause I had the band there, and all the new songs that I would do acoustically at random I had to compartmentalize and think about, "Well, should the band play this song first so if they play that one well they'll be confident when the one they don't know that well comes along, and they'll think that they're great and they might play it well without thinking about it?" (*laughter*) All these things that you have to think about are extra when you're dealing with a band that may or may not know the material.

So I picked the two *Trans* songs first. 'Cause if they were as into the groove as I was, or in the same way that I was, then it would have been a really great transition. David Briggs and I were talking about the show last night. And we feel it was like, we went up, we flew and we landed it. But the thing never should have left the hangar. There were things ready to fall off everywhere and we could have crashed very easily. (*laughs*) But we got enough so that on the report card it looks very good.

MUSICIAN: *Do you think the performance was altered by the fact of being a TV production?*

YOUNG: I don't think so. I think that particular venue for playing music and the way it was in there was as good as it can get. It was like a beautiful thing.

BUCK: That's why *Unplugged* is kind of pleasant, because it actually mimics a live show. So much other TV has nothing to do about anything except what goes on this little screen and comes out of this three-inch speaker. I hate to sound like Gloria Swanson in *Sunset Boulevard* but you've got a guy juggling plates and a guy teaching a bear to dance and Oprah over here and you're in the middle, and it kind of reduces you to that level. When we did *Saturday Night Live* I saw the show and it was like, "Oh, I'm not in that song, am I?" Kate Pierson was singing, and she's a great singer, dressed real nice, and there's one second where the camera pans past her and you see the back of this guy's head—that's me!

We did all these European TV shows where it's local and there's a Belgian synth pop duo and then some little kids singing a song about going to the beach and then a dance contest and then us. Just like amateur hour. I remember one show where they had to supply the drums and there were no cymbals. The guy said, well, you only said you wanted drums. (*laughter*)

MUSICIAN: *Is your opposition to current digital technology related to the fact that several of your records have yet to be released as CDs?*

YOUNG: No, it's not connected. The records that haven't come out on CD haven't because the record company doesn't want to put them out, usually. In the case of Geffen it's not worth the money to them. But we've mastered them all recently. And it keeps changing too, every three or four months there's a better way to master digitally. To get a little closer to the original sound. But digital is completely fucked anyway. We're in the dark ages of recorded sound. And there's no solution other than changing to a different thing that hasn't been invented yet, some kind of chemical-based computer, instead of being based on precious metals. Maybe a kind of chemical gas that does the same thing but has more variability in its computation so you get more colors. 'Cause we're not listening to music, we're listening to a reconstituted replica clone of music. We don't hear it anymore. Since '82 it's been gone. That's how I feel about it.

But I could go on about that for a long time. And if they ever put me in the Rock and Roll Hall of Fame they'll regret it, 'cause I will not stop talking about it, it'll go on all fucking night. So let that be a warning to all you assholes with your tuxedos.

MUSICIAN: *So what do you think about the Rock and Roll Hall of Fame?*

BUCK: Maybe when I'm 45 I'll dig it. It does kind of smack of this older rich boy's club. But for people who haven't seen that kind of financial reward, the Ruth Browns and Etta Jameses, it's a great thing. I went to the Grammys one time, and the Grammy show itself is a stultifying boring piece of shit. But if you go in the afternoon when it's not televised, and they give out the gospel and blues awards, for them it's often like a validation of their life. It's very moving, and people break down and cry . . . and it's beautiful. It's the real thing. So for that alone they should have the rock and roll hall, for the pioneers, the rhythm and blues folks. And maybe when we're eligible I'll like it. I've figured it out, that's in 2006 or 2007, depending if they count our first single. But right now the '70s are coming up. That's pretty grim.

It's pretty funny that they still haven't broken ground yet. It's like some really long joke where you keep waiting for the punch line. Maybe Andy Kaufman will dig the first spoonful.

YOUNG: You know, I think the Rock and Roll Hall of Fame was a great idea when it started out. But I think they ought to close the hall. I think it's full. I think it's too early for a lot of the people who are going in now, and they're just looking for people to go in because they're out of people! OK? They've got this thing going but let's face it—they've had the whole past to draw on for the first two or three years, and then they took all of that, what really *is* the hall of fame stuff. And now, they've got to come up with new stuff every year: "Let's see, what happened in 1968?" Before they had 50 years to draw from.

So they should close and reopen it. It just came to me. Closed "for renovations and repairs." Due to lack of interest. I think they can say they have enough people in for the foundation. Now they should wait 20 years. Or close it now and call it the "Original Rock and Roll Hall of Fame." Then they could have a grand re-opening.

And I say that in all sincerity. Close the doors. I think I'm developing an attitude about it.

NEIL YOUNG: OUR 1993 ARTIST OF THE YEAR

Greil Marcus | January 1994 | *Spin*

In June 1993 Young headed out on a European tour, backed by 1960s R&B legends Booker T. and the M.G.s. This was Young's first of many jaunts on the lucrative summer festival circuit, sharing stages in 1993 with the likes of Metallica, the Black Crowes, and Pearl Jam. He was also joined by the legendary Stax house band on a late summer US tour.

Chronologically halfway between the earliest and latest pieces in this collection, this piece by the dean of American rock journalists, Greil Marcus, serves as a critical overview of the first part of the artist's career, an overview that contextualizes Young's renewed relevance in the early 1990s. Young spends time discussing the failure of *Landing on Water* in the context of the Geffen albums, "coming out of an egg" with *Freedom*, and the revelation that the inconceivable complexity of pure sound that's he's chasing is God. –Ed.

Neil Young and I were talking in the deserted parking lot of the Mountain House, a restaurant on Skyline Boulevard in the mountains above Stanford University, near La Honda, where Young lives. Although I'd driven down from Berkeley, I'd grown up here, and as I headed down Skyline—a rambling two-lane shadowed by huge fir trees—I wondered if the radio was going to cough up any of Young's music: At the last minute it did—the radio standard "Rockin' in the Free World," the sonic assault that closed his 1989 album, *Freedom*.

It's a brutal, raging song about the free world as a black hole, throwing out the tale of a woman choosing between crack and her baby (it's no choice at all, despite those perfect lines juggling life and death and just life, "That's one more kid / That'll never go to school / Never get to fall in love / Never get to be cool"). I gunned the motor, sped past the Mountain House, turned the car around and drove back when the song was over. Pulling into the lot, though, waiting for Young, I thought about how you never hear the version of "Rockin' in the Free World" that opens *Freedom*: Young solo, playing acoustic guitar and harmonica, onstage at Jones Beach on Long Island, singing a song no one there had heard before. It's an altogether bizarre recording. In some ways it's much tougher, meaner, than the electric take, even if it lacks the last verse about "a kinder, gentler machine-gun hand," the fabulous, mindless rant about Styrofoam, the ozone layer, cars, highways, and the world going to hell. From Jones Beach you get not irony and controlled fury but a picture of a scorned prophet telling people what they don't want to hear—or, rather, what they aren't even listening to. Shouts from the audience wash over the song, seemingly at all the wrong moments. There's no sense of anyone listening to anybody else. It's more like someone's tossed a beach ball into the crowd and it's bouncing from hand to hand; people are cheering for *that*. Well, that's always been my fantasy of what was going on that night; I couldn't help asking Young what had.

He bore down straight off. "See," he said, "the challenge to me is to do the new song, to deliver the shit out of the new song, to immerse myself in the song—and whatever else happens is part of that. Because if I'm doing that, nothing else matters. So what you heard was part of the recording; it was even part of the event, it was part of the time when this went down. I loved the crowd noise in it; to me it sounded incongruous—'What's going on here?' The sound of the background, the distraction—you can't fake that. Where else can you get that, but in a crowd? You have to go into a crowd and do something they can't . . . some of them are hearing it and some of them aren't. The idea is the tension: the tension of the crowd, and me, the performance, everything at once."

"Incongruous" and "tension" do fine as words to frame the entire scope of Neil Young's career. Even in 1967 and '68, with the superb Los Angeles folk-rock band Buffalo Springfield, he stood out—or didn't fit, dotting their albums with songs of torment and paranoia ("Nowadays Clancy Can't Even Sing," the shattering "Out of My Mind") among the celebrations and reveries. In 1969, when he joined Crosby, Stills & Nash, he was hailed as the solid ground for the group's New Chipmunk harmonies (though, to be fair, it was only onstage with CSN that Young was able to get his "Southern Man" off the ground, even though you won't find the evidence on the live *4 Way Street*). In his solo work, beginning in 1969 with *Neil Young and Everybody Knows This Is Nowhere*, he crashed back and forth between oversensitive singer-songwriter greeting cards ("A Man Needs a Maid") and all but nihilistic explosions of doubt, fatalism, and guitar madness—an ability to get *gone*—a cycle that defines his work to this day. In 1977, he was Johnny Rotten's favorite hippie—or maybe he was the only hippie Rotten would suffer to live. But by then, the *National Lampoon* public service announcement, "The previous half-hour of no Neil Young music has been brought to you by . . ." was as much a staple of FM radio as the endless spins of "Sugar Mountain," "Cinnamon Girl," and "Heart of Gold" the spot was presumably meant to negate. It's possible that in the '80, however, the name "Neil Young" was heard on the radio more often by way of Lynyrd Skynyrd's "Sweet Home Alabama" than by DJs announcing his own songs.

Pairing a cool, folkie dream like *Comes a Time* with a cage-rattler like *re·ac·tor*, Young was his own most complete critic, no matter which side he was on, or you were. "Incongruous" and "tension" are, perhaps, not strong enough—with Neil Young, at least every other record sounds like his last word, a dried-up nothing-more-to-say, or a damned farewell. You don't exactly keep up with Neil Young; he'll hold your hand one minute and burst into flames the next.

He may look like a star today, when his presence is both ubiquitous and strong—tearing up the Bob Dylan 30th-anniversary tribute concert and releasing *Harvest Moon*, his highest-charting album for 13 years, in late 1992; in 1993 combining a solid *Unplugged* and an even better PBS *Centerstage* with a successful *Unplugged* release and a greatest-hits tour with Booker T. and the MG's, then again stealing the show at the MTV Video Music Awards, using Pearl Jam as backup for "Rockin' in the Free World"—but in fact, hits for Neil Young are as incongruous as anything else. He only seems like a star: On his own he's had precisely one No. 1 album and single, 1972's *Harvest* and its "Heart of Gold."

If the 48-year-old Young can be named Artist of the Year for 1993, it's not only because of what he's done over the last 12 months or so, but because of the extraordinary fusion of weight and grace in his work of the last four years. Beginning with the five-song non-US release *El Dorado* ("A declaration," Young says today)—spare, wild demos for songs that would turn up on *Freedom*—he moved to the 1990 *Ragged Glory* with his longtime bandmates in Crazy Horse (the album title reviewed the album), and from there to an alliance with Sonic Youth for the tour that was captured on *Weld* (two discs of songs) and *Arc* (one disc of orchestrated feedback). These records brought Young the title Grandfather of Grunge, and the nearly absolute credibility he currently enjoys.

"None of these old guys around know how to do it," Young told Terry Gross on the NPR radio show *Fresh Air*, when, in 1992, she asked him how it felt to play "that loud grunge sound . . . as somebody in your 40s who's been playing since the mid-'60s, playing a music that mostly people who are a generation younger then you know—" "I know how," Young said. "If they were as lucky as me, they'd be doing it too. I mean, it's fantastic. There's no sensation like it."

But Young is his own inheritor, and he makes sense as Artist of the Year less for what he's done than for where he is. On his own self-defined ground, he also occupies a certain public center—the unstable moral center of the most extreme contemporary white rock 'n' roll, from Nirvana and Bikini Kill to Bratmobile and Pearl Jam. At the same time, there is a recognition that Young has a capacity for a greater musical extremism—which is a kind of moral extremism, a picture of limits and of limits transgressed—than any of his erstwhile soulmates, no matter that most of them could be his biological (never mind musical) children. And as some of them now wrestle with the sort of commercial success Young has never quite known and is never likely to, there is also a recognition that regardless of how extreme Young gets, he can always get back from any edge he calls into being. He can open up a hole in the world turning over the first guitar solo in "Over and Over," on *Ragged Glory*, dive through it, and then find himself in the sylvan glades of *Harvest Moon*.

It all looks shining—but with Neil Young there is always a fine line between riding the wind and, as one character on Young's 1974 *On the Beach* says to another, pissing into it. Novelist John Irving once said the same thing slightly differently, talking about Young both as a fellow artist and as "one of my heroes—along with Bob Dylan. They're not afraid to embarrass themselves—and you've got to be able to do that."

Young has never been afraid to embarrass himself (or his listeners: I always try to mentally rewrite "On our foggy trips," the sappy line in "Like a Hurricane" that comes just before Young as a guitarist turns the metaphor of the song's title into fact), and his current ascendance is, among other things, merely a moment in a long career. Ten years ago, matters looked altogether different. Beginning with *Trans*, a proto-techno album, Young launched a whole series of records that seemed to connect with nothing: *Everybody's Rockin'* (a blend set of rockabilly exercises sealed with the deathless "Ronnie and Nancy do the boppin' along / Rockin' in the White House all night long"), the vaguely country *Old Ways, Landing on Water*, the stunningly pallid *Life*, and the stilted *This Note's for You*. The records rested briefly in the lower regions of the charts and then disappeared almost as if they'd never been. Early on, Geffen, Young's label from 1983's *Trans* through 1987's *Life* (Reprise was his label before and has been since), took the remarkable step of suing Young for not being who he was supposed to be, seeking both damages and compensation for Young's production of records "which were not commercial in nature and musically uncharacteristic of Young's previous records."

With 1986's *Landing on Water*, a strange ad appeared in the U.K.: a picture of British Prime Minister Neville Chamberlain, fresh from signing the Munich Pact with Hitler in 1938, giving his speech proclaiming "Peace in our time," but holding in his hand not the infamous "piece of paper" that sealed the Munich sellout to the Nazis, but a copy of Young's album. I asked Young what in the world that was supposed to mean—that

Young was Chamberlain and Geffen was Hitler? He responded with a demonic chuckle. "I didn't have anything to do with that," he finally said. "But I kind of like the concept. Whoever thought of that must have been a genius." "If I can find my copy of that ad I'll send it to you," I said. "Oh, I'd love it," Young said. "I'd frame it. Sounds like high art to me. It *does*.

"You see," he said after a moment, "the cover and the title of that album, it's directions on how to survive an insurvivable thing: how to land on water, in a jet that's crashing. The most ridiculous damn thing you've ever heard of. You're really landing on water where there's no clear floor underneath you: everybody dies. That title was there because I knew where that album was going. I knew the process and the thought behind the people who were putting the album out; what they wanted me to do. That was me doing their method. And my title for it. Geffen tried to force me to do things—the record company, not David Geffen himself—when they saw that I was on—tangents. Ultimately, 'Make a record that sounds like you.' That was a very tough thing to do. But I tried to do a great record. We put everything we had into making that a great record. But I was just starting to come out of the trees at that point."

I said I could remember almost nothing about the records Young had made in the mid-'80s, except the titles—when I could remember the titles. "I was doing things that didn't really commit me one way or the other," he said. "I think I was disillusioned with a lot of things—"

"With what was going on in music?" I asked. "With what was going on in the country?"

"With life," Young said. "For whatever reason, I chose to disguise the music, and keep everything inside the music, and not reach out, do things in styles that I knew would piss everybody off so nobody would even buy it or listen to it."

He looked combative for a moment. "I don't make excuses for those records," he said. "I think those records are going to stand up, in time. I don't feel the records are not as good as the records I'm doing now. I just feel that they're not aimed at success—in any way. Yet if you put them on a wall—I look at them as if you're walking through a museum. You see somebody's paintings. You go, 'Wow, look at this period here!

Is *this* weird!' Especially considering what came after it and what was before it. And then you have to look at 'Well, during that period, what was the artist doing?'—and even knowing what he was doing, no one knew what was going to follow. Obviously (in my case), people considered nothing was going to follow. This was the end."

The dynamic, Young insisted, was just as crucial today, when everything he touches seems to come to life. Onstage, now, he said, "I really try to do something every time I go out there that stretches my capabilities, that puts me on the edge of going too far—where it might not work. But if I deliver the song right,"—then, Young said, something new can happen, and the museum vanishes. "If I deliver the song right, then it'll make people forget who I am. What I'm doing and what I've done. Especially what I've done. That's the only way to the next step."

I said that for me, as a fan, the next step was when I saw Young on *Saturday Night Live* on September 30, 1989, a picture of a very dead-looking Elvis Presley on his T-shirt, flailing all over the stage, nearly down on his knees shaking bent notes out of his guitar for the then-unreleased "Rockin' in the Free World." Not catching a word, I was happy to be lost in the sound, and then thinking when it was over, "If he's been away, he's sure as hell back."

"That's when I was starting to get sonic," Young said. "I knew that I was starting to break out. That I was coming out of an egg. The egg started to crack, pretty soon pieces of white shit were flying everywhere, and—there I was again. I could break out of the shell that I'd put around myself. I don't know how this happened, or why it happened, but it happened. Maybe it had to do with the fact that I'd already been making records for 17 years before it happened.

"It's that old expression you hear," he said, "'How can I miss you if you don't go away?'"

He lost me there: How can you miss *yourself*?

Young grinned. "Right," he said. "How can you find yourself if you don't lose yourself? How can you be renewed if—if you don't get old? You can't. You *have* to do that. There have to be peaks and valleys, or it's boring. If I've done that, I guess it's because I believe in that part of life, and I believe that's the way things are. Even if it means temporarily sacrificing success. I don't really give a shit."

For some reason I wasn't buying Young's up-is-down and down-is-up philosophy—maybe because somewhere in the back of my mind I figured it meant I'd now have to go back and really listen to all those albums I'd so happily dismissed. I argued for the present not just as a peak, but as a world. "In the last four years," I said, "it seems like you've been everywhere at once. It seems like there's been no place in the world of pop music where you weren't welcome, or comfortable. . . ." But if I wasn't buying Young's point of view, he wasn't buying mine.

"Look," he said, "this'll be history at some point, too. A point where people will be saying, 'Well, there was a time when Neil Young could have done anything—and *now* look at him. Can't do shit.' That's down the road. I know that. But I don't care. Because I know it's coming. By then—who knows? Record companies may be paying millions of dollars for any one of my records, no matter what the fuck it is. Or I may not be able to get a contract. I don't know these things. Right now, everybody thinks I'm great. But I've been there before.

"I know that the sacrifice of success breeds longevity," Young said. "That's an axiom. Being willing to give up success in the short run ensures a long run. If you're really doing what you want to do. I think that works. I don't know. I won't know for 20 years." He broke off laughing.

It wasn't as if, Young had said earlier, that the present was any sort of utopia. He wasn't referring to crime, or pollution—he was referring to digital recording.

We'd been talking politics. No, Young said, he couldn't see himself playing the White House, were Bill Clinton to invite him. While Young liked the Clintons' health plan, he saw nothing in Clinton's response to the Farm Aid programs Young has supported for years. It was no denunciation; one sentence into a thought about the preservation of the family farm, Young talked circles around himself. "It's like interstates against two-lane blacktops," he said with weary disgust. "Route 66 is dying—and yet it's an American tradition. Is this progress, or are we going to be saying in 20 years, 'Oh, we should have kept Route 66 alive, and kept all of these beautiful little motels going, and charged people a certain something for traveling on the road, because it's a piece of history?"

This took us quickly enough to the death of vinyl—but immediately Young's regret turned into anger and his vagueness into specifics. It was a question, he was saying, of the fullness of sound—the fullness, really, of the picture a musician could draw of the possibilities of life. "Someday," Young said, "the digital age will be seen as the Dark Ages of recorded sound."

We were talking about "Cowgirl in the Sand," from 1969, as explosive as anything Young has ever done on old vinyl, but dead on its CD reissue: Turn up the volume, the bass, lock the doors, set fire to your speakers, you can't make it *sound.* Analog recording, Young said, "produces real emotion, because there are so many possibilities for the sound in that recording, so many variations in sound that are recorded, that it's almost like real life." He didn't mean like a live show; he meant the way you can walk down a street and never begin to exhaust the possibilities of light and shadow, noise and quiet, that one street holds. Digital, though, is a single, stable picture. Young described the record industry sitting in a room, changing the picture: "'We don't really need to see the sky in all its detail—just paint that in blue. Now, look'"—Young pointed up through the trees around the Mountain House to the clear Bay Area sky—"'that's *blue.* There are really no nuances to that that we need to put in so—it's blue. Fine. *No one will know.*'

"The hardest thing for me now," Young said, "is to listen to my own records. Because I know what's not there. I know that when people go out to buy a record, today, that it doesn't resemble what's really going on in the studio." He doesn't use analog tape anymore, not even for himself, Young said, "because it's too depressing. You hear it, and then it's gone. I don't want to hear it. I wouldn't be able to make records anymore. I have to know what's gone right away, and just deal with it. Rather than make the record, having it sound great, and then lose it, at the last minute, when it goes to the consumer, and go, 'Well, the consumer got one-tenth of what I heard'—which is what I think they're getting.

"Give us another 10, maybe 15 years," Young said, "and we'll be into some other kind of recording. Maybe something chemically based—computations made with chemicals, as a transporting agent, instead of hard metals." Young pointed at a six-paned screened window on the front of the Mountain House. "Look," he said, "imagine that window is a drumbeat. The digital drumbeat is six big panes. And the analog drumbeat is somewhere smaller than every one of the tiny little screen squares—that's the amount of detail that's missing. You have a universe of possibilities—averaged out to one color. And the way those possibilities, those sounds, bounce around the room, is another thing altogether. That's why you can listen to old records over and over again—and wherever you're standing in the room, it's different."

"There's a sense of surprise in the song," I said. "No matter how many times you've heard it, you still aren't ready for what's coming."

Young glared at the window again. "That's right," he said. "Because your mind cannot conceive of the—that, that, I think, is God. That's it. Things were created with such detail that the human mind can never understand it. Can't encompass it. Therefore, it's like every time you hear a pure sound, it's like being washed with the water of heaven. You're completely renewed."

Having thus solved the mystery of life—if not exactly the question of how to get that mystery down on tape—there seemed little more to say. There was one more thing I had to ask about, though: Young's car, an old surfer's Woodie, a station wagon paneled in gleaming wood. I hadn't seen anything like that for over 20 years. "What is that?" I asked. "That's a '47 Buick Roadmaster Estate Wagon," Young said in one breath, as if the 13 syllables were one word. "I got it in Hollywood. I paid 1,500 bucks for it. That was a lot of money—it was a mess." We looked at the pristine, slatted-wood ceiling inside. "That was all painted with orange construction paint." Really, it was something.

"It's a cool car," Young said, getting in. "Let's see if it'll start."

There was the groaning sound of a motor wheezing, not even coughing: pure emphysema. Young tried again with worse results. "It doesn't always do this," he said. He gave it one more try and the engine barely made a scratching sound. "Okay," Young said. "Now we wait." We waited. "I might have to go into 'Come on, Baby,'" he said. "You know, sing to it."

I had to ask: "All right, Neil, tell me: What song does this car respond to?"

"'Long May You Run,'" he said. "It likes that."

"You can do better than that," I said—I'd always hated the song. "Okay," Young said again. "I *feel* that this is it." He turned the key, there was a lumbering noise, then a horrible clatter, and the engine turned over.

Young drove off, and I drove down Skyline and then down Old La Honda Road, a steep, twisting, narrow stretch that leads to Sandhill Road, a great circle that runs through the Stanford foothills. Buzzing along, I realized I was coming up on the local Dead Man's Curve—the spot where, in September 1959, my first week of high school, two cars full of drunk teenagers met, head on.

All eight people were killed; the impact was so strong the two cars were stuck together by their tangled front grilles; the dead were thrown right out of their shoes. Knowing an educational opportunity when it saw one, the school board had the two cars loaded onto a flatbed truck and taken to every high school in the district. You got to climb up on the truck and look inside: the shoes were still there and the windows were smeared with dried blood. I remembered one kid wondering out loud if the radio still worked; I tried to remember what would have been on it. But then "Rockin' in the Free World" came back on my own radio, and I drove on back to Berkeley, pressing my luck, running the dial across the stations in search of my favorite Neil Young song, "Surfer Joe and Moe the Sleaze," from *re·ac·tor*, which I've never heard on the radio, not once.

NEIL YOUNG ON

The Meaning of Americana

"Well, there's a feeling, for sure. There's the space, and the wide-openness of–and it's a real abstract. It's real hard to describe that. But it's a collection of thoughts and a collection of images. I guess the most obvious one is the highway. And the cool car. But those are material things, and . . . there's a sense of leadership and tragedy and loss and everything that goes with that–with being a world leader and also having made incredible mistakes that cost a lot of lives. Things like that, that's in there, too. That's kinda like hanging in the landscape."

–from an interview with Dean Kuipers, *Ray Gun*, August 1995

I BUILD SOMETHING UP, I TEAR IT RIGHT DOWN: NEIL YOUNG AT 50

Nick Kent | December 1995 | *MOJO*

Neil Young and Crazy Horse recorded from late 1993 until late winter 1994. An album was mostly completed when Nirvana front man Kurt Cobain committed suicide on April 4, quoting Young's "it's better to burn out than to fade away" in his farewell note. Young quickly wrote and recorded the LP's new title track, "Sleeps with Angels," as a response. The album was released August 16, 1994.

Young didn't tour to promote the LP and kept a low profile the rest of the year, appearing at the usual benefit shows then on the Oscars to play "Philadelphia," his Best Original Song nominee. He lost to Bruce Springsteen's "Streets of Philadelphia," also from the Jonathan Demme-directed *Philadelphia*.

In January 1995 Young and Crazy Horse played two Voters for Choice benefits in Washington D.C. Before you could say "Even Flow," Young and Pearl Jam joined forces to record *Mirror Ball*, released in August. In March, Young recorded the soundtrack to Jim Jarmusch's *Dead Man*. The LP would be released in February 1996.

The August 1995 release of *Mirror Ball* coincided with a Neil Young and Pearl Jam European festival tour. After playing the standard fall Farm Aid show (solo) and Bridge School Benefit (with Crazy Horse), Young celebrated his fiftieth birthday on November 12. Two weeks later, on November 26, Young's long-time coproducer David Briggs died. This is one of the first interviews Briggs is given much consideration.

This article melds interviews from 1992 and 1995 to offer a rich overview of Young's musical life, with a focus on his recent work with Pearl Jam. Most of subjects and themes have necessarily been covered to this point, but the interest here is not only the depth of this interview, but the contrast between the immediacy of earlier responses and the more considered, retrospective answers here: "Look at how the time goes past." –Ed.

"IN THE FIELD OF opportunity/it's ploughing time again" crooned Neil Young back in the late 70s. Yet at no time have those eager sentiments seemed more appropriate to the Canadian singer-songwriters mercurial career than in the 90s. Right now, in fact, in 1995—the year he celebrates his 50th birthday this November 12.

In the first two months alone he was inducted into the Rock & Roll Hall Of Fame, playing there backed by Crazy Horse, then recorded an entire album of new material in four days backed by Pearl Jam in Seattle. He also re-signed to the troubled Warners record division in a prestige deal that, as a spin-off from the divisive boardroom squabbling that has so publicly embarrassed the company of late, ended up netting him (according to *Vanity Fair*) many more millions of dollars than he might otherwise have merited on previous record sales alone.

The new head of Warners who inked this extravagant deal was Danny Goldberg, previously the manager of Kurt Cobain, the haunted young rock star who'd quoted Young's line "It's better to burn out than to fade away" in his suicide note back in April 1994. Young was apparently devastated when he heard about it, and since has staunchly refused to address the subject directly, even though Cobain's ghost hangs heavy over his last two albums, *Sleeps With Angels* and *Mirror Ball.*

In early spring, he sat down in the studio with just an electric guitar and thumbed a series of melodies and themes, some familiar, some brand-new, to provide music for *Dead Man*, New York director Jim Jarmusch's black and white cowboy drama starring Johnny Depp and Robert Mitchum. Young had never heard of Jarmusch before, but, when approached via his management, fell in love with the movie's rough cut.

Not only did he soundtrack the film, but he turned up with Depp and Jarmusch at the Cannes Film Festival in May to promote it.

Next, he regrouped with Crazy Horse, cut a couple of new songs he'd written for the group, and played lead guitar for the band's soon-to-be-released album featuring songs written by the other members. He also found time to cameo on new albums by Bobby Charles and his old Canadian guitar hero, Randy Bachman.

By this autumn, Goldberg was no longer Warner Bros Records President, but Neil Young, fresh from an ecstatically received tour of European festival gigs, was very much part of the rostrum—indeed, now suddenly boasting his very own record label, Vapor, and a list of upcoming releases including the *Dead Man* soundtrack and a West Coast rock band called The Stonecutters.

Most interesting of all, Young and his manager Elliot Roberts have signed one of the few rock iconoclasts perhaps even more bloody-minded than he is himself—Jonathan Richman. A new record is finished for imminent release.

As if all this was not enough, Young devotes his spare time to an alternative vocation. Inspired by his quest to communicate as fully as possible with his severely retarded and crippled 17-year old son Ben, Young invents devices, including, this year alone, a specially modified electric wheelchair and computer—"Ben is my assistant; he's my tester"—that can help the handicapped to express themselves. He is also involved with, and partly funds, the Bridge Foundation, a special school for handicapped children run by his wife Pegi. "I don't really do much" he'll shrug; "I'm just a figurehead, public relations kind of guy. My wife does all the work." Most recently, Young made a take-over bid for Lionel Trains, a toy company beloved by he and his son.

At six-foot-two with a weathered face and suspicious, penetrating eyes, Young is an imposing figure at the best of times, and his renowned antipathy toward journalists (his first ever review, back in Canada in 1964 described his songs as "just a string of clichés," and he seems to have borne a grudge ever since) can make him a nerve-wracking interview. But during the two sessions (October 1992 and June 1995) from which this interview is culled, when his frosty veneer cracks, you feel his warmth, sincerity, argumentative idealism and generosity of spirit rise to the fore. He is, above all, a very, very funny man with a dry sardonic wit bubbling just under the surface whenever he speaks.

Young's 11-year-old Amber accompanies him to our 1995 interview in San Francisco. The youngest of his three children (his eldest Zeke, now works for a record company in Los Angeles), Amber is the only one not to suffer from cerebral palsy. She has her mother Pegi's blonde hair, a glowing West Coast complexion, and a pair of remarkable eyes the living spit of her father's. During a short-filmed interview with Young for MTV, she manages to get herself filmed briefly standing next to her father, and then spends the rest of the afternoon haranguing him to make sure she appears in the finished report. He, of course, has other ideas. "Listen honey," he mutters, "Take your old man's word for it, OK? You don't need the exposure."

On one of your most poignant and best-loved songs, "Helpless," you sing about a town in North Ontario which you keep returning to in your mind for comfort. I've always presumed you're singing about the town in which you were born?

Well, it's not literally a specific town so much as a feeling. Actually, it's a couple of towns. Omemee, Ontario, is one of them. It's where I first went to school and spent my formative years. Actually I was born in Toronto . . . "I was born in Toronto" . . . God, that sounds like the first line of a Bruce Springsteen song (laughs). But Toronto is only seven miles from Omemee.

Was there a lot of music in the house when you were growing up?

When I was growing up, I remember guys like Frankie Laine. See, around the same time as Elvis, there was also *Rawhide* and all that cowboy stuff. I loved that stuff—I even covered one of his songs on the *Old Ways* album. "The Wayward Wind." It was one of his biggest hits up in Canada. See, I used to walk by a rail-road track on my way to school everyday. There was even a real hobo's shack there. The song and the image have always stayed with me. When I hear it, I always think of being five or six walking past that old shack and the rail-road tracks gleaming in the sun and on my way to school everyday with my little transistor radio up to my ear.

Another song from that period that I loved, and also ended up doing a version of with Crazy Horse and Jack Nitzsche on piano, that's going to end up on *Archives*—it's a country waltz called "It Might

Have Been" recorded by Jo London. It was a big hit in Canada though it didn't mean anything in the States. Great record. Real, real soulful rendition. Unfortunately on my version, I screwed up almost all the words (laughs).

Were your parents musically oriented?

Well, of the two of them, my father was definitely more musically oriented. Mom and Dad used to listen to the old big bands, Lena Horne, Della Reese, Tommy Dorsey, Glen Miller Orchestra, Cab Calloway . . .

When you were just beginning your teens, your father Scott Young, a well-known Canadian journalist, left your mother to live with another woman. At 16 you decided to drop out and become a full-time rock musician. How supportive were your parents?

Well, as my Dad wasn't living with me at the time, he didn't have the perspective on it that my mother had. If he had, he'd have seen how into the music I was, but at the same time he'd have been pushing me to stay on at school, just like my mother was. And I definitely think he'd have certainly been stronger at persuading me to stay on, but the classic thing that happens in family break-ups . . . the perspective gets changed. The father will always have a negative reaction to what the mother does particularly if she's being soft on the child. Without the true understanding of what's going on, he'll just say that "it's wrong." It's a reaction created out of frustration over not being able to really voice an opinion. So . . . to say that my father was less into my music than my mother would be unfair. Although my mother was more supportive.

You started playing at 14. What was your first guitar?

My first was this little plastic Arthur Godfrey ukulele, then I seem to remember a baritone uke, then I had a banjo. So I had all these different-sounding instruments which I played the same way. I played electric lead guitar first. Then I started rocking out in a community-club teenage band. First we were called The Esquires. Then we changed it to The Stardusters. And after that we settled on being called The Squires. Kinda like Spinal Tap's early days!

Legend has it that "Don't Cry No Tears" from *Zuma* is the first song you ever wrote . . .

No, that was only one of the first 30 or 40 songs I wrote! Oh yeah, there were a lot of them from back then. Unfortunately, we only have glimmers of most of them but we do have actual recordings of five of them which you're going to hear when the *Archives* finally appear. I really love these tracks, by the way. I'm not embarrassed by them or anything because I'm so young. I mean, some of them I wanted to hear over and over again, whereas others were clearly not so successful. I think it's real interesting when you hear the bad ones with the good ones . . .

After The Squires, you joined a band called The Mynah Birds in '65 and apparently even recorded an album with them that never came out . . .

Yeah, there are tapes of me and The Mynah Birds but I've not been able to get hold of them. I only sang a little bit in that group . . . Rick James and Bruce Palmer were in the group also. Right after I left The Mynah Birds I took up as a solo folk singer. Come to think of it, I did a bit of that before The Mynah Birds also. After I arrived in Toronto I tried to keep my band going and then tried to work with several others. But it just never worked out for me there. I could never get anything going in Toronto, never even got one gig with a band. I just couldn't break into that scene. So I moved instead toward acoustic music and immediately became very introspective and musically inward. That's the beginning of that whole side of my music.

From the outside, it looked like Canada in the early '60s had a very creative scene going for it, with people like Leonard Cohen, Joni Mitchell, Gordon Lightfoot, Ronnie Hawkins and The Band. But from the inside, was there really a "scene" at all and were you a part of it?

Not really, no. They were all way above me at that time. The Hawks were the best band in Toronto which is the biggest city in Canada, musically. And I'd just come from a place called Thunder Bay which is between Winnipeg and Toronto. We'd done really well there but couldn't get a gig to save our lives in Toronto. All we ever did was practice. So I ended up cruising around by myself on acoustic guitar, playing my songs at coffee houses for a while, just showing up at these places. It was quite an experience! I remember it now as . . . Wow, this is really out-on-the-edge! Walking around in the middle of the night in the snow, wondering where to go next!

Robbie Robertson once said that the power of the songs he wrote for The Band about America came from the fact that he had the perspective of a foreigner arriving in the promised land. Did you feel that way when, at the very beginning of 1966, you left Toronto and drove to Los Angeles in an undertaker's hearse. Is the drive a good memory?

It's pretty good, yeah, but I got burnt out somewhere around Albuquerque. I just collapsed basically. We'd met a bunch of hippies and ended up crashing in their pad. I slept for a couple of days, then went to the hospital for exhaustion. They told me to eat, sleep and rest—the usual. In retrospect, I'm really not sure what it was that kept me up for so long. I'm not sure if any chemicals were involved.

You drove down with Bruce Palmer, looking for Stephen Stills and Richie Furay, whom you'd met playing in a folk revue in New York City. Legend has it you bumped into each other in a traffic jam . . .

Yeah, that's true. Well, it took us about 10 days to find them but we knew Stephen and Richie were down there. I was looking to hook up with Stephen in particular. When we met them in February '66 The Buffalo Springfield began the same day.

It's been said that at that time, Stills was a folkie who was just beginning to rock. Meanwhile, you were a rocker who was starting to get interested in folk-music . . .

Yeah, that's pretty accurate but I'd been into Dylan since '63 when I heard his very first album; that left a big impression on me. And later, the Byrds were great. What they did was deeply cool. They really impressed me.

What made you want to work with Stills?

His voice. He was a really great singer. He had the beginnings of being an electric guitar player too. Somehow we could play lead guitar parts simultaneously and not get in each other's way. And that's real rare. It gave the sound a real edge. And it has absolutely nothing to do with what he does by himself and what I do by myself.

Apparently, just as The Buffalo Springfield was starting to get successful, your epilepsy began . . .

Well, I had been that way before but yeah, I started to have big seizures when the Springfield started to happen.

You actually had a fit on-stage while playing. Can you remember what triggered it?

(After long pause) I'm not sure. Now when it happens, I can control it. I don't know whether I just couldn't control it or whether there just weren't too many new things happening to me. Whatever it was, I'd just get this feeling inside of me and I'd just go . . . Now, when I get that feeling, I'll lay back or turn off everything. Close off the input for a while. It's a little hard to do that when you're on-stage in front of a lot of people. Although I still do it I haven't had any "events" for almost 20 years. None of any real consequence anyway. But I have had . . . y'know, tremors. I sense it's still there.

Buffalo Springfield played the fabled Monterey Pop festival in 1967. You didn't.

No, I was out of the group at that time. Actually, the reason I initially left the group was because I didn't want to do the *Johnny Carson Tonight Show*. I thought it was belittling what The Buffalo Springfield was doing. That audience wouldn't have understood us. We'd have been just a fuckin' curiosity to them.

At that time you were linking up creatively with arranger Jack Nitzsche, as well as a group called The Rockets who'd become Crazy Horse. Were you actively looking for other people to work with at this time?

Yeah . . . Well, I just liked these people. I wasn't looking, I just found 'em. All of a sudden, there are these other people and I'd sorta go back and forth between them and the Springfield.

Jack taught me a lot: I mean, he'd already worked as an arranger for Spector and had played piano on recording sessions with The

Rolling Stones. I met him in a club in Hollywood right when the Springfield first started. We were introduced by Greene and Stone who were our managers then. We just liked each other and always had a great time together. I love listening to all his ideas. Plus I liked hanging out with him because he always got all the new records sent to him every week and he'd sit and listen to them, forming his opinions . . . He worked as an independent arranger back then. He was a very sought-after guy.

When I quit the Springfield, I was living at Jack's house with him, his wife Gracia and his son, "Little" Jack. 45s would be coming in every week and I remember the day we got the first Jimi Hendrix Experience single—this was way before the first album had been released—and all of us were just awe-struck at how raw the guy sounded. That first album of mine was basically just Jack and me.

Six months after your first album comes *Everybody Knows This Is Nowhere* in which you introduce the world to Crazy Horse—and also the sound of you playing guitar in D modal tuning. It gives your songs a very singular power and tone best represented on "Cinnamon Girl," for example. Did you actually discover that sound and tuning from playing with Crazy Horse?

Actually, no. Where it comes from originally is . . . Stills and I on "Bluebird." We discovered this D modal tuning at around the same time in '66, I think . . . We'd play in that tuning together a lot. This was when ragas were happening and D modal made it possible to have that droning sound going on all the time, that's where it started. Only I took it to the next level which is how "The Loner" and "Cinnamon Girl" happened. You make a traditional chord shape and any finger that doesn't work, you just lift it up and let the string just ring. I've used that tuning throughout my career right up to today. You can hear it on everything from "Fuckin' Up" on *Ragged Glory* to "War Of Man" and "One Of These Days" on *Harvest Moon*. Lots of songs.

You recorded another album with Crazy Horse in '69 straight after *Everybody Knows This Is Nowhere*, that also had Jack Nitzsche on piano. It was apparently a sort of country-rock affair and most of

the tracks were recorded live. Then you scrapped it all of a sudden and put out *Gold Rush* instead. Why?

Well, it wasn't really scrapped (pauses). It exists (longer pause). See, things were moving very quickly at that time so it's hard to say . . . exactly why I went for *Gold Rush* instead of that project. I just remember thinking that *Gold Rush* was the next logical step after *Everybody*. Just after I'd begun playing with CSNY, I went out on the road and did some really funky things that indicated that our next album would be in that particular vein. We recorded "Wonderin'," "Dance Dance Dance," "It Might Have Been," "Winterlong" and several others. They'll appear on the *Archives*, I've had them transferred to digital.

Let's move on to *After The Gold Rush*, then. Many of the songs were inspired by a film screenplay written by the actor Dean Stockwell. What was the film actually about?

It was all about the day of the great earthquake in Topanga Canyon when a great wave of water flooded the place. It was a pretty off-the-wall concept, they tried to get some money from Universal Pictures. But that fell through because it was too much of an art project. I think, had it been made it would stand as a contemporary to *Easy Rider* and it would have had a similar effect. The script itself was full of imagery, change . . . It was very unique actually. I really wish that movie had been made, because it could have really defined an important moment in the culture.

With *After The Gold Rush* you became incredibly successful. At the same time, you had this image of someone very confused, isolated, emotionally fragile and introspective. Was that a fair evaluation of your condition?

No, not really, I didn't see myself like that, I always thought there was a funny side to my music. But see, my sense of humor hadn't really been appreciated at that point in my career. Shit, it hadn't even been noticed (laughs). I mean, "Last Trip To Tulsa" . . . that's my idea of a really funny song and that's just one of 'em.

Were you concerned about this image?

What image? Listen, there was nothing to be concerned about. I really just wanted to make music . . . My only concern was to make the fuckin' records sound right. When I finally got the studio together and played, I think, "Running Dry" (on *Everybody Knows This Is Nowhere*), that was my first live vocal. As was almost the whole of *Gold Rush* after it . . . Things like "I Believe In You"—that's when I started recording live.

Yes, but an image is created when you stand in front of an audience and perform and they treat you like a counter-culture icon . . .

Well, it's like a mirror. And you can't get away from a mirror if you stand in front of it all the time, right. But if you step away from it, you don't notice it anymore And that's what the stage is like for me. See, an image becomes meaningless in as much as it's always temporary.

After the overwhelming success of *Harvest*, your next new music was *Time Fades Away*, an abrasive-sounding live album from a 1973 stadium tour that you'd apparently rather forget. Over 20 years later, the memory of that tour and the subsequent record still seems too uncomfortable for you . . .

Well, we didn't put any of *Time Fades Away* on *Decade*, if that's what you mean. See, *Decade*'s good for that reason. It makes a statement about my work from my point of view. Things were added in abundance and omitted. There's different angles in there. It's not like an even editorial.

But "Don't Be Denied" for example is one of your best songs. It's also your most openly autobiographical . . .

Yeah, certainly. It's one of them, anyway. The other one's called "Hitchhiker." It's a contemporary of "Don't Be Denied" from 1975 and it was all about all the different drugs that I took. I started at the beginning and ran right through my years of drug usage up to that time, drawing parallels with other stuff. It's a very interesting song (laughs). Eventually I mutated it partly into a song called "Like An Inca" (on *Trans*). Only the chorus lived, though all the verses were gone. "Hitchhiker" is now probably bootlegged 'cos I played it six or seven times on some acoustic tour I did in the '90s.

Then in 1973 you went out to record *Tonight's The Night*—meditation on life, hard drugs and death that's gone on to stand as one of

your greatest, if bleakest albums to date. I've always been fascinated by the rumor that you wrote and tried to produce a Broadway play based on the record . . .

Yeah, we did. The plot was about a roadie who made it and then OD'd on drugs. *From Roadie To Riches* was the name of it (laughs). For Broadway in 1974 it was a little ahead of its time, as you can imagine.

Straight after recording the album, you took it on the road for a series of extremely controversial gigs . . .

Oh, that was a fabulous tour, one of my best. Over in England, The Rainbow . . . Bristol was the best ever . . . the Festival Hall . . . those were magical gigs. I did an encore at the latter with nobody there but Ahmet Ertegun who owns Atlantic records. I said, "Ahmet, I played so good tonight I think I deserve my own private encore." So we went out and played "Tonight's The Night" for the fourth time that evening (bursts out laughing) with no-one left in the theatre.

Actually, you didn't release *Tonight's The Night* till 1975. Instead, you put out *On The Beach*, a record you are still cagey about releasing on CD. Are a lot of your previous albums too personal to listen to comfortably now?

I'd say so, yeah. There are several records like *On The Beach* and *Time Fades Away*. See, that's something you have to understand: I don't make a habit of listening to my old stuff. Ever. I listened to *Weld* once since I've finished it. *Freedom* I've heard once. I spend so much time making them that when it's over, I just never want to listen to 'em again. I just send 'em out into the world like an evil father. "OK get out of here now. Be sure to write if you find a home!" (laughs)

At exactly the same moment *On The Beach* was released, you chose to relocate with CSN for a financially lucrative but musically unbalanced tour in '74.

Well, 1974 was the swansong of Crosby, Stills, Nash & Young for me.

On that tour, you performed a number of excellent songs you've still never released. I'm thinking of titles like "Traces," "Love-Art Blues"

and "Pushed It Over The End." What happened to those songs? [*All on 2014's* CSNY 1974. *—Ed.*]

Well they'll probably be out on the anthology too. Listen, if they'd had new songs with the authority that their old songs had, we could've knocked off four and five of mine so that just the best two surfaced . . . That would have truly been CSNY. But it wasn't to be, so the record never came out.

Let's move on to *Zuma*. After that dark stretch, it sounded like you'd suddenly been liberated. The most renowned composition on *Zuma* has to be "Cortez The Killer." I've always been intrigued about your personal opinion of the great explorer. Where did you get your information from?

It was a combination of imagination and knowledge. What Cortez represented to me is the explorer with two sides, one benevolent, the other utterly ruthless. I mean, look at Columbus! Everyone now knows he was less than great and he wasn't even there first (laughs). It always makes me question all these other so-called icons (smiles).

Another musical venture you embarked upon in the mid-'70s was a short tour of West Coast bars with a group called The Ducks . . .

Oh, The Ducks was basically me having fun and taking a musical vacation. It was a great band and a friend of mine managed them, so I got into them because it presented me with a perfect vehicle for playing in a band without being the leader or having to sing too many songs. I wrote a few songs with them but I was really just the lead guitarist.

After that, you returned to the studio to make *Comes A Time*, your most mellow, middle of the road recording since *Harvest* . . .

Well, I was going one way and then needed to move in entirely the opposite direction just for some kind of release. My career is built around a pattern that just keeps repeating itself over and over again. There's nothing surprising about it at all. My changes are as easy to predict as the sun coming up and down.

It's become something of a cliché to say that *Rust Never Sleeps*, the raucous follow-up to *Comes A Time*, was very influenced by the UK punk-rock scene at the time . . .

No, I wasn't really influenced by that scene. Most of the songs on that album had been written well before the Sex Pistols were ever heard of. "The Thrasher" was pretty much me writing about my experiences with Crosby, Stills & Nash in the mid-'70s. Do you know Lynyrd Skynyrd almost ended up recording "Powderfinger" before my version came out? We sent them an early demo of it because they wanted to do one of my songs.

Surprising, that. After all, Lynyrd Skynyrd put you down by name on "Sweet Home Alabama," their first hit single . . .

Oh, they didn't really put me down! But then again, maybe they did! (laughs) But not in a way that matters. Shit, I think "Sweet Home Alabama" is a great song. I've actually performed it live a couple of times myself.

After the major critical and sales success of *Rust Never Sleeps*, you embark on yet another long unsettling journey away from the mainstream. A journey that begins with *Hawks & Doves*.

Well, it's what you might call a transitional album for me. But that's not to say there aren't some really interesting things on there. "Comin' Apart At Every Nail" is good and I really like "Union Man." It's no big thing: just a funky little record that represents where I was at and what I was doing at that time.

***re·ac·tor* reunited you with Crazy Horse again. But the music on that record sounded so willfully primitive and brutal.**

We didn't spend as much time recording *re·ac·tor* as we should've. The life of both that record and the one after it—*Trans*—were sucked up by the regime we'd committed ourselves to. See, we were involved in this program with my young son Ben for 18 months which consumed between 15 and 18 hours of every day we had. It was just all-encompassing and it had a direct effect on the music of *re·ac·tor* and *Trans*. You see, my son is severely handicapped, and at that time was simply trying to find a way to talk, to communicate with other people. That's what *Trans* is all about. And that's why, on that record, you know I'm saying something but you can't understand what it is. Well, that's the exact same feeling I was getting from my son.

You seem to feel *Trans* is particularly underrated?

Underrated! Well, let's say I don't underrate *Trans*. I really like it, and think if anything is wrong, then it's down to the mixing. We had a lot of technical problems on that record, but the content of the record is great.

The release of *Trans* began your ill-starred liaison with Geffen Records. Actually, hadn't you already offered them an album entitled *Island In The Sun* which they refused?

Yeah, I offered that to Geffen just before *Trans*. It was a tropical thing all about sailing, ancient civilizations, islands and water. Actually two or three songs ended up on *Trans*.

Then came *Everybody's Rockin'*, a curious and underwhelming collection of '50s rock pastiches and easily your most mystifying record to date. You lost a lot of your audience with that record, I reckon . . .

Well that was as good as *Tonight's The Night* as far as I'm concerned. The character was strong, the story was great but unfortunately, the story never got to appear on the album. Before I got a chance to finish it—I got stopped from recording. Geffen cancelled a couple of sessions where I was going to do two songs—"Get Gone" and "Don't Take Your Love Away From Me"—that would've given a lot more depth to The Shocking Pinks. But if you didn't see the shows you wouldn't be able to get into it fully. Of course, it wasn't anywhere near as intense as *Tonight's The Night*. There was very little depth to the material obviously. They were all surface songs. But see, there was a time when music was like that, when all pop stars were like that. (Ardently) And it was good music, really good music. See, when I made albums like *Everybody's Rockin'* and everyone takes the shit out of 'em . . . I knew they could do that. What am I? Stupid? Did people really think I put that out thinking it was the greatest fuckin' thing I'd ever recorded? Obviously I'm aware it's not. Plus it was a way of further destroying what I'd already set up. Without doing that, I wouldn't be able to do what I'm doing now. If I build something up, I have to systematically tear it right down before people decide, "Oh that's how we can define him".

Peter Buck once told me that you and R.E.M. had been planning to record an album together in the mid-'80s (possibly using material that ended up on *Landing On Water*), but you couldn't enter a studio with them without being sued by Geffen . . .

There was certainly something like that going on back then. Actually it's funny: R.E.M. were going to go with Geffen, then they heard I was being sued and everything, they just dropped all contact with Geffen and signed with Warner Bros instead. Geffen actually lost R.E.M. simply for suing me over *Everybody's Rockin'*!

At the end of your problems with Geffen, you got back together with Crosby, Stills & Nash to make *American Dream*. The experience was not a happy one. Yet you still talk about possibly reuniting with them in some form.

Damn, you'd have thought our performance on Live Aid would have been enough to finish off any wave of nostalgia, wouldn't you? (laughs) Seriously though, I think CSNY reminds people of a certain feeling. Our audience want to see it alive again because somehow it verifies the feeling that they're alive too. CSNY—when it works—can make music that is very committed, heartfelt and sincere. It's not easy to get it out and it's not easy to overcome some of the bullshit around it. *American Dream* was an attempt that failed to reach anything like its true potential. But that's no reason for me to not try it again sometime.

After that, you suddenly seemed to get back to a state of real creative focus. Firstly with *Eldorado*, then *Freedom* shortly followed by *Ragged Glory*. What changed for you?

I really can't say. Just life—I've been doing this a long time. When the '80s started, I'd been making music for 15 years professionally. Now the '80s are usually the period that people tell me they lost me or I lost them. What happened was that I just wasn't being accessible. See, as far as I'm concerned, those records (*Trans*, *Everybody's Rockin'*, *Old Ways*) are as good as any record I've ever made. Maybe my '80s music should just be looked at as one record. Maybe it would be easier for people to understand.

You regrouped with Crazy Horse for *Ragged Glory* in 1990 with spectacular results—Yet after the *Rusted-Out Garage Tour* in '86–'87, you publicly vowed never to work with them again . . .

Well, that was a bad period for us. We weren't playing well then. Overall the material wasn't up to much. I made a film about that tour, the legendary *Muddy Track*! (laughs) I still want the films I directed to come out in a special six-pack: *Human Highway*, *Rust Never Sleeps*, *Journey Through The Past* . . . *Muddy Track* is really my favorite of all of them, though. It's dark as hell. God, it's a heavy one! (laughs) But it's funky.

On *Ragged Glory* I notice a real jazz feel to the way you improvise now. In fact, the way you operate puts me in mind of Miles Davis and John Coltrane.

Miles and Coltrane, yeah, they're two of my favorites. My guitar improvisations with Crazy Horse are very, very Coltrane-influenced. I'm particularly taken by work like "Equinox" and "My Favorite Things." Miles I love just because of his overall attitude toward the concept of "creation," which is one of constant change. There's no reason to stay there once you've done it. You could stay for the rest of your life and it would become like a regular job.

One person we haven't mentioned who has been an almost constant musical cohort of yours is your producer David Briggs, whom you've been working with for 25 years. Could you define your working relationship with him?

I'll show you how we work, OK. He told me what was wrong with my performance at Bob-Aid. Everyone else was telling me how great it was. He didn't belabor the fact that it was great. His opinion was: "Yeah, it was great, OK. It was great BUT forget about that because what was wrong was . . . this, this and this. You sang it in the wrong key, your voice was too low, the drums weren't tight enough till half-way through . . . No-one'll probably notice but . . . It's not usable." (Laughs) And I always listen to what he has to say and take note of it.

It was great to hear the return of Jack Nitzsche in your music on *Harvest Moon* . . .

Yeah, on "Such A Woman," that's our sound (smiles). "Expecting To Fly" has that sound too. That's what that track is supposed to relate to.

Didn't you have a serious falling-out sometime in the '70s though?

Yeah, we did. We get on great now but, at a certain point, Jack made the call on me that I had copped/sold out. Maybe it was something I did in the early '70s, during *Harvest* or *Goldrush*—I don't know when exactly it happened, but somewhere along the line it happened. It was his opinion that I wasn't living up to my potential even at that early stage. He was one of the guys who could see how fucked up I was compared to what I could really do. He was one of my earliest critics. He was a trailblazer in that respect.

Before your current union with Pearl Jam, there was apparently serious talk about you recording with Sonic Youth, possibly for the album that became *Sleeps With Angels*.

With Sonic Youth? Well, that sounds like it came from a news story that was in fact wrong. Hell, if they wanted to play, I'd be there. It sounds like too much fun to pass by. Sonic Youth are great. Same with R.E.M.: I'd love to work with those guys if the right conditions prevailed.

***Sleeps With Angels* seems deeply haunted by the specter of Kurt Cobain and his sad end . . .**

Sleeps With Angels has a lot of overtones to it, from different situations that were described in it. A lot of sad scenes (pause), I've never really spoken about why I made that album. I don't want to start now.

Has it anything to do with the similarity of Kurt Cobain's death to Crazy Horse Danny Whitten's death in 1972? They both looked so much alike . . .

I just don't want to talk about that. That's my decision. I've made a choice not to talk about it and I'm sticking to it.

Let's not discuss Cobain's death then. But what about his life? Did his music inspire you?

He really, really inspired me. He was so great. Wonderful. One of the best, but more than that. Kurt was one of the absolute best of all time for me.

"Scenery" on *Mirror Ball* seems equally haunted by Cobain's doomed image. It's like there's OJ Simpson on one side and Kurt Cobain on the other: two very different victims of celebrity madness?

Well, the problems with celebrity and rock 'n' roll start with the fact that nowadays it gets way too big too fast. Back in the '50s and '60s, rock 'n' roll was "big" but it was only "big" to people who cared about it. Now it's big to people who don't care about it. So they can't begin to understand it. They just make ill-informed judgements on performers without first comprehending why or what it was that made the person famous in the first place. In the '60s there was a bond between the artists and the audience. It's harder to see now because so much these days is simply down to image projection. But today's pessimistic bands have a vision and an attitude that's unified their generation just like the "peace and love" groups helped unify the '60s generation.

This brings us neatly to the subject of Pearl Jam and Eddie Vedder. I can't help wondering whether you truly sympathize with Vedder when he moans on and on about the price of fame. Doesn't it all come with the job?

The way most people seem to regard Eddie—it's a little out of perspective. No matter what he says, it all gets taken down and quoted back at him. Who else do you know who's his age and going through the things he's going through because he just wants to make music for a living and travel around a bit? Hopefully though, he'll get used to it. People will get used to him being around and they'll leave him alone a little more.

Surely you're no stranger to obsessive fans yourself. Have you had your share of stalkers and lunatics running all over your property?

Oh, yeah, I've had all kinds of people trying to get to me over the years. I've had some real nutcases looking for answers that I couldn't begin to give 'em. There's only one way to deal with them: ignore them and escape them as quickly as possible. Because the more you dwell on those people and their problems, the worse it gets for you. You just end up being the dickhead all your worst critics think you are anyway. (Laughs) You need to surround yourself with regular people—people who can treat you like a human being. If you don't have any of those in your life, you're finished. But by the same token, if you have a good situation and can make music whenever you want with a whole bunch of people who are cool and you have nothing else to do, then it's ultimately going to get shallow. Because there's not enough challenge going on in your life. That's why I went out of town over to Seattle to make this record. Recording *Mirror Ball* was like audio verité, just a snapshot of what's happening. Sometimes I didn't know who was playing. I was just conscious of this big smoldering mass of sound.

The whole record was recorded in four days and all the songs, barring "Song X" and "Act Of Love," were written in that four day stretch. I played "Act Of Love" with Crazy Horse in January at The Rock & Roll Hall Of Fame. Then, the following night, I played it with Pearl Jam at a Pro-Choice benefit concert and the version was so powerful I decided there and then to record it with them as soon as possible. On a purely musical level, this is the first time I've been in a band with three potential lead guitarists since The Buffalo Springfield. Plus there's Jack Irons, their drummer, who was just unbelievable. He just played his ass off on every take at every session. I can't say enough good things about him.

I didn't even think about recording a whole album when we went in to cut "Act of Love." I had two days with Pearl Jam initially. Two days and just two songs—that wasn't enough for me so I had five written by the time I went in. Recorded five of them, left one out. Then I came back for another two-day session with two more new songs. Plus I re-recorded the fifth one from the first session again. Then the day after that, I wrote another two new songs. "Throw Your Weapons Down"—maybe. Maybe not, though there's a large part of making this new album that's pretty foggy . . . (laughs)

The song "Act Of Love" is about the issue of abortion. It throws together images like "Rockin' In The Free World" did . . .

Yeah, there's no bias so you have to make up your own mind, finally. See, personally, I'm pro-choice. But the song isn't! This isn't an easy subject to confront head-on. People who say that human beings shouldn't have the right to dismiss a human life—they have a point. You can't dismiss that point. But then there's the reality. There's idealism and reality, the two have got to come together yet there are always major problems when they do. Maybe that's the crux of what I'm trying to say in this new album. It's also a commentary of the differences between my peace and love '60s generation and the more cynical '90s generation. Like this term "love." We hear the word so much it gets devalued and you need to—if not redefine it—then at least re-examine what it really stands for. We all need to get back inside ourselves and take another look. You can't just keep coasting along on the previous analysis because it isn't working any more.

"I'm The Ocean" strikes me as one of the most blatantly autobiographical songs of your career. The line "people my age don't do the things I do/They go somewhere whilst I run away with you". The "you" is your audience, the people who listen to your music . . .

(Pause) I think so. Definitely. I'm referring to the people who listen to music—they don't have to be there with me but they're still out there listening. We're together because we're both escaping through the music. It's like that line "I'm a drug that makes you dream." That's me trying to define the power of music.

Now you're 50, how do you physically manage to do what you do?

I just work out a lot. Make sure I stay in good shape. If you'll notice, I'm not exactly that skinny-looking guy from the '60s and '70s any more. I weigh over 40 pounds more than I used to back then. And none of it is fat—it's all muscle.

After the *Ragged Glory* tour, you started suffering from tinnitus and had to stop playing electric rock music for a couple of years. How's your hearing now you're confronting the heavy volume of Pearl Jam?

I made *Harvest Moon* because I didn't want to hear any loud sounds. I still have a little bit of tinnitus but fortunately now I'm not as sensitive to loud sounds as I was for a year after the mixing of *Weld*. My hearing's not perfect but it's OK. I'm not sure what's going on but the point is I can still hear well enough to get off on what I'm doing. There's still a lot of detail I can pick up. I'm a fanatic for hearing detail and that's not been lost, though I've got these other sounds I have to deal with too.

Joni Mitchell recently admitted she suffers from a wasting disease known as post-polio syndrome . . .

I've had that too. It affected me particularly in the mid-'80s, when I couldn't even pick up my guitar. My body was starting to fall apart on me. That's when I started working out. It's proven to be my salvation too. Lifting weights and exercising have completely changed everything for me, with regard to my health.

Let's return to the forthcoming *Archives* project. How has it been sifting through your past so meticulously?

In a lot of ways, it's been a real inspiration to me. It re-orientates me to the things I've done. In certain ways, it's been a lot of fun though I wouldn't want to spend a lifetime doing it. Plus it's woken me up to certain things about my talent.

Such as?

Well, it's weird. The things I thought weren't very good are really good. And things I thought were really good—where I thought I was really at the top of things—aren't so good. They sound more shallow somehow. Maybe when you think you're being real good, that's when you're not. At least that's what doing this project has got me thinking.

Is this the right time for that kind of thing?

Well, there is no right time for this kind of undertaking, I believe. It was just something that had to be done. I need to get up to date. I want to catch up to now. I'm doing the *Archives* so my work will be organized so that people will know what I thought. They won't have to guess. Everything'll be in there. There'll be grades and chronological orders.

In the end I want to leave a record of what I've done that's definitive and organized. Not because I want it out of the way. I want to get up to date. I've been 30 years behind myself.

Finally, how easy is it being as prolific a songwriter as Neil Young?

Oh, it's pretty easy (laughs). Just as long as I don't try.

NEIL YOUNG ON

What Happened in the 1980s

"At a certain point in my life I felt lost, I didn't know what to say. I recall that I was very reserved at that time. I didn't dare to touch what was inside of me. I was hiding it. Maybe a question for the psychiatrists? Now I look upon this period like an artist looks at his pictures. Looking at this period I am often surprised by the personality I find."

–from an interview with Thomas Wördehoff, *Zurich Weltwoche*, July 4, 1996

NEIL YOUNG ON

Doing Interviews

"Even yesterday I didn't know if I wanted to meet you. But when I'm talking to you it's different from talking to ten anonymous journalists who come from all over Europe. Now, I do just one interview. I'm sitting around with you and having a proper conversation. But doing this ten times a day? I can't. I don't have to and I won't do that. I've talked to you and if anybody is interested, they have to read what you write. If you ask the right questions, you will get the information you want. If not, you're the idiot, not me."

–from an interview with Thomas Wördehoff, *Zurich Weltwoche*, July 4, 1996

NEIL YOUNG ON

The Go-Go Dancers at Whisky a Go Go

"It was great! We knew them all. We would look up there and say hi to them—they were right there while we were playing. [*Laughs.*] It was an inspiration."

—from an interview with Sylvie Simmons, *MOJO*, July 1997

NEIL YOUNG ON

Jimi Hendrix

"Hendrix is the best, nobody can touch him. I'm a hack compared to him, a hack. That guy . . . it slipped off his hands, he couldn't help himself. I've got to go in there and hack away with a machete to get through what he just walked through. I can aspire to be able to play that way and to approach it sometimes, so I'd get half way there sometimes; but when it comes to really playing . . . I mean, I've got a lot of emotion and very little technical ability. Jimi had them both. He was so smooth and so great and so special—and what a great attitude his music had. He can't be touched."

—from an interview with Sylvie Simmons, *MOJO*, July 1997

THE *SILVER & GOLD* INTERVIEW

Jody Denberg | April 2000 | KGSR - Austin City Limits Radio

After a ferocious first half of the 1990s, the tail of the 20th century was a bit of letdown, ending not exactly with a whimper, but certainly not with the bang of '69, '79, or '89.

During March and April 1996 Neil Young recorded a new LP with Crazy Horse. *Broken Arrow* was released July 2, two weeks into another Crazy Horse European tour. The album was poorly received and the tour had the feel of a nostalgia show, as mentioned in contemporaneous reviews. The *Broken Arrow* tour continued in the United States and Canada from August through November.

The epic tour rendered the *Year of the Horse* album and the Jim Jarmusch-directed film, both released in 1997. 1997 also saw a continuation of Young's live work with Crazy Horse, including a headlining gig on the jam-band friendly H.O.R.D.E. tour alongside such artists as Beck, Primus, and founding act Blues Traveler. Fine performances, but artistically, Young was treading water.

1998 was quiet, save a few solo charity appearances and guest spots with Phish, who turned down an offer to back Young. In the studio, Neil continued recording with a new band and CSNY. He would feature these new songs on two spring solo tours in 1999. The year would end with the October release of CSNY's *Looking Forward*. He also continued archival work, including a renewed look at the Buffalo Springfield catalog.

January 2000 saw the start of the 41-date CSNY2K Tour, which featured old songs, high ticket prices, and mixed reviews. As the tour ended in April, Young released the *Silver & Gold* studio LP and a DVD culled from May 1999 solo shows in Austin, Texas.

This radio interview aired to coincide with the *Silver & Gold* LP/DVD release. Young talks at length about these recent events–the new products, CSNY, Buffalo Springfield, the Archives, CD production–sounding like a man rejuvenated. –Ed.

Jody Denberg: Neil, as the first song on *Silver & Gold* says, good to see you.

Neil Young: Thanks. Good to see you, too.

Denberg: The songs on *Silver & Gold*, they're as intense as any rock and roll that you've ever done, but they're in the style of albums like *Harvest* and *Harvest Moon*. When you were writing most of these songs, did you know you wanted to produce them this way or did you try various settings?

Young: Most of these songs were written in the last couple of years, maybe the last three years. And I recorded them fairly soon after I wrote them. And the guys playing on them are the same guys playing on all of them, basically. They're just, the right guys for the tunes. And I was into playing that way at the time and had the band come—I'd write two or three tunes and then they'd come—they'd fly in and we'd try to do those two or three tunes and the some other ones that I already had that I had tried to record before that didn't get or something. I've got quite a few of them that's kind of hovering out there. So I add a couple of those into the mix so that we got a lot of songs to play. And then they'd come for three days and we'd just play all the songs and that's it. And then try again when I write some more new ones.

Denberg: Does your personality have to change in some ways when you're playing with, say, Crazy Horse or Pearl Jam as opposed to when you're in the mode of *Silver & Gold*?

Young: Well, I don't know if my personality changes, but maybe it does. What changes is the songs. The songs drive the whole thing. And I have no control over what the songs are going to be like. I just—they're just a reflection of what's going on. And I have no control over what's going on! [*Laughs.*] So it keeps changing. What can I do with it?

Denberg: The first song on *Silver & Gold*, "Good to See You," it sounds so direct. It sounds like you had the feeling and you just sat down and wrote the song. Is it ever that simple?

Young: Yeah, because that's how that one happened. I wrote that one in my bus in Florida somewhere. There was a thunderstorm and the

H.O.R.D.E. tour was playing. And we had to shut down for half an hour or something. And so I went to my bus and I was in the back. And my voice was real low 'cause I'd been playing with Crazy Horse and screaming and yelling and carrying on. So my voice was real low. And I wrote these—a couple of songs. "Good to See You" was one of them. And "Without Rings," I think, was one—the other one that I wrote, either that day or somewhere along in there—on a big piece of newspaper. I remember I had a piece of newspaper with all this felt-tip marker pen stuff written over top of the other writing. I like to see the writing on top of pictures and other stuff, so when you look at it it's not too imposing. It just looks like a big—there's nothing there, really. It's just all jumbled looking. It's comfortable to leave it around like that. You don't have to hide it. Where if you write something on a piece of paper, it's like a note. Anyway, that's probably more than you want to know about that. [*Laughs.*]

Denberg: Neil, a couple of the songs on the new album date back to the early '80s. One is the title track, "Silver & Gold." Why would a song like that go unrecorded all these years?

Young: Well, "Silver & Gold" I think I wrote back in—I don't know 1981 or '82. And I did record it several times. I tried it several ways. And it was such a nice—it's just such a song. It just kind of lives with the guitar. It's just there. And it's always a kind of song you do it the first time, it's fine, it sounds great. And then you do it the second time and it's like, why are you doing it again? You just—you've already done it. It's such a simple thing that either you—I would get it right the first time and then by the time the band knew it, it sounded so contrived to me that I could never get it. So I really recorded, I think, a total of 11 times with different people in all kinds of different configurations. And we got 'em all, none of them are worth listening to. But this one here finally just got back to the roots of it and just sat down with my guitar and played it and said, "That's it." Because I love the song and I feel the song now and it means something to me now. And so I just did it. When I got back from the H.O.R.D.E. tour a couple of years ago, I went in the studio, sat down, and did this one the second day after I was back, I think.

Denberg: "Silver & Gold," it's a direct love song. It reminds me a little bit of something like Paul McCartney would have done on his very first solo album. And a little bit more than a year ago, you inducted Paul into the Rock and Roll Hall of Fame. Is it only fans who fantasize that, you know, our heroes would collaborate, or would you be open to working with someone like Paul?

Young: Oh, I'd love to work with someone like Paul. I'd love to work with Paul. I mean, I love Paul's music. Paul's like—his potential is great. I mean, he's right there. He doesn't—he can do what—basically whatever he wants to do. I'm available to play with Paul McCartney any time he wants to play. He knows it, too. I already told him. I said, "Listen, if you want to do something with me, I'm ready. So . . ."

Denberg: When you've written a love song like "Silver & Gold" is your wife, Pegi, the first one to hear, it or is it easier to play it for other folks first?

Young: I think she heard that one first.

Denberg: "Silver & Gold" is the title track of your brand-new album. It's a song about the joys of love and family. And one thing that's a family affair for you and yours, Neil, is the Bridge School. Most music fans know about the annual concerts, but can you explain in a nutshell what the Bridge School's mission is?

Young: Well, the Bridge School's mission is to bring communication to children, young students that are—that can't talk and have communication problems, have to use an interface, some sort of an interface to communicate. And we try to supply the interface so that they can—so the kids can communicate and do the things they need to do, go to school and get up to speed on being able to use their devices so they can navigate the world that we navigate. And it's a big challenge. And it's a great school. And it's a model for other schools. There is a program where we share our information that we've garnered over the last 15 years of existence in teaching kids how to use computers to communicate. It's a great idea that my wife had. And we had our son, Ben, is the inspiration for the school. And he's one of the first students. And so it's been a real family thing for us. And all the musicians who have come to help by playing at the concerts have all come away with a good feeling about it. And it's been a great thing. I think my wife has done a great thing there.

Denberg: I'd imagine it takes up a lot of your time, maybe almost as much as the music sometimes, keeping up with the Bridge School?

Young: Well, Pegi does that. She's the one. I can't keep track of stuff like that. I, I support it 100 percent. But if they relied on me for anything, they'd be in big trouble. She's the organized one.

Denberg: And it is like you said, the diversity of the musicians who have played the Bridge School benefits over the years, you've had everyone from Green Day to Brian Wilson to R.E.M. to Sheryl Crow. Has it made you feel closer with the music community at large?

Young: Yes, I think it has. I've met a lot of people. And just the way they keep coming. Every year we just get these amazing bills of people. And there's always—we're looking for new people, but we want to keep—maintain our roots with the past with people like Brian Wilson. I mean, he was unbelievable at the show. I mean, he was just staggering. I couldn't—I couldn't believe my ears.

Denberg: The thing about the Bridge School and the Bridge School concerts is that it closes this great divide. And your new song "The Great Divide" and "Buffalo Springfield Again" were a couple of the final songs that you wrote for *Silver & Gold*. It was my understanding that you wrote these new songs for *Silver & Gold* because you let your friends, Crosby, Stills, and Nash, cherry-pick some tunes for the latest CSNY disc, *Looking Forward*. And we're going to hear "Buffalo Springfield Again" in a moment. Was your reunion with CSN, was it sparked by putting together a Buffalo Springfield project that you were working on?

Young: Well, the project was pretty well complete, and I wanted Stephen to come up to the ranch and check it out, see what we'd put together and see how he felt about it and what perspective he could bring to it. And we also had Richie Furay come in and listen to it. And so it—we listened. It's a four-CD box set. And it's—like all of my box sets I'm working on, it is in chronological order. So it doesn't go in the order that the records were released in. It goes in order of the recordings. So you have—at the beginning, you have all these demos that we did when we first came to L.A. for the first Buffalo Springfield record. And then it goes into the—I believe, the mono masters of the Buffalo Springfield record that we made—that Stephen and Richie and I mixed. And then it—and then there's a lot of—a fair amount of unreleased Buffalo Springfield things in there. But it's chronological. So the thing is, you hear us, you hear us as just, we're just kids. You hear us coming together and you can hear the sound growing. And then you can hear it kind of breaking up and falling apart. It's kind of a sad thing. And then at the end the group—they sound pretty watered down and it's pretty obvious that it's not the same group as it was in the beginning. And people come and go, changes and stuff. And so when Stephen and I listened to it, we realized—I mean, we're laughing and crying and carrying on, talking to each other while this thing's playing. And we realized that we really didn't reach our potential at all. So that was a dawn on us: that we both knew that we hadn't reached the potential of what we could do together. And so we—he played a song for me, a new song that was a great song and asked me if I wanted to play on it. So he—when I went down to L.A. a couple of—oh, a month or so later, I played on the song and I played on a few other ones. And I just kept listening to the tapes and I played on them. And it was like, not really the way I like to do things. I like to play all at once and everything, so . . . But these songs that they had were done. And so I played on them. And then we played on some new ones where we played all at once. And that's more fun. But it's kind of like a process of coming back together again. I mean, working on each others' tapes and then creating new stuff and then finally we had what we thought was an album. But in the making of it, I—I only worked on their songs at first. I played on about 12 or 13 of their songs before I played any of my own songs. And then I just played them the 14 songs or so that I'd recorded for *Silver & Gold*, which had no title at the time or anything. And I said, "Just go ahead, just take whatever ones you want. Just take however many. Just take 'em. We'll sing on 'em and we'll, we'll see what else they need, if anything, and then we'll put them on this record. They'll match everything" 'cause that's the way we did this record, basically. So it'll work. So they chose the ones they chose.

Denberg: And then what happened in the meanwhile to the Buffalo Springfield box set?

Young: We finished it and it's—I believe it's coming out pretty soon.

Denberg: You know, it's good to hear you sing about playing with Buffalo Springfield again. So many of us, we think of Neil Young as being in the moment. And yet, this is kind of a nostalgic song. Could Buffalo Springfield really ever play together again?

Young: Well, I'm sure they could, but I don't know if they will. I mean, I don't know if that'll ever happen. It's more like a musing of situation, just reflecting. Sunday afternoon philosophy.

Denberg: Neil, the live version of "Looking Forward" doesn't appear on the studio album *Silver & Gold*. But it's part of a digital video disc concert release that's also called *Silver & Gold*. It's recorded here at Austin's Bass Concert Hall. Isn't it a little confusing that the CD and DVD have the same title but they're two, they're two different projects?

Young: Well, it is kind of confusing, but look at the money we saved on artwork. I mean, we passed the savings on to the consumer. [*Laughter.*]

Denberg: I was watching the DVD and actually was at the shows here in Austin. You're onstage and you're surrounded in that semi-circle of guitars and a banjo. And when I watch you, I was wondering, what goes through your mind when you're, you're changing guitars and choosing a song?

Young: Well, the show's got kind of a structure to it. And the songs are interchangeable. So I'm not really sure what songs I'm going to be doing when I go out there. Although there's a pattern that develops. And sometimes I deviate from it and sometimes I don't. But when I go out there and sit down with the guitars all around me and everything, it's very comfortable. And on the floor to my left there's generally a big loose-leaf binder with about 600 songs in it or 400 or something. And they're all in there alphabetically so I can go through and—if I can't remember a song or something, I can skim through it. And after I just take a glance at it, I can remember it. And then—I mean, it's pretty straight ahead. I've been playing acoustic solo shows since the mid '60s. And I've always gone back and forth between playing with a band and playing acoustic solo. This is just—a lot of the songs—the reason why we called the DVD *Silver & Gold* is because I think there's eight songs on it that are from the new record. So what it is—and there's older ones, too. There's a couple of—there's "Philadelphia" and "Harvest Moon" and "Long May You Run" and something else might be on there. But the thing is that it's primarily the same material that's on the album, but it's a live performance of it. And in this era that we're in where you have to format—your songs fit into a format or they don't. There really isn't much of a format that my songs fit into on—that are on this record. So the idea of me releasing the DVD of my performing these records is, I'm trying to create another way for people to become familiar with this music because, in case they don't hear it on the radio. I mean, we're playing it here tonight because that's what we're doing. But—and that's a great thing. But in reality, when you listen to these songs, they're so subtle that they may never make it on the radio. I mean—so you've got to do everything that you can do to let people know. There's so much going on so if I don't do anything, people won't even know that the record came out. And I love this record. So I put a lot of my heart and soul into it. So I'm supporting it as much as I can within the boundaries of good taste. [*Laughs.*] Hopefully?

Denberg: Last spring, you did the solo tour. This spring you did the tour with CSNY. What do you enjoy about playing with a band versus playing, as you say, solo, which you've done for 30 years?

Young: Well, there's another one, too. There's playing in the band that I lead. There's three things here. And playing by myself is simple, but—and it's great and it's direct and it's really rewarding. But, after playing about 40 shows like that, I can hardly—I get, I get kind of boxed in. I feel like everybody's looking at me all the time. It's kind of like you're—you sit out there for two hours and you're the only one out there. And after a while, that kind of adds up. So it has a—even though it's fun, after a while I think my nerves get a little shattered. So I stop doing that. Then, the playing with CSNY, when I was doing that, it's really great. I mean, because I'm part of a band. I'm—I don't have to be in the front line all the time. I'm not always singing the lead. Sometimes I don't even sing in the song. I just play my guitar. And that's a lot like the way Buffalo Springfield was. And I like that, because that's where I really feel comfortable is in a band where I'm not the leader of the band. Then you have Crazy Horse where I am the leader of the band. And I like to get down and play with them. So I have to have—keep changing from one thing to another to keep it—to keep the balance going. And also, as long as the songs keep going, that's what dictates the pace of the change, is the arrival of the new tunes.

Denberg: Neil, how did you and David and Stephen and Graham come up with a set list for the CSNY reunion tour shows? Seems like that was a big challenge.

Young: Well, we rehearsed a lot and we learned a lot of songs. And then it was—we had to—we worked on an acoustic set. We worked on—we decided on the form of the show, having that opening set an electric set, and then taking a break. It just all kind of came together one night. We had to pace it because we knew it was going to be long. So we had to figure out a way to—you don't want to come out—we were thinking of coming out acoustic, but we nixed that idea of playing acoustic when we came out in favor of playing with the band so that we could introduce the band and kind of get everybody loosened up. It was almost like an opening act, our first set. It's about an hour long. And then we took a break and then played the acoustic set, about an hour-long acoustic set. And then instead of—our problem was taking the break, another break. We didn't want two breaks. So we came up with this seventh inning stretch, which was kind of a fly by the seat of the pants kind of concept thing for the audience to get into. And it worked. So we got Harry Caray singing "Take Me Out to the Ballgame" and everything on the videos. And we're all out there just hanging out, while they're changing the set. And Crosby's out there carrying on. And it's just—we've got these little tents we can go into that are out there like the Dead used to have. So we managed to put it together, put their songs in there. It wasn't that hard, really.

Denberg: Did the set list vary at all throughout the tour?

Young: At first we stuck with pretty well the same set list. And then we varied it a little bit. And then we kind of got into another groove for a while. And then we started adding new songs after we started getting really confident. We added "Eight Miles High." That was the first one we added, which really rocked. And it was cool to be playing that with Crosby. It was like the Buffalo Springfield and the Byrds playing "Eight Miles High" with the Hollies singing along. [*Smiles.*] I'm telling you, that was pretty good. No, we just—we try to, we try to mix it up as much as we can, but it's a long show. And soundchecks are—they take a little bit out of you. So you want to save what you have for the show.

Denberg: How did you feel about the public's response to the new songs from *Looking Forward* and the album?

Young: Well, I think the album was a disappointment because I don't think it reached out. For some reason, it didn't, it didn't really get the acceptance that I hoped it would. But as far as the music goes, my songs that they picked from my selection from—that I had recorded for *Silver & Gold*, they took three of my songs. I thought they came out really well. I like the way they sang on 'em and everything. It sounds really good to me. And the funny thing is, when those songs were taken from the mix, were taken from the other songs, they—the songs that were left were—there were too many songs. And they were all—originally there were too many songs for *Silver & Gold*. And they were all struggling and kind of holding each other down. And when CSN picked those three songs out and then I was left with the other ten or eleven, they suddenly just fell into place. It was really a great feeling, because I was struggling with trying to put it together. And when they took those three songs out, it just—everything else was left. I mean, I just wrote them out in order of what I wanted to hear and that was it. It never changed again. The running order was right. Everything was right. So there was something about it that was really right, where you give something away and you get something back. It's like a reward for sharing or something. I don't know. It's a good feeling.

Denberg: Do you think you'd ever tour again with CSNY or make another record?

Young: Sure. No reason not to. It's like returning to the mothership now.

Denberg: You alluded to this earlier, Neil, but for so many years, we've been hearing that you're putting together some sort of retrospective box set from your archives. We talked about the Buffalo Springfield box. But this is different. This is the Neil Young—well, what is it and where is it happening, because we've heard about a lot of incarnations?

Young: Well, it's almost ready to come out, actually. It's in its final phases of production—of post-production. And its form is—it comes in a box—in a square box, tall box. And it has the package of CDs. There's eight CDs. And it's—the music is chronological from the beginning of my recording all the way through. And it's—there's selections. It's not every song. But there's a lot of selections from different—from different periods and some, a lot of unknown ones and unreleased ones and different versions of things. But the thing that makes it interesting is the chronological order that it's in. You can really sense a growth and a change as it goes through it. And it reveals things about where songs actually fit, because a lot of times I'll record songs and just hold on to them for three or four years and then drop them into a record. So as this thing unfolds, it kind of puts my earlier records in another perspective. And then there are a few performances in there of one live record that I did with Crazy Horse at the Fillmore East that was never released. And it's in there. And some other early performances. So I—of—at the Riverboat in Toronto where I played in a kind of folk acoustic, little, small coffeehouse setting where you can hear the glasses tinkling and there's only about 20 people there. And I'm singing really soft and it sounds very young and very open. Anyway, there's a lot of chronological—it just goes from, I think, 1962 or '63 to something like 1972 or something like that.

Denberg: So this is going to be Volume One then?

Young: Yeah, it's Volume One. And along with that, there's a book that comes in there that's got all kinds of—it's a different approach to a book. What it is is, it's all the things that people wrote about us, about me and about the songs and everything. Negative and positive. They're just all in there. Everything that we could find we just crammed in. It's like a scrapbook of comments and stuff. And that's all it is. It doesn't draw any conclusions. And then on top of that, there's a DVD of the—of all of the film and video, et cetera, that I did back in those years. And so that's a chronological DVD also that covers the same period. And there's a lot of stuff in there with—that's never been seen. The original *Harvest* recording sessions that we filmed and the recording "A Man Needs a Maid" with the London Symphony Orchestra, the sessions. "There's a World" with the London Symphony. All this stuff. And there's just a lot of information in there that has never been released before. And that's in one DVD. And the other DVD in there is a film that I made back in, I think, 1971 or '2, called *Journey Through the Past.* And that has—it's kind of a collage film.

Denberg: And this box ends around '72. Are we expecting this around the end of the year this year?

Young: I think we are expecting it in the early fall.

Denberg: And then after '72, there's a series of your records, albums like *On the Beach, American Stars 'n Bars.* And for some reason, you've never chosen to release these half dozen records on compact disc. Is there any reason why these certain discs weren't released on CD and are they ever going to be?

Young: Well, that's a deep question, because I was hoping that technology would come along to the point where it obviously could be at this point. We have—the record companies have a huge problem right now with—they have the DVD audio standard, which we worked for years to establish. And it's—the quality is just unbelievably better than the CD. I mean, it is—it approaches what you expected from digital in the first place. And it's much better. But someone cracked the code after we set it all up and there was all these committees and everything and we got it all together. And I was working with Warner Brothers and their representatives in that working group for—that was called to make the DVD audio standards. And it's a wonderful standard where the artist has creativity, has control and you program the DVD so that when you put it in, it configures your system to play it back optimum for what's on the disc. I mean, if you had 40 minutes of music on the disc, you could have a higher sampling rate. You might decide you want to listen in stereo or you might want to listen in 5.1. The artist decides. And the format keeps changing as the artist programmed it to be. So you get to take advantage of all of the digital information that the DVD has, the storage. By configuring your information to fit—to maximize it, much like on an old RPM record that you would—a vinyl record that you would have to keep the length down to 18 or 19 minutes if you wanted the thing to really hammer when it came out of the radio. So if you get too long, the tone goes away. So if you try to pack too much stuff into a DVD or a CD—well, not a CD. CDs don't sound good no matter what you do. But DVDs you can put so much information into them. But if you only have like—suppose I made a record that was 39 minutes long. That thing would kill on DVD. I would use all of the computing in the DVD and focus—and raise the level of quality of the sampling and the rates and everything to the point where the shorter it is, the higher the quality is. So the artist can control the quality vector—the quality level. And that's—that was a great thing. So what happened? We got it all together and then somebody figured out how to crack it, so that, of course, now it could be duplicated and so nobody—the record companies couldn't make any money off of it. But, that's already happened with the CD, so what's the big deal? Why not put out the quality? If there are people who are going to crack—if they're going to crack it and send it around on Napsters and whatever, MP3, who cares? I say, just let it go. We've got to work it out. It's music. If people can't afford music—if they can't afford it but they can get it with a Napster, they can get music. Around the world, people who couldn't get it and have it in their houses and listen to it over and over again are going to be able to do it. Now, what's the difference—why doesn't the record companies come out with the higher quality? And then they'd have something to—well, OK. We've got the higher quality, but maybe the Napster or whatever can't transfer the DVD quality or whatever. Maybe it's only a CD quality. The MP3 is less than CD. I mean, MP3 is dog. The quality sucks. It's all compressed and the data compression—it's terrible. They've—it's—that's not good. But the DVD stuff was approaching the way it should be. And it was frustrating to me. So the answer to your question is: I didn't really see things in CD because they don't sound good. So I like the original analog masters. And I don't want people to have CDs to listen to for the rest of time. I want to wait until these things are ready to be dumped into a format that I can understand is really relative to the original format in quality. [*Laughter.*] There you go?

Denberg: I'm never going to hear *On the Beach* again.

Young: You might hear it. You might hear it. I'm sure that—I mean, now—I mean, that's why I waited so long. I had to—but they're coming out now HDCD. I mean, it's the best CDs you can make.

Denberg: Neil, you're always been interested in making movies and videos and the DVD of *Silver & Gold* comes out Tuesday, the album comes out. And you've done—you've done films before, *Rust Never Sleeps* and *Year of the Horse*. They both featured Crazy Horse. First of all, do you ever think you'll ride the horse again?

Young: Sure.

Denberg: But *Silver & Gold* is—it's so far removed from what you do with the Horse. Was that your vision for this video?

Young: For the DVD?

Denberg: Yes.

Young: Well, the DVD is a—basically, it's just me playing. It's the way I play acoustic. It's a performance. And it was a good performance. It was here in Austin and it was played—it just was a good night. And the crowds are great. You come to Austin and it's like a music church or something. They listen to the music. People don't yell and scream through the whole song and they don't feel compelled to show their enthusiasm while the song is happening. They're more musically sensitive. I think basically the people in the South and the people in Texas are just—they're moving at a pace where they can—where they have time to listen.

Denberg: And speaking of a music church, one of the songs you do on the DVD, "Long May You Run," you play on some sort of church organ. Is it a pipe organ?

Young: It's a pump organ, actually. I bought it in a junk store about 15 years ago in Redwood City. It's a funky pump organ. You just pump it. It's got a good sound.

Denberg: Neil, our conversation is taking place close to Earth Day. And as a supporter of Farm Aid, you told audiences on your solo tour about some real ways that the family farm is good for our environment. Could you tell me what those were again?

Young: Well, the fact is that family farms, today, a lot of them are—in able to survive, are turning to organic agriculture and providing organic food. So if you want to help the family farmer and if you want to make a good contribution toward the future of our farming lands, you can buy organic food and that would be good statement to make for Earth Day, I think. And you could just continue doing it all year long and feel good about the food you're giving your children or feel good about what you're eating yourself. Because the organic food is safe, it tastes better, and it's good for the planet.

Denberg: Thanks, Neil, those are some good words to remember this Earth Day. And thanks for joining us.

Young: Thank you for having me. I enjoyed myself. Thanks.

NEIL YOUNG ON

The Patriot Act

"My heart wants one thing, my mind wants another. Benjamin Franklin said that anyone who gives up essential liberties to preserve freedom is a fool, but maybe he didn't conceive of nuclear warfare and dirty bombs."

–from an interview with Edna Gundersen, *USA Today*, April 11, 2002

NEIL YOUNG ON

Staying Passionate

"I was born this way. It's never been a problem for me. The only thing that I do that makes it possible for me to keep on going is, if I have to change something, I change it. A lot of people won't make changes out of loyalty, out of their perception of what loyalty is."

–from an interview with Tom Lanham, *Pulse*, April 2002

NEIL YOUNG ON

Viewing Movies

"I'm very uneducated. I used to think Abbott and Costello were really funny. I loved Jerry Lewis movies. I thought they were fine art. But I also like the long shots and ambience of the early Federico Fellini and Jean-Luc Godard pictures."

–from an interview with David Fricke, *Rolling Stone*, September 4, 2003

YOUNG AND FREE

Patrick Donovan | November 21, 2003 | *The Age* (Melbourne)

Neil Young embarked on the late summer 2000 Music in Head tour with *Silver & Gold*'s Friends and Relatives musicians, plus his wife Pegi and sister Astrid. In a quick turnaround, a live CD, *Road Rock Vol. 1*, and a live DVD, *Red Rocks Live*, were released on December 5.

Young and Crazy Horse's summer Eurotour '01 featured a handful of new songs. The fall found them playing the usual charity shows, plus a performance at the *America: A Tribute to Heroes* Telethon for the United Way's September 11 Fund. There was no album of new material, but the Young-curated *Buffalo Springfield* box set was released in July.

Inspired by the events of 9/11, Young wrote the totemic "Let's Roll" and, in political mode, hit the road with CSNY from February to April 2002, backed by Booker T. and the M.G.s. The Stax band mostly featured on the mellow *Are You Passionate?*, released April 9–this author's pick as Young's weakest album. The year rounded out with the recording of *Greendale* with Crazy Horse.

2002 also saw the release of Jimmy McDonough's *Shakey: Neil Young's Biography*. McDonough had access to Young for six years to create an official biography. Young got cold feet and tried to stop the publication and was sued by McDonough. A measure of détente was reached, and the tome, brilliant but incomplete, hit the streets.

Greendale was the word for 2003. After a late spring European solo tour playing the album and a few hits, Neil and Crazy Horse brought that album out for over 50 shows in the United States, the Far East, and Australia. The LP was released August 9, with Bernard Shakey's film version out October 9.

The interview contextualizes Young's reawakened political concerns in George W. Bush's USA, while Young discusses the political aspects of *Greendale*, relating the American story to a global audiences, and deciding to work with McDonough. –Ed.

Neil Young has followed his muse across a wide musical landscape, leading most recently to the fictional town of Greendale.

"Well, yeah, the older you get the mellower you are. A lot of things that would have got me into trouble, I just don't bother with any more. But the important things are still there—last time I checked, anyway." Neil Young is talking over the phone from Fukuoka, Japan, having just arrived from Osaka by bullet train. Speaking in a deep drawl—in stark contrast to his falsetto singing voice—he's commenting on how he gets on better with his old bandmates from Buffalo Springfield these days, but every fan who has followed Young's zigzag path can relate to the sentiment.

Young's music affects listeners to a degree few other artists can match, whether it's Kurt Cobain quoting him in his suicide note, Bob Dylan—who rarely mentions contemporaries in his songs—namechecking him in his song *Highlands*, or Australia's biggest band, Powderfinger, naming themselves after one of his songs.

But if people like his music, it's a coincidence, because Young says he doesn't write to please the fans.

He works on the theory that the first thought is the best. In his biography *Shakey*, he told author Jimmy McDonough that playing music is a pure expression of the soul—the truth—but that lyrics are contrived and adulterated. So he waits for thoughts to come to him, whether in a dream or on a long drive, and his songs represent snapshots of different phases of his life.

"I don't want to put any thought into it if I can help it; I'd rather just have it come out and try not to edit it."

Young is in town tomorrow for his first Melbourne show in 14 years, and his first here with the legendary Crazy Horse. The show starts with a stage production and performance of the new album, *Greendale*, followed by a set of old favorites. This is when fans will finally witness the dynamics of the band that in one day wrote "Down By the River" and "Cowgirl In the Sand."

"It's just a natural thing with us," says Young. "We're just happy to be here. We still enjoy it and it's always fun, and now we've got all this new material, so when we play *Greendale* you get a feeling for us, that we're still alive, not just re-creating old stuff."

On his last tour of Australia, Young showcased both his gentle acoustic work and his brutal, cathartic rock-outs. He says the two sides of his music don't represent extremes of emotions for him, even if they elicit extreme reactions from some of the audience.

"It's just folk music and rock 'n' roll. It's pretty straightforward. It's all the same emotions, just different ways of expressing them."

After he opened, on that last tour here, with the relatively obscure "Ordinary People," people were yelling for hits off *Harvest.* How does Young handle his legacy and his fans' expectations of him?

"Well, they're used to me now. I can't surprise them any more with any of that," he says with a laugh. "I really don't see the need to go out of my way to make people happy. I don't think that's what I'm here for. I'm just here to do what I do and play my songs, and a lot of people like them, which is cool, but if they didn't like them, I'd play them anyway.

"It's not that I don't appreciate them; it's just that I don't feel anything other than 'Thank you.' I don't owe them changing what I do to accommodate them."

The Canadian-born Young struggled to make a living out of music in his home country, but found fame in Los Angeles with Buffalo Springfield, who had a string of hits in the 1960s. He became a star in his own right in 1972 with *Harvest, Billboard*'s top-charting album of that year. However, he alienated many of his new fans when he followed it with dark, jagged albums such as *Journey Through the Past, Time Fades Away, On the Beach* and *Tonight's the Night.*

It was considered commercial suicide at the time, but these days the latter two albums are considered classics.

Does he believe this credibility justifies the direction he chose to take back then?

"At the time all I was doing was what I thought I should do. I was only doing it because I had the idea. The idea came to me, so I did it. So it's pretty straight-ahead. There's no planning or thought that goes into it—'Is this cool?' or 'Is this going to be good?'. I really don't care. All I want to do is what naturally comes out of me. When I first started out I tried to spend a lot more time trying to fix things, and as I started to mature a little more, say, with *Everybody Knows This Is Nowhere*, I started getting a little more loose and just letting things happen, not judging what I was doing and really respecting the fact that I had a gift, that these things would come through me if I let them."

In much of his work, Young's music is defined by simple strumming or jamming on a couple of chords, given meaning by his heartfelt delivery. But for *Greendale*, Young offers in-depth liner notes, a film (which he wrote, shot and directed under his alias, Bernard Shakey) and stage play.

Young says the concept was born out of one song, but then the same characters kept re-emerging in other songs, and soon he had created the fictional town of Greendale (based on many places he's known, he says) for the cast to live in.

There's stubborn old-timers Grandpa and Grandma Green; their Vietnam veteran, psychedelic painter son-in-law Earl; hippie activist daughter Sun; and her gun-toting cousin, Jed, who shoots and kills a policeman, Carmichael. The media descend on the Green household for an explanation, causing Grandpa to have a heart attack, which spurs Sun into action.

It's not rocket science—Bruce Springsteen did it better in one song, "Highway Patrolman," on his *Nebraska* album—but it gives Young the platform to voice his feelings about the arrogance of Western society and the loss of community values.

I explain that with the current Howard Government, many Australians can relate to *Greendale*'s themes: the erosion of personal freedoms, trial by media and the destruction of the environment.

"Well, I'm glad it has, because a lot of changes need to be made. It's too bad that Australia went along with the coalition, but I guess the leaders felt that by co-operating with Bush's agenda they were making the right move. They were probably acting on the same information that America had, which has turned out to be a bunch of bullshit."

Steve Earle, the Dixie Chicks and Michael Moore have been slammed in the US as being unpatriotic for questioning their president, but Young says he's had a mostly positive reaction to *Greendale*.

"I've had more emotionally charged reactions to *Greendale* from the audience. When people come up and talk to me, they sound different about it than they have about anything I've done."

Are the problems in *Greendale* limited to the West?

"I think they relate to the entire free world, particularly Australia and Japan—anywhere where people are on the edge of co-operating with the US agenda and trying to figure out what they should be doing. All the governments seem to be polarizing rather than bringing people together, which I think is interesting."

Like Bob Dylan's previous two albums, *Time Out of Mind* and *Love and Theft*, Young seems to be pining for simpler, more innocent times when he namechecks *Leave It To Beaver* and sings: "When I was young, people wore what they had on."

"There's always room for reflection on what's going on," he says. "You can always find things that are wrong and things that are right at any time. And right now the seeds for revolution—not a huge, violent revolution, but like the one they had in the '60s—are a very ripe environment for it. I don't think the youth have had a target like Bush since Nixon, so we'll see what happens in the colleges. It's got to start with the young people."

The visual extension of his work isn't an attempt to capture some of the younger TV-fed generation, he says. It's simply to help tell the story. The music, though, still comes first.

"That's what makes the whole record work."

As the tour progresses, so, too, does the *Greendale* show, and Young says Melbourne, being the last show on the tour, will see it in its most evolved form.

The album has polarized the critics. Some say it comprises little more than hippie clichés and student sloganeering atop plodding blues. Believers say it's Crazy Horse at their grooviest, and that a line such as "A little love and affection, in everything you do/We'll make the world a better place, with or without you" is appropriate for such troubled times.

Young does use clichés—they were all over *Harvest*—but they're honest ones, and he believes that sometimes they're the purest form of communication.

Physically, Young has been dealt a horrid hand that has also left scars on his psyche. He suffered polio as a child, which left him rake-thin and shy, which was compounded when his parents divorced. As a teenager he suffered epileptic fits and migraines, and he was so spaced-out that a doctor warned him never to take LSD or "you'll never come back".

As a parent and husband he has also had his share of heartache—both his sons were born with cerebral palsy, and his wife Pegi survived surgery for a brain tumor after being given a 50/50 chance of pulling through.

Young isn't the only artist to endure such trials, but he's managed to overcome his obstacles with compassion and truth. Even if it's a cliché, fans believe him.

He says some critics have changed their mind about *Greendale* and are seeing it in a more positive light. I suggest that although some of his albums appear to offer their wares up front, some, such as *Silver and Gold*, take a few listens to fully reveal themselves.

"I just try to perform the songs so that I feel them when I'm singing them. Lately we've tried to not worry about the mistakes; we don't even fix them up, because it seems like a mistake is almost a feature in today's sterile world, the way that people make records these days."

Young says plenty of young people are attending his shows, and I suggest that some of them should buy 1974's *On the Beach* (recently released on CD for the first time, along with *American Stars 'n Bars*, *Hawks & Doves* and *re·ac·tor*), as it covers similar themes to *Greendale*, such as environmental destruction and intrusions from the mass media.

"*On the Beach* is a record that reflected what was going on at that time, and what was going on in my life at that time, and I think, like anything, if it's true in the first place, it'll be true forever. It should just ring differently, but it will still ring. If you're contriving it or working too hard to create something, then it's not going to ring true later on. So I'm glad *On the Beach* is happening now, and I hope people get something out of it."

He says he has remastered all of his other albums, so fans can soon expect to hear *Journey Through the Past* and *Time Fades Away* on CD.

Those curious about the meanings behind Young's songs were enlightened by the release of the 800-page *Shakey* last year.

Was it a big decision to let someone into his life, or was it just an extension of his songwriting?

"I think it was a mistake, but I did it, and I chose him because I like Jimmy and he's a great writer, but I think it was a mistake to put it out."

After giving author Jimmy McDonough unprecedented access to his personal life, Young then tried to block the book's release, and McDonough, fearing that eight years of research and 300 interviews would go to waste, sued Young for $US 1.8 million.

Young, though, says he was just trying to delay its release until his daughter was old enough to read it.

"My daughter wasn't even 17 when they wanted to put it out, and I didn't get a chance to go through it before they handed it in to the publisher, which was the way I thought it should be. So I was a little upset about it, so I did what I could to hold it up as long as possible, which was 18 months, which made everything work out fine, because she was over 18 then, and if she was going to read it, then fine."

Many of this year's best albums, from bands such as Songs: Ohia, My Morning Jacket, Grandaddy, Will Oldham and the Autumn Defense, have their roots in Young's soulful country sound. But Young says he's too busy with his own work to keep tabs on new music.

"I listen to the radio, where you only hear what the corporate people decide you should listen to, so that's not rewarding. Hopefully now with the implosion of the record business, the radio waves will open up a bit. I just listen to stuff at parties, but I don't have time to go out and check on things."

In his 34-year solo recording career, Young has meandered between rock, folk, blues, country, psychedelia, grunge and electronica. He says that after this tour he will continue to take *Greendale* on the road in the US in the lead-up to the next election. But what kind of music does he think he will dream up next?

"I haven't heard anything in my head that I felt like I wanted to grab. I don't like to write a song if I can't record it straight away. I don't go looking for songs. I want to feel fresh about it."

NEIL YOUNG ON

Making Movies

"I wanna do it impulsively and I wanna do it at my own pace, which is fast. And I don't like getting hung up on technical difficulties. I don't give a shit about the technical aspect of it. We try to use what some people might consider to be mistakes to create a sense of urgency about what we're talking about. It's realism."

—from an interview with Jonny Leahan, *IndieWire*, February 26, 2004

NEIL YOUNG ON

Fans Sharing Music

"I can't control what people do. I don't want to. If they want to sell my music to someone else or send it to their friends, they can just as easily tape it off the radio as the Net."

—from an interview with Ted Greenwald, *Wired*, March 1, 2004

NEIL YOUNG ON

Taking Guitar Lessons

"One. Maybe two. I either quit after the first one and didn't go back for the second one, or I went to the second one and that was enough. I don't think the guitar lesson hurt me—I just realized I didn't need it. I figured out what to do with a guitar pretty quick on my own."

—from an interview with Josh Tyrangiel, *Time*, September 25, 2005

NEIL YOUNG ON

Failure

"It's more important to get down what you want than it is to succeed at it. You don't want to fail to do something for any reason other than that you decided not to do it. If you fail to put something out there because people are telling you it's no good, or that it won't sell, or something like that, then you're already listening to too many people."

–from an interview with Russell Hall, *Performing Songwriter*, December 2005

NEIL YOUNG: "I'M NOT READY TO GO YET"

Jaan Uhelszki | September 2007 | *Uncut*

The *Greendale* tour returned to North America for more shows in early 2004. The rest of 2004 was filled with a dozen charity performances and Young's first straightforward best-of collection, *Greatest Hits*.

Young completed work on *Prairie Wind* in March 2005. Soon after, he suffered a brain aneurysm that incapacitated him for a short time. He was back on stage by the middle of May and, in August, filmed two Nashville shows that formed the basis of Jonathan Demme's 2006 movie *Neil Young: Heart of Gold*. The *Prairie Wind* LP/DVD was released in September 2005.

Young recorded and released the politically charged *Living with War*, a response to US President George W. Bush's policies, in spring 2006. In July he cranked up the protest machine, CSNY, and set out on the 35-date Freedom of Speech '06 Tour, featuring a mixture of *Living with War* tunes and classics.

November 2006 also saw the long-awaited first music from the Neil Young Archives, *Live at the Fillmore East*, culled from two Crazy Horse shows from March 1970. The same month Young also released a "straight-to-the-board" version of *Living with War* called *"In the Beginning."*

2007 was dedicated to working on the Archives, and recording, releasing, and touring *Chrome Dreams II*, a follow-up to the unreleased 1970s album *Chrome Dreams*.

This interview, the first of two with *Creem* magazine cofounder Jaan Uhelszki, finds Young reflecting back but still "looking forward." He breaks down the *Chrome Dreams II* and *Archives* creative processes, ponders organized religion and spirituality, and, combining these themes, considers deceased friends and relatives who inhabit this LP. —Ed.

He might be one of the wealthiest rock musicians in the world, but Neil Young still retains something of the untamed savage. Maybe it's those prodigious sideburns, fuzzy as twin albino Amazonian caterpillars. The scarecrow-cum-woodsman look that he's sported in recent times has been toned down, mind, but that could be because on this Indian summer day in Manhattan—September 11, to be precise—it is far too warm for plaid.

Today, Young is wearing too-large jeans and a black Willie Nelson T-shirt. A pair of silver-rimmed aviator shades dangle from the neck of his shirt, much like the mirrored reflector glasses that he used to keep the world at bay with in the 1970s. The hair is less unkempt than usual, still damp from a shower, and brushed back neatly from his high forehead. Two months from his 62nd birthday, Young's features are chiseled and defined and, if you take a step back and squint, he resembles no-one so much as James Garner.

Nevertheless, he still cuts a wild figure in this over-decorated suite at the Carlyle Hotel, a luxurious home-away-from-home for diplomats, bejeweled matrons and top-tier rock stars.

He is not, historically, the easiest of interviewees: fastidiously guarded, his slate-blue eyes traditionally grow narrow and dark when he is angered or distraught. But this time he is less wary, teetering somewhere between suspicion and amusement, but never landing on either. As he embarks on a meticulous journey through his past, in the wake of a string of bereavements and a near-fatal aneurysm, it seems as if this stoical figure has finally made an uneasy peace with both his mortality and his career.

The interview is running 90 minutes late, postponed so that Young could fit in his daily workout routine on the Power-Plate, a fashionable form of exercise also favored by Madonna and Clint Eastwood. A piece of equipment developed by Russian scientist Vladimir Nazarov to help prevent astronauts' muscles suffering atrophy, the Power-Plate emits a series of high-speed vibrations that give your muscles an accelerated workout, making them relax and contract up to 50 times a minute.

It's akin to standing on a tumble dryer, and there are critics who think that all that high-powered jiggling could possibly harm the brain. But that's not something that bothers Young. After having suffered that aneurysm in 2005 and subsequent corrective surgery to implant tiny platinum coils in his brain, he has a sense of freedom nowadays. Two days after he was released from the hospital, Young collapsed in Central Park, a vascular complication leaving him bleeding and unconscious. "I just knew I wasn't ready to go," he says today, still more than a little bemused.

The Power-Plate has worried Young in one way, though: he feared it could affect the songs he was recording for what has become his extraordinary 43rd album, *Chrome Dreams II*, a sequel of sorts to 1977's legendary unreleased *Chrome Dreams* (the original home of "Like A Hurricane," "Powderfinger" and "Sedan Delivery").

"I reviewed how the songs ended up sounding the way they did, by looking at other activities that I had done during the period on the same day," he says, adjusting his body into an architecturally challenging wing chair that looks like a woolly plush animal. "I have a certain exercise regime that I go through, and I wanted to know if there was any correlation. So I look back at that. But really, this music just started coming out."

"All it takes to get me started is a good environment and then I'll start thinking about music," he explains, shaking his head back and forth a few times, as if the process amazes him as much as it does us. Eighteen months ago, he told me, "Accessing creativity—it's like approaching a wild animal in a hole. If you try too hard, it's gonna get away. You can't corner it, you can't scare it. You consistently stay there with it, and wait for it to come out."

The trouble is, Young just doesn't know when that will be. Sometimes it descends on him like a willful ghost, or an unplanned pregnancy, causing havoc with the best-laid plans. For a while, the urge stayed away. "*Greendale* (2003's equivocally received environmental concept album-cum-community musical) was such a huge thing that it just drained me, I didn't pick up a guitar for almost 18 months. I don't sit around and practice. If I don't feel like it, I don't do it. And if I do feel like it, I won't do anything else."

Since 2005, songs have come hurling out of him, like one long bout of projectile vomiting. After he was diagnosed with the aneurysm, Young finished the eight songs that would form the basis of *Prairie Wind* in just four days while awaiting surgery. With last year's barnstorming, audacious *Living With War*, it was much the same. He wrote and recorded it in a blistering nine days—and then released it a month later, testament to both an unruly muse and the level of his moral disgust over the war in Iraq. It has been a hectic period, also notable for two tantalizing teasers of his endlessly promised Archives set: *Live At Fillmore East*, capturing his marauding 1970 tour with Crazy Horse; and *Live At Massey Hall*, a 1971 acoustic show in Toronto that would presage *Harvest*.

Living With War was only released in spring last year, so no-one, least of all Young himself, suspected there would be another album hovering on the edge of his subconscious. "I really wasn't planning anything," laughs Young. "I don't know what it is, but I'm thankful for this bout of hyperactivity. I just let it happen."

Before *Chrome Dreams II* materialized, Young was actually occupied with a couple of other things. He was due to travel to Nashville with Pegi, his wife of 29 years—the bartender of his favorite bar near Santa Cruz in the early '70s—to help get her eponymous debut LP off the ground, originally slated for 2005. In a New York hotel room prior to setting off, he spotted something in his eye while shaving—a first sign of the aneurysm, but he carried on to Nashville after diagnosis, as his doctors couldn't operate right away.

"I had planned to do it then," Pegi says, "and the next thing you know we're in Nashville making a record, and it's his record. So at any rate, I had to wait my turn again to work with the band, and obviously the priority was to get him back." Even Pegi Young is mystified by her husband's creative vagaries, though. "Neil does what Neil wants," she adds, "and if he's not ready, not a thing in the world will make him do anything that's not his idea."

Besides Pegi's album, Young was spending an hour or two on the Archives, his long-promised "Audiobiography" project that has been on and off the release schedules for the past 15 years. The first volume of this massive collection of his life's work might just come out next February, though rumors suggest it may be pushed back yet again to autumn 2008. *Volume One* covers the period from '63–'72, stretches across eight CDs and two DVDs, and features myriad unreleased studio and live recordings, rare photos and personal letters, plus a 150-page booklet. Young has been hands-on from the start of the project, most recently unearthing all the reviews—good and bad—that ran at the time.

The mythic archives are currently housed in a charmless, windowless industrial outpost just north of San Francisco airport. One day, though, Young found himself on a part of his 1,800-acre Broken Arrow ranch, 35 miles south of San Francisco in the hills of San Mateo County. He was wandering through the yawning corridors of his car barn, a massive structure that he'd just built to house his 50-odd gleaming vintage motors, thinking about anything but making music.

"I got some old cars I was going to put in the building, and when I was walking around I realized the floor was cement. I didn't like the way it felt on my back," he says, pausing for the briefest second and unconsciously running his hand along the left side of his body: *Harvest*, remember, was recorded with Young in a back brace.

"I said to myself, if I'm going to hang out in here and look at these cool old cars and stuff, it's not going to be fun if I'm going to be tired from walking on cement. So I went out and bought the thick, spongy rubber flooring they put behind bars for people to stand on. I covered the entire floor with it. And I walked on it, and it felt great. It was amazing.

"And then I realized that after I put the stuff down, it sounded incredible in there. It went from being a tank, a terrible-sounding place where you'd never want to play music, to a very interesting-sounding place. It had a corrugated roof and corrugated wainscoting and wooden walls and glass windows, so it had a lot of high-end loud. When I put the rubber down, it dampened it like 80 per cent. So it was instantly loud from the ceiling, and then gone, instead of bouncing around.

"That's what you want. You want the big new sound, the big fresh sound to be real loud. And big. Usually a big sound will have so much power that it'll start bouncing around and overcome the next sound, so the sounds wash together. But the rubber on the floor seemed to dampen it completely. I noticed the holes had the cement still coming through them, so I filled up the holes with sawdust. And then it sounded incredible. It's the best sounding place I've ever played in."

So because you changed the sound in your car garage, you started getting the inspiration to write?

"That's how it happened. Called it Feel Good's Garage. Then I thought, well, I'm going to get together some guys that have never played together before, put together a different combination, and go in this little room and see what it sounds like. And then when we started playing, I started grooving and having more and more fun, and started playing more."

Young had no songs written, but he and his pals—one-time Bluenotes bassist Rick Rosas, Stray Gator guitarist Ben Keith, and Crazy Horse drummer Ralph Molina—began re-recording a few old songs that had never quite fitted onto an album.

"After we did the older stuff, we just kept playing," recalls Young, "and I went, 'God, you know, this is good. And if I keep going, I might have an album.' So I'm going to keep on going till I stop, until I run out of songs. And that's what happens, when I get started I just keep going until the songs don't come. And every day I come to the studio, I have a new song. And if I miss a day, then the next day there's one and it starts coming again, I have two or three more. And when you miss two or three days, four days, well, that's it. We're done."

But how did this bunch of old and new tunes become not just one of Young's most varied and compelling sets in years, but also a sequel to an album that had never been released?

"I started thinking about the fact that when I made *Chrome Dreams*, I also had some old cuts on it that I drew out to fill it out," he explains. He pours himself a cup of steaming black coffee from a sculpted china jug rimmed with gold leaf, a study of good taste and opulence, then sticks his index finger into the white cup to test the temperature and quickly retracts it with an abashed grin. I get the feeling that it's not the first time he's gone through this ritual.

"Quite often I'll record things that don't fit with what I'm doing, so I just hold onto them for a while. Some of them are so strong that they destroy what I'm doing. It's like if you have a bunch of kids and one of them weighs 200 pounds and the other ones are 75 pounds, you've got to keep things in order so they don't hurt each other. So that's why I held certain things back.

"This gave me a vehicle to go back and grab those things, and either re-record them or just grab the originals and see how they felt now. 'Beautiful Bluebird' was actually recorded originally for Old Ways, and that was back in the '80s somewhere. The record didn't take me where the song took me, so I left it off. So then I re-recorded it. I'll do that when I'm recording and I don't have that many new songs. I'll start by recording some old songs, not expecting to use them. There's no pressure. It just gets everybody going, then I start writing more songs. But these came out well. 'Boxcar' came out really nicely. I've got a few other recordings of it, but they're not as good as this one."

Besides "Boxcar" and "Beautiful Bluebird," Young dusted off "Ordinary People," a remarkable 18-minute song that was destined for *Freedom*. Even he admits it isn't exactly a perfect fit, but he still wanted it to come out now, rather than just being subsumed into *Archives*.

"Today that song rings maybe even more true than it did then, so I felt that that's a good example of a song without a home, a strong song that destroyed other songs when you put it with them," Young says. "When I recorded it, it would have gone on *Freedom*, but it blew away *Freedom*. Somehow it just didn't work.

"It's relentless, there is a lot of energy in that song. And it's a little bit abusive as a listen because it is long. I mean, 'Ordinary People' is so overbearing that you might want to skip it every once in a while, just go 'I can't go there right now'. And if you do, that's fine. 'Ordinary People' wasn't able to coexist with any other records until this one. It was always there. I said, this has got to come out and it's got to come out before the Archives because it has too much in it to be held back for 20 years."

Three Picasso prints hang in Neil Young's luxurious Carlyle suite, below which the singer sits easily, his battered, buckled brown shoes resting on the 288-knot Persian rug that covers the expanse of his room. In the adjoining suite, on a well-gnawed leash, his dog, Carl, a 12-year-old champagne-colored Labradoodle waits patiently to be taken on one of his nightly prowls through Central Park. Young doesn't routinely choose this hotel because it has housed every US president since Harry Truman.

He's not here for the Upper East Side location, the white-gloved elevator operators, the world-class original art, or the bar that used to be home to pianist Bobby Short. Young stays at the Carlyle for one good reason: he can keep his dog there.

Young's demands aren't quite in the same class as another rock personage "of the same stature as Mr. Young," according to the front desk at the hotel. This unnamed star insisted that the entire staff not make any noise around his fourth-floor suite before noon. Ever accommodating, the Carlyle suspended some ongoing room construction until 12:01, even instructing the maids not to start their shift until the star awakened. But unlike Young, that rock personage didn't pen a song like "Ordinary People."

The funny thing is, if you don't listen to this admittedly fantastic 18-minute rant, *Chrome Dreams II* does feel more cohesive. It becomes the focused tale of a man on a spiritual quest, rather than a gripping odds 'n' sods record searching for its own center. Taken together, the songs seem to describe Young trying to find his way home, weirdly reminiscent of Dorothy in *The Wizard Of Oz*. Instead of a pair of ruby slippers, though, Young's talisman is a hood ornament from a vintage Lincoln Continental.

"I have to say, that it's the first time I've explored my own beliefs and it was just a natural thing," he says. "It just happened this way. Usually, I find it hard to talk about those things as I don't like to judge anyone else's beliefs. I'm just into nature, that's what I believe in.

"If I was to be classified now and you had to put me in a box, my favorite box would be pagan. I feel natural with it. And of course it was a huge threat to Christianity, so it took a bad rap for centuries, and that reputation still lasts. Like 'pagan' is considered a bad word, but it's really not a bad word. It's a good word. It's a beautiful word.

"I respect people who are dedicated to organized religion, and I respect their way of life, but it's not mine. And so I feel grossly underrepresented in the current administration, but I feel I'm doing the right thing for me. The Great Spirit has been good to me. My faith has always been there, it's just not organized, there's no doctrine, there's no book I follow. To me, the forest is my church. If I need to think I'll go for a walk in the trees, or I'll go for a walk on the prairie, or I'll go for a walk on the beach. Wherever the environment is most extreme is where I will go. If there's a moon, I'll try to get out and walk under the moon."

The spiritual path of *Chrome Dreams II* was prompted when Anthony Crawford—"a singer that I play with and sing with sometimes from Nashville"—was visiting Young's ranch. Crawford took a photo of the ruined automobiles that take up about 200 yards of Broken Arrow.

"It all connected in a weird way," explains Young. "The way it really started was that Anthony Crawford took some photographs of an old car graveyard on my property. They're all great old American classics, but they're all totaled. They're the best cars, in the worst condition. Although they're in a state of decay, they still have their classic lines. He took this one picture of a hood ornament, and the hood had moss growing on it and all this crud, and the paint was peeling. It was all tarnished and starting to come apart, looking really bad, but also looking really good.

"I related to the fact it was something great that wasn't in its prime. I went, 'Oh, my God, this looks like me!' You know, because I just feel a little bit weathered and beat up a bit by things that have happened, but I feel good. And this thing looked strong and I felt good when I looked at it. I thought the title of this picture would be *The Pursuit Of Excellence*, but that's not too good a name for an album. Then I started thinking of *Chrome Dreams*, as the picture made me think of those words. I went on the Internet and started looking for *Chrome Dreams* to see if there was anything there. And sure enough, somebody in Germany had found an acetate, a couple of years ago.

"So naturally, I remembered a sketch that my friend David Briggs (Young's long-time producer, who died in 1995) made for *Chrome Dreams*. If you turned it vertically, it looked like a beautiful woman. Turned sideways, it looked like a Chrysler. So it was amazing, just a hand sketch, and I could never duplicate it. It was destroyed in a fire, but I still remember it." Young looks at a spot over my left shoulder, as if the ghost of Briggs is sitting there, egging him on.

What stands out most vividly about recording the first *Chrome Dreams*?

"I remember when I was living on the beach in LA in Malibu, and Carole King lived up the beach. I said, 'Carole, why don't you come over and let me play you my new album.' About halfway through she went, 'Neil, this isn't an album. It's not a real album. I mean, there's nobody playing, and half the songs you're just doing by yourself.' She was just laughing at me. Because she crafts albums.

"I was out there, you know, using all these different techniques, and I recorded 'Will To Love' on a cassette player in front of my fireplace and then overdubbed a bunch of instruments on it in one night. That's the way I like to make records. I have the original tapes of all of those songs. Probably *Chrome Dreams* will come out in the Archives, but it won't have its cover, which is heart-breaking."

Besides David Briggs, much of *Chrome Dreams II* seems inhabited by other spirits of those have passed on, from Neil's own mother, who died in 1990, on "The Believer," to co-producer Niko Bolas' wife, who died right before they started recording. It's an album about those who have gone, and what remains of them. Of questions asked and not answered and roads taken and those discarded.

Did you mother really say she wanted to be on that windy road for eternity, like you sing in "The Believer?"

"Yeah," says Young, with an unwavering, almost dead-eyed stare; the kind of small flash of warning when you know you've gone a little too far with him.

What did she mean by that?

"We're driving out near her house in Florida, and she said, 'Stop the car, I want to get out.' I finally stopped and she got out. She was just standing there in the wind and she had her trench coat on, and the wind's blowing about 40 miles an hour, and the sleeves of her coat are billowing out, and leaves are falling and things are happening on this hilltop; this ridge road, with eucalyptus trees on both sides of the road for a mile and a half. Giant trees. And the wind is coming off the ocean. After a few minutes, she opened up the car, got back in and said to me, 'That's where I want to be.' I just believe that's where she wanted to be, so I put her there. I spread her ashes there when she died. Went out in the wind and threw 'em up and drove away."

Does David Briggs haunt any of these tracks, since he produced the first *Chrome Dreams*? He seems to be the missing friend "whose counsel I can never replace" on "No Hidden Path."

"I think I know the part you're talking about," says Young non-committally, his moment of uncharacteristic candor having passed.

Is it Briggs that you miss?

"I think everyone misses somebody here," says Young quietly.

So you're not going to tell me who it is, right?

"Right."

The 2005 album, *Prairie Wind*, was haunted by his father, sportswriter Scott Young, and singer Nicolette Larson—something he admitted during the recording of the Jonathan Demme-produced documentary, *Heart Of Gold*. But there are many more disembodied spirits that flit through Young's life, from Crazy Horse guitarist Danny Whitten, to roadie Bruce Berry, to his second wife, Carrie [Snodgress], who died in 2004. Like Emily Dickinson said so chillingly in "Poem 670," "One need not be a Chamber to be Haunted/One need not to be a house." All one really needs is a past, and at 62, Neil Young has a long and often messy one—something that he plans to disgorge with the release of the *Archives*.

While they may be revealing for fans—who've waited long enough for them, after all—they are even more valuable to Young, forcing him to look at things he might not want to and find some patterns in the arc of his long career.

"I've learned a lot about the trail that I've left, the debris behind me, going through this. It's a process. And then I learn so much, and then I get tired of it, and then I'll do something new and it will distract me completely. And then I'll stay focused on that, and then it takes a long time for me to let go. Very difficult to let go.

"But when I do finally let go, I'm never happy. I'm always going, 'I could've done this, I could've done that.' But I've got to stop. I'm just obsessing. And it doesn't matter if 'Boxcar' is first or 'Beautiful Bluebird'. You know, it does, but it doesn't. I'm still going back and forth on that."

This wavering may be one of the many reasons Young has repeatedly stalled the release of *Archives* for the past 20 years. Always willfully inscrutable, and a world-class contrarian, "I'm a walking contradiction," he tells me—as if that explained everything. Falling silent, he seems to think about it for a moment.

"I think the most profound thing I realized while working in the Archives is that I'm not careful. I've been too concerned with moving on. So I leave a lot of unfinished and unreleased stuff, as it doesn't fit with where my head is then. I forget about all the work that went into it. And I just forget about it. But they're still there. And I say, well, gee, maybe I should put that out. Or why didn't I finish this? Or that was real good, why didn't I do that all the way? Stuff like that.

"I just found that I'm careless because I'm always only interested in the new thing. If it's taking too long to finish the old thing, and I have something new happening, I'll abandon the old thing. Because I don't want to lose the new thing."

So why is Young—who told me in 2005, "My best work is ahead of me. It's always in front. It can't be behind you. It's just a question of getting to it"—spending so much time thinking about the past? Is this the end of the line for him?

"I'm fascinated by time travel and things like that," he says. "So really *Archives* is a super-deep and long filing cabinet. Visually, that's what it is. I mean, you press a button and the files keep coming, flying out of this big file cabinet, and the drawer goes on forever. And it goes through 45 years of music.

"If you're going to listen to, say, 'I've Been Waiting For You' from my first album, there's a mix on there that was never used, that's better than the mix on the record. I don't know why we didn't use it. So in *Archives*, we take that and make a collage, blow up the lyrics so they're as big as the wall. Spread 'em out and use 'em for a rug. And then put an old vintage '70s tape machine on the floor. And so when you choose 'I've Been Waiting For You,' then you get that image.

"We developed it as we went along. The idea of having places to go all the way along, things to read and look at as you go through time.

You can read all the newsprint. You can see manuscripts, photos from the period. And it just keeps coming."

Won't you feel some sense of loss once you've put out a retrospective of your whole career? It seems like an end of something, not a new beginning.

"Yes, sometimes I do, and then I don't put it out. Did that with *Tonight's The Night*, I waited two years before I put it out. I thought maybe *Decade II* would come along (a sequel to his '77 compilation, *Decade*), but I'm such a collector that I have so much stuff.

"To tell you the truth, I don't even know how that's going to happen. I'm making the template and I'm creating the new songs as I go along. I have the choices to make, what fits and what doesn't. And I've been able to do that for the first, and now almost all of the second volume. The third and fourth are going to be easier. There are less songs that I didn't put out, because when I was younger I wrote so much more than I do now. The whole thing has a life of its own. And when it comes out I think people will find it a different experience."

One person who doesn't think that *Archives* will ever come out, is Crazy Horse guitarist Frank "Poncho" Sampedro. Back in 2003, Sampedro told Paul Cashmere at Undercover News that he'd be surprised if the collection ever emerged—a collection that would eventually unleash over 150 Crazy Horse tracks on the world.

"I think Neil just has a feeling that putting out a boxed set like that is kind of marking the end of your career, like a tribute to yourself," said Sampedro. "He would never say that, but he just doesn't want to do that until he is done. That's what I feel."

What does Young think of that?

Is there a part of you that thinks that if you put this out, then it will make the end of something. Your life? The world?

"Ultimately I hope that I'm around to see it through, the whole thing. But no, I don't want to go. I'm not ready for that. Mostly you can see yourself changing. See the ups and downs physically, feel them in the music.

"It leads to an inevitable end," reflects Young. "But I don't dwell on that too much. I don't know what that means. I'm not ready for any of that. But in another sense I am ready. I'm just on a journey."

NEIL YOUNG ON

Getting Old

"I'm 61 years old and there are a lot of things starting to crop up. Different parts of my body don't work the way they used to. And there's pain and stuff. The older you get, the closer to the end of your life you get. It seems like there are a lot of things to do now."

–from an interview with Burhan Wazir, *Guardian*, October 4, 2007

PODCAST INTERVIEW

Michael Goldman | January 2008 | *Digital Content Producer Magazine*

Young, as Bernard Shakey, premiered the 2006 tour documentary *CSNY/Déjà Vu* at the Sundance Film Festival in January 2008. This interview digs deeply into Young's political and creative thinking behind the controversial film, one of the few times in this volume in which the focus is exclusively on filmmaking. –Ed.

Michael Goldman: Hey, Neil, it's Michael Goldman.

Neil Young: How are you?

Goldman: I'm great. Thanks for making time for this I really appreciate it.

Young: Thank you.

Goldman: I did want to talk to you about the movie, and I thought to start maybe you could just give me a little bit of background on the how and the why. First of all, you decided to make this a documentary at all, and second of all why you decided to have yourself direct the piece, make the movie, rather than going the route of like the Rolling Stones and finding a great filmmaker, somebody like that to do it.

Young: The whole subject matter of it was pretty personal and I had an opportunity in doing the videos—I met Mike Cerre and I saw all his footage. He called me when the *Living with War* album came out and he wanted to do a special thing on MSNBC, a half-hour special on the album and the war in Iraq, and then I saw some of his footage and I did say, "I don't really wanna do the television show on this album." I'm really not looking for a way to promote the album. I think it would be in really in poor taste to promote or to try to put something together and get publicity for it—just let it speak for itself. It wasn't made to be a commercial album, really, it was made to be a statement of sorts and so it's kinda distasteful to promote something when you're singing about the subject matter that was there. But in the long-run I saw his footage and I wanted to make videos of every song on this and make a DVD of all the songs and the videos. So we ended up making all these videos and putting them on the website and I used all of his footage and a lot of stock footage and everything.

And then I was doing that and then I decided, who can I go out and play with and do these songs? I had made a plan to do a CSNY tour even before I started recording the *Living with War* album, so that was still sitting there. I made this commitment to do the tour. So then I played them the album and I said, "Listen, let's go in this direction." And then as I was doing that, I was finishing the videos and I was taking with Mike Cerre, I said, "Mike, why don't you come with us? You know all these guys who have been over there and all these women that have been over there fighting for us and fighting for the country and carrying out the President's orders and doing this this. Why don't we have them come and see what they think about our music and what we're singing about 'cause we're gonna be singing about what they're doing and we're singing about the predicament that they're in following these orders and let's see what they say. I think that'd be an interesting film." It never really ever was intended to be anything other than a documentary about the reaction of the country to the music.

So we filmed. Of course we shoot every night and we put it up on the screen so we have a lot of footage we could use, and a couple of nights we shot with a few more cameras. So we just started putting it all together. But that's how it happened. I saw it as a final thing I could do to wrap up the *Living with War* project. So, when the film comes out, it'll be kinda telling a story of a point in history where the country was at a turning point with regards to supporting the administration on the war.

I think that we're very supportive of the troops in our position, in the songs we sing, I think, are sympathetic to the troops and not necessarily sympathetic to the administration. It's just the way we feel, but we didn't think that the way we feel is the way everybody else should feel. We just wanted to get it out there—this is how we feel. The guys supported me on these songs and we used a lot of their older songs to kinda offset it with giving ourselves a place in history and a reference point. So we did that and then we recorded the reaction of the people around the country. We tried to get as much reaction, pro and con, in every way that we could. Collected all the reviews, made a chart of all the reviews so that we could see—we got about maybe two-to-one positive reviews. We got a couple of hundred positive and about a hundred negative. So we chose the best reviews and the worst reviews and put them up against each other in the film and tried to give them equal opportunity and in that way we actually skewed. We used relatively a few more bad reviews that we were actually getting, but they were all real reviews—everything was real. And we just tried to find people in the audience, interview people in the audience, and tried to find people who had—the whole thing—not just people supporting our point of view. The whole thing from about *Living with War* and the record that I made a coupla years ago starting this thing was to spur debate, to get people talking about, it because it had become so unpatriotic to even question anything that was going on and that was kind of the status quo and we wanted to play our part in breaking that.

Goldman: During the course of that whole thing, was it intentional in terms of the story, or did it just evolve that way that you also were able to, sort of, give an indication of the story of the history of the band sort of bookended between Vietnam and Iraq, needing to do this to be protesting? I got out of it that you guys yourselves can't keep doing it forever and other people had better start picking up the torch.

Young: Well, if they want to. This is us. This is what we do and maybe the further into history . . . I'm an optimist—maybe we won't have to. Maybe we'll evolve to a point where we don't have to, but we have to get out of this mess first and then, who knows. We didn't learn after Vietnam, but that doesn't mean we can't learn after this one. All we need is the right people running the country that feel that way to, basically, give peace a chance, like Lennon said. It's very idealistic and there's all kind of opinions on both sides about what we're doing and whether it's right or wrong. We tried to give the people who had strong convictions that we are doing the right thing over there and America should be having a preeminent war against a regime like Saddam's. It's hard to say post-9/11 world exactly how to act, but we found out that what we did certainly didn't garner much sympathy around the world for us. I really wanted to stimulate the discussion and let the chips fall where they may. My only regret in the whole thing is that there is that was a tour that was out there about the same time as ours, it was kind of a patriotic American celebration kind of a tour that was—I thought our tour was patriotic also—but I think that we really could have benefited from filming that. They had Toby Keith and they had some other artists that were pro-administration artists that were basically on the other side of the fence from us on this subject. We were not allowed to go in there with our cameras and film that so we could use it and juxtapose it against this, so what we ended up with was, we used everything else we could find that represented that opinion. I wish we had had a little more of a level-headed voice on that side, someone who really made sense and wasn't just purely emotional, but we couldn't find it, we couldn't find enough of it and we were not allowed to go into where it was really happening. I would have loved to have gotten into the Young Republicans and found out what the kids were saying, what the Young Republicans—the twenty-five-year-olds—I would have loved to have gotten their opinions about what we were doing and the other side of, representing the other side of the discussion, but we couldn't get that. So we used what we had. We used what we came around with naturally and we didn't try to skew it one way or another. We tried to give an equal balance to it so that at the end of the day you'd have this feeling about what we're doing and how different opinions, how many different opinions there are about him in the country, just to start a discussion on the way home in the car about what we're doing.

Goldman: Once you decided to do this as a filmmaker, it then creates all these technical and logistical issues about putting a crew together and what kind of cameras and how you're gonna edit it and all that stuff. I know you've done film work before and you made *Greendale* into a movie and all that stuff—what was this filmmaking experience like? How involved did you get in it?

Young: I was very involved in the structure of it and very involved in the editing. Initially the shooting—my concept for the shooting—was that I directed Mike Cerre to go out there, and I said, "I want you to give me 10 or 15 different stories—shorts subjects, like TV episodes—of your covering of this tour and the people and just give them to me and I will decide how to use them." So I did 'em and I got those and I took 'em and I took 'em and put them in the order I wanted 'em in and decided what songs we wanted to use and I picked all the music and the tunes and the performances and then kinda put it together. But I had a lot of help from Mike because he constructed a lot of these vignettes, the episodes, and then in some cases I edited the episodes heavily and in other cases I left them alone. Deciding what order they were in and how to juxtapose the music to them and what to use and what not to use was—that's really the MO that we had on this.

Goldman: And so when Stephen Stills is out campaigning and you're following one of the veterans around: was that Mike sending a crew out there, or how did that—

Young: Well, we knew that Stephen was doing that so we made sure that Mike covered it, and Mike was, Mike, he was all over it—we told him everything. I just said, "Listen, I want you to shoot everything, everything that . . . I want you to find the people who don't like what we're doing and give them a voice, get out there and ambush them, catch them when they're leaving the venue."

Goldman: And did they shoot with HD cameras or how did all that work?

Young: Yes, HD.

Goldman: How did this experience compare to sort of making *Greendale*, which was a structured, stage piece that you then put on film?

Young: Oh, it's a completely different structure.

Goldman: The editing: were you able to see dailies and rushes while you were on the road or—

Young: No, I didn't do any of that. We didn't do anything until we got home. Well, actually, that's not true 'cause we saw a couple of Mike's episodes, and I put 'em on the website while we were on the road. We used parts of them in the film. We just wanted to give people an idea that we were filming it and that there was gonna be more to come. So we used a little bit of it on the websites and we cut that up and used a little of it in the film. But we had many episodes that weren't on the website. I just put it together in a way that it told a story of the tour and the country's reaction to the tour and that was our purpose. Our purpose was to try to give everybody an equal voice and to represent what really happened, and that's why we were careful to capture all of the reviews, then we had the reviews read, and we did what we could with it.

Goldman: Was there a particular structure for the look or the palette of the film? Was there a digital intermediate done, did you spend much time—

Young: We did some, yeah, we did a lot of color things with it. We did some reframing on the footage. Since it's HD, we had a lot to work with—we tweaked it here and there. At one point we were gonna have all the interviews be real solid video look and then put a little film look on the performances, but we abandoned that halfway through. We had some TV-like graphics on the interviews and we took those out. We did a lot of stuff that we tried and then we just dumped it because we thought it was really strong and we didn't want to be kitschy with it.

Goldman: Yeah, 'cause I'm curious—I'm not sure how interested you are in being a filmmaker beyond something that's real personal to you, much like your music. But, in terms of how this digital technology has made it easier, or changed things, much like it has in the music world—I'm just curious, your thoughts . . .

Young: It's lean and mean . . . to get content. It's pretty good. I like film myself, but for this project, it worked real well to use the HD. I personally enjoy shooting film. And if the film we're doing now, the picture we're doing now, it's also, it's a blend of formats, but it's mostly HD, the next picture, as is the picture after that. We're working on two other ones right now. One of them has nothing to do with music and everything to do with transportation and fuel. And the other one is a music one.

Goldman: Do you foresee yourself doing a lot more filmmaking?

Young: Yeah, definitely. I enjoy doing it.

Goldman: How does the process compare to making a record and stuff like that?

Young: It's gratifying. It's new. Hey, I'm sixty-two years old—the fact that I'm doing something new is gratifying and I like it.

Goldman: Yeah, I wish you a lot of luck with that.

Young: All right, thanks a lot.

Goldman: Glad to do it.

NEIL YOUNG ON

Changing the World

"I think the time when music could change the world has passed. That's not just an opinion, I think it's a reality. It's time for science and physics and spirituality to make a difference and to try and save the planet."

–from an interview Stephen Dalton, *Scotland on Sunday*, February 24, 2008

NEIL YOUNG ON

Writing Songs

"Just being there and staying open. I think staying open for me would mean–no one has ever asked me that before–but I think it is like what I said. If I feel it, I am open to it. That is like the boss. That is where it is coming from. So I go there. So I am open to it."

–from an interview with Charlie Rose, *The Charlie Rose Show*, July 2008

NEIL YOUNG: GOLD RUSH

Richard Bienstock | September 29, 2009 | *Guitar World*

There was no new studio music in 2008, but Young released archival and CSNY live LPs and, from June until June 2009, toured Europe, North America, Australia, and New Zealand with His Electric Band. He also worked extensively on preparing the first *Archives* and on LincVolt, his energy project that revolved around his hybrid 1959 Lincoln.

Echoing the LincVolt auto vibe, in April 2009, Young released the vehicle-oriented studio LP *Fork in the Road* and, finally, in June, released *The Archives Vol. 1 1963-1972*. The innovative collection is discussed at length in this June 2009 interview. And, as expected from this guitar-oriented source, the article also explores his axe playing, including Young's lead playing, which he says "sucks." –Ed.

"How're you all doing?"

It's June 2009, and Neil Young is standing center stage at the O2 in Dublin, an ultra-modern, orb-like arena that seems as much a food court and concession stand as it does a music venue. He's wearing baggy blue jeans, sneakers and a corduroy button-down over a faded black T-shirt. His hair is grey, and wild as ever, with bushy mutton-chop sideburns framing either side of his face. Young is nearing the end of a European tour in support of *Fork in the Road*, which is, roughly speaking, the 34th or so album of his solo career. Taking into account live discs, soundtracks, projects with other bands, and the nebulous nature of what exactly constitutes an "official" album in Young's catalog, it's probably closer to being his 50th. Last year Young turned 63, but tonight he's been stomping the stage and flailing his body with abandon, all the while coaxing some incredibly gnarly, earsplitting tones—even for him—from "Old Black," the heavily modified 1953 Les Paul Goldtop that in its own way looms as large in music history as Young does.

"We got one for you," he continues from the stage. "May not be the one you wanted." Young moves away from the microphone to cue the next song. Then he changes his mind and steps back up. "Or," he adds, "it might be."

With that, Young and his band launch into the jangly, upbeat "Burned," a not-quite-unfamiliar, but certainly not well-known, tune he first cut with Buffalo Springfield back in 1966, and which he once identified as his "first vocal ever done in a studio." Since that day more than 40 years ago, the song has rarely, if ever, been played live. But Young's been in a different kind of mood lately.

Last year, for instance, Young took to performing "The Sultan," a twangy, Hank Marvin–inspired instrumental that he recorded in 1963 while a teenager in Canada, with his first real band, the Squires. The reference was probably lost on all but the most devoted fans in attendance, and Young added an extra layer of absurdity to his performance by having a man dressed as a sultan bang on a gong to introduce the song.

Discussing this episode today, Young finds it all rather amusing. "We had one lying around backstage," he says, referring to either a sultan's outfit, or perhaps an actual sultan. "So we wanted to get him out there."

But beyond an easy laugh, there's another reason Young has been unearthing songs like "The Sultan" and "Burned" on recent tours. He's been knee-deep in a journey through his past, and now, with the release of the long-delayed, nearly 20-years-in-the-making *Neil Young Archives Volume 1, 1963–1972*, so are his fans.

The first of what Young envisions will ultimately be four or five installments (each spanning roughly a 10-year period of his career), *Archives Volume 1* is, to put it lightly, massive. Issued in three formats—as a 10-disc Blu-ray or DVD collection, each with a 236-page book, and as an eight-CD set—the retrospective boasts more than 120 songs from Young's first decade as a musician, beginning with the Squires and continuing through Buffalo Springfield, his early solo work, Crazy

Horse, and Crosby, Stills, Nash & Young. The tracks are grouped by era: for example, the Buffalo Springfield period resides on a disc titled *Early Years (1966–1968)*, while the *Harvest* record is chronicled on *North Country (1971–1972)*. The *Archives* set features many of Young's biggest and most enduring songs, from acoustic standards like "Sugar Mountain," "Tell Me Why," and "Heart of Gold," to Buffalo Springfield and CSNY classics like "Mr. Soul," "Ohio," and "Helpless," to Crazy Horse barnburners like "Cinnamon Girl," "Down By the River," and "When You Dance, I Can Really Love."

Practically half of these performances are unreleased recordings, live cuts, outtakes and alternate mixes. In addition, the Blu-ray and DVD sets house an excess of visual ephemera, including concert performances, TV appearances, photos, letters, newspaper articles, original manuscripts, audio and video interview clips, and the full version of *Journey Through the Past*, Young's 1972 feature film directorial debut. These materials are organized around two primary tools: a virtual filing cabinet in which each song and its relevant audio and visual documents are gathered in their own individual folder, and an interactive timeline that runs through all the discs and places Young's music within the appropriate personal and historical context.

To call *Archives* merely a "box set" would be to miss the point entirely; it is, in essence, the most panoramic, comprehensive-to-the-point-of-obsessive audio-visual product ever issued by a recording artist.

"What we've done is something that's never been done before," Young says matter-of-factly, sipping a Guinness in the lobby of the Four Seasons hotel in Dublin on the afternoon prior to the O2 show. "'Necessity is the mother of invention,' I guess is the phrase. And that's where this came from. I *needed* this."

The invention that Young refers to is Blu-ray, his preferred platform for viewing and listening to *Archives*. In addition to offering superior sound—state-of-the-art 24-bit/192kHz ultra-high resolution, compared with DVD's 24-bit/96kHz and CD's 16-bit/44kHz standards—the format allows two additional features unavailable on any other platform. Unlike DVD, Blu-ray lets users listen to music and scroll through documents simultaneously. This means that while playing the audio track to Crosby,

Stills, Nash & Young's "Ohio," the listener can also peruse, among other things, recording information about the track, photos of the band onstage at the Fillmore East in New York, Young's original handwritten manuscript of the lyrics, *Time* and *Life* magazine covers about the Kent State University shootings that inspired the subject matter, and a copy of the 45 single and sleeve. There is also audio of Young discussing the song in a radio interview, and video of CSNY performing it at a show in Boston, with the audience singing along to every word.

The other technological development at the center of *Archives* is BD-Live, which enables Blu-ray users to download free updates in the form of additional songs, videos and other documents, as Young makes them available. Once downloaded, these materials appear in their appropriate chronological spots on the interactive timeline.

As Young explains, BD-Live makes it possible for *Archives* to be an evolving, ever-growing project. "It takes a certain kind of organization to come up with that stuff," he says. "These aren't things that somebody kept; these are things that *everybody* kept. And we had to find each person. We had a scanning network out there. And the reason it's so detailed is because we took a lot of time. A *long* time. So new pieces of material are always being uncovered. And because of BD-Live we'll be able to continue getting it out there forever. It's never finished."

That said, Young has already moved on to the second installment of *Archives*, which will take him into the early Eighties. He expects it to be assembled in less time than *Volume 1*. "It'd be hard to not be quicker." He laughs. "That one was, like, 20 years. I think we'll see *Volume 2* in about two or three years, tops."

Young recently sat down with *Guitar World* for his first, and only, comprehensive interview about *Archives Volume 1*. In the following wide-ranging discussion, he expounds on the classic songs and great musicians heard on the collection. He also delves into the guitars, amps and recording techniques that went into creating the timeless music, and speaks candidly about songwriting and his own instrumental abilities.

Most of all, Young was eager to talk about the *Archives* project itself and in particular how, in his view, the benefits of the technology offered by the Blu-ray format will reverberate far beyond his own music.

"People don't understand the value of sound anymore," Young says. "But somebody's going to have to have the nerve to rescue an art form. My responsibility here is to show that music can be supplied at a higher quality, and with deeper content. I'm making it available."

He continues. "Where I came from, music was God. So I must be a dinosaur, you know? Like my day is over. But the fact is, my day is still ahead of me."

GUITAR WORLD: You've been talking about the *Archives* project for close to two decades, and countless release dates have come and gone. Now that it's finally here, one of the things I find amazing is that as far back as the early Nineties you were adamant that certain technologies—such as the ability to scan documents onscreen while simultaneously listening to the music—needed to be in place in order to deliver the project as you saw fit. You knew what you wanted, but you needed to wait for the technology to catch up.

NEIL YOUNG: I knew that it had to be this way, and I believed it was gonna happen. I just thought it would happen sooner. I actually thought DVD would do it. But DVD didn't cut it. So Blu-ray came along just in time. It was only about two years ago that we really saw what we could do with this format. And then it was only more recently that we discovered the BD-Live feature and the possibilities there. That was something that we uncovered while putting together the timeline that binds all the discs together. And new discoveries keep popping up. It'll continue to grow as the Blu-ray standard grows.

The thing with *Archives* is that you're not just getting a music Blu-ray; you're getting something that no movie Blu-ray has ever done, that no educational Blu-ray has ever done. On a broader scale, we're trying to create a new flow of information. In my case, the music is the glue that holds it all together. But it could be anything—it could be art, it could be film, it could be history. As far as I'm concerned *Archives* is a great opportunity to build this platform, and we've pushed the walls of the technology already. And the developers love that. We're helping.

GW: So how many *Archives* sets are we looking at?

YOUNG: Maybe four, maybe five. It depends on how much cutting and paring down we do, and how much we get into using BD-Live, which is really a great thing. It's tremendous. It's remarkable because we really only saw that aspect of it for the first time six or seven months ago. And even then it was cobbled together and the software was buggy. The developers didn't show me too much, because they were still working on the technology. I'd say, "Is it working yet?" And the developers would say, "No." So all right, I don't have to look at it. And then finally it got to a point where they said, "We think it's working pretty good, you oughta check it out." And even then we were just looking at the technology: How does it work? Can you listen to music while you're scrolling around? What types of updates can we do with BD-Live? How are the updates going to sit on the timeline?

One thing that we figured out is that we're going to be able to do progressive download updates. So for instance, around 1970 I played a show at The Cellar Door club in Washington, D.C. That show was taped, but we don't have enough great takes to release it as its own disc. Instead, I'll probably make the songs available as downloadable updates to *Archives*. We'll drop them onto the timeline, one at a time. So one day you may receive an update that will allow you to download the first song from that show, and then maybe a week later, you'll get an update with the second song. And then the third song will come the next week. Before you know it, you have 40 minutes of music in high-def sound that you didn't have to pay for, and that no one's ever heard before.

GW: On a more personal level, why did you feel the need to gather your work in this manner?

YOUNG: Well, my music and the way it's presented here are really inseparable. I have this thing that I'm doing—I'm telling a story. It's something that I've wanted to do for a long time, and in doing it I've become part of the creation of a technology platform that is so much more far-reaching than what I originally envisioned. And I'm fascinated by that. My music has become a way to demonstrate a navigation system through time. And really, my life, my own content, is almost secondary at this point. I look at *Archives* and I go, "Well, there's a hell of a lot about me in there." If you're interested in that, then great. If you're not interested in me, then just listen. Because what you'll hear is better than any record you've ever had. And there's an era coming up in which this level of sound quality, and this level of interaction, is going to be the standard. Much like the CD was the standard for the previous era.

GW: Assembling *Archives* afforded you the opportunity to view the contents of your musical life fairly comprehensively. Was there any overall pattern of behavior that revealed itself to you in the process?

YOUNG: One thing that really surprised me is how ruthless I've been in pursuit of the music. And for how long I've been like that. I always knew I was callous—if I had to do something I had to do it, and I didn't make any excuses. That might mean changing musicians midstream, or dropping a project to go somewhere else entirely. If that's what I had to do to keep the songs coming then that's what I did. But when I saw it, and I remembered what happened, and thought about how I dealt with things in immature ways, it gave me a lot of pause. But nonetheless, I continue on, and keep doing it anyway.

GW: Why change now?

YOUNG: [*laughs*] Yeah, right. Why change. So it's good.

GW: Something that became apparent to me was the incredible pace at which you were moving. To take just one span of time, say, mid-1968 through the end of 1969, you played your final show with Buffalo Springfield, released your first solo album, paired up with Crazy Horse for *Everybody Knows This Is Nowhere*, began working on *After the Gold Rush*, joined Crosby, Stills & Nash, played Woodstock and cut *Déjà Vu*. That's all in about 18 months or so.

YOUNG: I was definitely doing a lot of multitasking. At one point I was recording with Crazy Horse in the mornings at Sunset Sound, cutting stuff like "I Believe In You," "Oh Lonesome Me," the original "Helpless," "Wonderin'," "Birds," all kinds of things, and then in the afternoons I'd go play with CSN. And the only thing I really remember about that is that it bothered them that I was doing both things.

GW: It bothered Crosby, Stills and Nash?

YOUNG: Yeah, a little bit. But I liked playing with them, and I would always be there on time and ready to go. So I didn't see a problem. But I was also playing with Crazy Horse. It wasn't like I was gonna *choose.* Because playing with Crazy Horse brings a whole other thing out of me that never happens anywhere else. And that was maybe hard for them to understand. So it was busy, but it's been really busy all the way through. Maybe in the last 10 years or so the pattern's finally changing.

GW: In what respect?

YOUNG: There's less waste now. I had massive amounts of waste all through the Seventies and Eighties. The most wasteful period is coming up in the next *Archives.*

GW: Define "waste."

YOUNG: Things that were unfinished, things that never really got started, things that were finished and never used. There's just so much music and nowhere to go with it.

GW: What you characterize as waste is to some fans your most valued material—unreleased songs, out-of-print albums . . .

YOUNG: That's true. One thing I'll tell you about the next volume of *Archives* is that *Time Fades Away II* is in there (the original *Time Fades Away*, a long out-of-print live album from 1973, is among the most sought-after releases in Young's catalog). And it's interesting, because the whole thing has a different drummer than what was on that album. I switched drummers halfway through the tour—Kenny Buttrey was in there for the first half, and Johnny Barbata came in for the second. It's a completely different thing, with completely different songs. So that's interesting. There's lots of stuff like that that I'm working on right now for the second volume.

GW: Among the many revelations on *Archives* is the wealth of material—recordings, photos, documents—of the Squires, the band you led in the mid Sixties while still living in Canada. While songs from this part of your career have been unearthed previously, this is by far the most complete picture fans have ever had of what was a pretty significant part of your development as a musician.

YOUNG: The Squires was a very real thing. In one of the document folders on the first disc there's a list that (bassist) Ken Koblun kept of all the shows we played. And it's a lot of shows. I mean, that's a band's life right there. And *Archives* brings that into focus.

GW: Overall, the material gathered on the first disc paints a picture of an artist in search of his own style. You move pretty rapidly from the instrumental surf-rock of the Squires to the Jimmy Reed–style blues of "Hello Lonely Woman" to a solo acoustic version of "Sugar Mountain," which you cut as an audition for Elektra Records in 1965. That song would become one of the defining tunes of your early career, but on this version you sound very unlike yourself, as if you're approximating what you believe a folksinger is supposed to be.

YOUNG: That was probably what was going on. I was just trying to find who I was. And it was very uncomfortable for me to hear some of this stuff. In the case of "Sugar Mountain," I couldn't listen to it. I knew what it was and I listened a little bit but I just thought, God, that's terrible. Because I can tell I was very nervous. I was just trying to be . . . something. But I didn't know what it was.

GW: At what point do you think that changed?

YOUNG: When did it kind of consolidate into something real and I found some little bit of footing? I actually think there's some showing of it earlier than the Elektra demos, on the Squires songs where I sing lead and that we cut for CJLX radio in Fort William in Ontario with (producer) Ray Dee. There's two songs on the *Archives* from those sessions: "I'll Love You Forever" and "I Wonder" (Young eventually reworked the latter song with Crazy Horse as "Don't Cry No Tears" for his 1975 album, *Zuma*). Those are both pretty good.

GW: Speaking of your time in Canada, in a recent interview with *Rolling Stone*, Bob Dylan told a story of how, while on tour last year, he made a pilgrimage of sorts to the house in Winnipeg where you lived during the Squires days. He said he wanted to see your bedroom.

YOUNG: I read that. Jack Harper, the original drummer for the Squires, sent me a copy of the article. It was a big deal in Winnipeg. That was remarkable.

GW: Do you think he found what he was looking for?

YOUNG: Absolutely. I'm sure he found it. I don't know what it is, but I'm sure if I went to his house I'd find it there too.

GW: Maybe you should go.

YOUNG: I think I'd better. I've actually been through Hibbing (Minnesota, Dylan's birthplace), but I've never been to Bob's house. It might not even be there anymore. But there's something to finding out where people came from. It's interesting archival stuff. And you know, Bob's a real musicologist. He's a guy who could do something like *Archives.* I'm sure that he has his thing organized to some degree.

GW: As far as your development as a songwriter and a guitar player, there's some information to be gleaned from the versions of "Everybody Knows This Is Nowhere" that bookend the *Topanga 1 (1968–1969)* disc. The first one, from early 1968, was recorded with the backing musicians you used on the *Neil Young* album and is a breezy, acoustic take, accented by woodwind instruments. The version that closes out the disc, cut the following year with Crazy Horse, is in the ragged country-rock style you became known for with that band.

YOUNG: Yeah that first one is very . . . organized. What's going on there is the difference between recording in a very contrived manner and just playing with a band. One is built, the other just happens.

GW: So with Crazy Horse it just "happened."

YOUNG: Well, I knew those guys. I knew them for a while, from back in Laurel Canyon, and I used to jam with them when I was still in the Springfield and they were still called the Rockets. And after doing that first solo record they were what I needed—I needed to play. I needed to go out and do things. I knew it was gonna be good with Crazy Horse. It was free.

GW: Is that around the same time Old Black came into the picture?

YOUNG: I think so. That'd be about then. I traded Messina for it. (As legend goes, former Buffalo Springfield bassist and producer Jim Messina, who also played on Young's first solo album, gave up the 1953 Gibson Les Paul Goldtop in exchange for one of Young's Gretsch guitars.)

GW: How essential was Old Black to the development of your guitar sound?

YOUNG: I don't know. I really don't. I mean, that guitar was a different guitar then than it is now. It had a different treble pickup. The Firebird pickup went in after the first one got lost, and that happened a few years after we did *Everybody Knows*. The first pickup had a really bad buzz, and I sent the guitar to a shop to be fixed. When I went to get it, it was gone. And by that I mean the store was gone. The whole place just wasn't there anymore. So that was the end of that. When I eventually got it back I tried a Gretsch pickup in there for a while, and then around the time of *Zuma* the Firebird went in. And that's been the sound ever since.

GW: People think of the Crazy Horse sound as this brute force, but the guitar interplay between you and (Crazy Horse guitarist and vocalist) Danny Whitten was actually a very nuanced and subtle thing.

YOUNG: That's exactly it. If you listen you can really hear how intricate it is, especially with the hi-def sound on the Blu-ray.

GW: On "Cinnamon Girl," to use just one example, your stylistic differences are more pronounced. You're doing these voice-leading-type lines with a fairly dirty tone, while Danny has a much cleaner sound, and plays nice, ringing arpeggios across the neck.

YOUNG: Danny's tone was *always* much cleaner than mine. And what you're hearing with the Blu-ray is basically the way it sounded to us in the studio. It's almost as good as what we heard. It's not quite as good, but it's as good as it can be. Right now, at least.

GW: What guitars did Danny use?

YOUNG: He was playing a Gretsch most of the time.

GW: Through any specific amp?

YOUNG: Umm . . . Probably not. Probably just through one of my amps. Maybe a (Fender) Twin or a Bandmaster.

GW: Did the two of you ever discuss what you were going to play, or work out your parts together?

YOUNG: We never had to. We just started playing, and that's what it sounded like. Danny was a great player. Phenomenal. And that part of Crazy Horse is now lost forever (Whitten died in 1972 from a heroin overdose). The Crazy Horse that came along with Poncho (guitarist Frank "Poncho" Sampedro, who joined Crazy Horse three years after Whitten's death) is a different band, and a completely different approach. You don't hear that same interplay. You only get that on the things Danny was on.

GW: On "Down By the River" you can hear how Danny continually alters his rhythm part behind your solos.

YOUNG: It's unbelievable. His work on that song is a masterpiece. The rhythm guitar position is a very powerful slot. You have to understand you're part of an orchestra. You're the backbone. You're putting horn parts in. Opposition. Changing the groove. Every time you change the groove it changes what the lead guitar does. And with Danny and me it just happened. We never talked about any of it.

GW: There's great video on *Archives* of CSNY performing "Down By the River" on ABC-TV's *Music Scene*, in 1969, and you and Stephen Stills are trading solos on a pair of big Gretsches. In terms of dynamic, how was playing with Danny different from playing with Stephen?

YOUNG: Well, Stephen is a lead guitar player, but he can also be supportive. And Danny was a guitar player, and he was *always* supportive. He was totally confident in his role. Stephen and I are a little more competitive, in a brotherly kind of way. Then there's the jacked-up part of CSN, which is the drums and bass aren't as open. It's more of a big deal. But the original is Crazy Horse. Everything else is just a version of that.

GW: How would you evaluate Nils Lofgren, who joined you for *After the Gold Rush*?

YOUNG: Nils I had known for a long time as a musician. I met him at the Cellar Door when he was 17. Then he came out to California and played on *After the Gold Rush*. He had a lot of energy—he practically walked from the airport to Topanga Canyon! And I just loved his guitar playing. When we're matching up and playing dual guitars on "Tell Me Why" it's fantastic. But he played too well to play with me. So for most of that album I put him on piano. He doesn't play piano, but he was more challenged that way. It controlled all the extra playing, put everyone on the same level. Because I like to keep things simple.

GW: With songs like "Down By the River" and "Cowgirl in the Sand," which feature extended instrumental breaks, how many takes were cut in the studio?

YOUNG: Maybe three or four overall, and the final version was usually an edited take. So, you know, maybe what you hear on the record would be take one, but with a couple pieces of something else in there. I could look it up. We have all the track sheets. All that information could be made available through *Archives* updates. We could make it so you could go in and figure out exactly what take you're listening to of a specific song.

GW: *Archives* features tons of great photos of you onstage with the Danny Whitten–led version of Crazy Horse, particularly on the *Live at the Fillmore East 1970* disc. But one thing I noticed is that there's no video footage of the band.

YOUNG: That's because we can't find any, anywhere. But if people want it in the *Archives* it can be there. They just have to come up with the stuff. And also realize that once they get it to me it's probably gonna be given away for free, but that doesn't mean they lose it. It just means that I get the chance to duplicate it, create the best possible copy of it for mass distribution, and place it where it belongs in a timeline, with stories and information about what it is. That's what I can do that would be hard for anybody else to do.

GW: One thing you can't be accused of is cherry picking the archival documents. There are some less than complimentary reviews scattered throughout the set, including one about a show at the Cellar Door that you read out loud in a video clip. The reviewer describes your onstage demeanor as being "as stimulating as watching your nails grow."

YOUNG: [*laughs*] I think it's good to have that stuff there. When you see it in perspective it's just as interesting as anything else. It's a valid reaction. I mean, people wrote negative reviews about my Massey Hall concerts, because they were upset that I was playing songs that nobody knew. (For these shows Young debuted much of the material that would eventually make up the 1972 album *Harvest*.) What the fuck are you gonna do with that?

GW: In that respect, the show documented on the *Live at Massey Hall 1971* disc features what is in effect an embryonic version of what would become your biggest hit, "Heart of Gold." Here, however, it's merely a small piece of the song "A Man Needs a Maid."

YOUNG: Right. That's the way it originally came out. It was just a little piano thing in the middle of a larger song.

GW: How did it become its own composition?

YOUNG: It just morphed. It grew. It's interesting, because there's another version of that song on *Archives* where I'm playing it live on acoustic. I put that version on there because that was the first time I ever used the harmonica onstage in front of people. But I have to think: did that version precede the recorded one?

GW: Well, it appears in the track listing before the studio version.

YOUNG: So then it happened before. That's good to know, because I wasn't playing the harmonica very good on that live take! It's much better on the recorded version. And that's probably why—it was later on. And you're able to establish which came first because of the *Archives*. Things like that, as simple as they may be, they're difficult to perceive without all the information laid out in front of you.

GW: To bring up another instance of the *Archives* affording deeper insight into a song: On the *Live at Massey Hall* disc there's a great video interview of you and your ranch hand, Louie Avila, shot at your Broken

Arrow ranch in 1971. Even casual Neil Young fans tend to know that you wrote the song "Old Man" about Avila, but few have ever seen him or heard him speak before.

YOUNG: And now you have. It's like, "I believed that. But now I *believe* it." It's good to have evidence.

GW: At one point in that video, the interviewer asks about the song "Old Man," and Avila says something to the effect that it's "really nice." You sit there silently, and eventually say, "That's really an amazing tape recorder you have there."

YOUNG: [*laughs*] That's good.

GW: Which reveals a greater truth about you that, in my opinion, has been displayed in countless interviews over the years: You don't like to talk about specific songs, or the act of songwriting.

YOUNG: It's not really worth talking about, as far as I'm concerned. It's so hard to nail down. It's something that happens. It's like breathing. It's like a wind change or something.

GW: But people do wonder about your process.

YOUNG: Well, I can't say what it is! Because it's different for all the songs, and I can't remember half of them anyway. They all have their own little story of how they came along, but I don't know . . I will say that the best ones come really fast. And they're complete. There's no editing or anything. You just get it.

GW: In your introduction to "Mr. Soul" on the *Sugar Mountain—Live at Canterbury House 1968* disc, you identify that song as one of the "fast" ones. You say it took five minutes to write.

YOUNG: Yeah, that was one like that. And that's how long it should take, about as long as it takes to write it down. So, I mean, what's the process? The bottom line is there is no process. The process is, *there it is.*

GW: How about your process as a guitar player? In particular, around the time of *Everybody Knows This Is Nowhere*, were there other guitarists who influenced you as far as your pursuit of the louder, noisier side of the music? Jimi Hendrix would be an obvious point of reference, but anyone else?

YOUNG: Not really. I mean, Jimi certainly. I liked him. He was on my radar. But not too many others. (Producer and occasional Young collaborator) Jack Nitzsche and I used to listen to the early Jimi Hendrix Experience 45s that came out of London before we did my first solo album. He was the latest, greatest thing from over there, and we were checking it out. Wanted to see what was going on.

GW: What about any of the metal players? For example, you were getting pretty thick, detuned tones on songs like "Cinnamon Girl" and "When You Dance, I Can Really Love." Were you aware of, say, Tony Iommi from Black Sabbath, another guy who tuned down his guitar?

YOUNG: Not so much. But I love that music. It's like classical rock and roll. The Scorpions, Iron Maiden . . . That whole thing is quite strong. It's an art form in itself. That's the thing about metal: some people think one band is great and another is just shit, while a normal person standing there couldn't tell the difference between the two. So I was never a metal*head*, but I'll listen to a guy like Zakk Wylde play the guitar. And I know a lot of metal guys. They come to our shows because there's something we do that I guess they connect with.

GW: But there was nothing directly influencing you at the time you were first getting loud with Crazy Horse?

YOUNG: Well, you know . . . when you really listen to it, Crazy Horse didn't get very loud. Not until (1979's) *Rust Never Sleeps*. The early Crazy Horse, with Danny, is not a big, whomp-'em, arena-rock sound. That happened with the second version of the band, when Poncho joined. "Cowgirl in the Sand" and "Down By the River"—when you listen to 'em, they're not that loud. Though they *can* be, especially when we do them now.

GW: Much of the "bigness" that's associated with Crazy Horse, I suppose, is a result of the grit in the guitar tones, and also the space between the instruments.

YOUNG: Yeah, there's *a lot* of room in those records. Those songs were written to be explored forever. There's no finished version.

GW: How would you characterize your lead playing?

YOUNG: It sucks! It's just a fucking racket. I get totally lost when I'm playing guitar. I'll just play a melody over and over again and change the tone, bend a string, do all that. I'm totally engrossed in what I'm doing. At one with it. But I suck. I've *heard* myself.

GW: Some people would beg to differ.

YOUNG: Well, I have *moments* where I really express myself on the guitar. But I can't play acoustic like Bert Jansch, and I can't play electric like Hendrix or J.J. Cale, who are probably the two best electric guitar players I've ever heard. And Jimmy Page, he's a great one. I really love the way he plays. He's so slippery. He's very, very dangerous. Those are three classic guitar players to me.

GW: What would you say are your strengths?

YOUNG: I have melodies, and I have a sense of rhythm and drive. But it's not about me, anyway—it's about the whole band. It's about everybody being there at once. When I play I'm listening for everything, trying to drive it all with my guitar. My guitar is the *whole fucking band.*

GW: Perhaps an example of what you're describing would be the famous "one-note" solo in "Cinnamon Girl," which encompasses everything you're talking about: lead, rhythm, melody, drive. Though my contention has always been that it's not really one note . . .

YOUNG: It's not! Everyone says that, but there's about a hundred notes in there. And every one of them is different. Every single one. They just happen to have the same name. (*laughs*)

GW: Does it amuse you that people spend so much time evaluating the things you do?

YOUNG: You know, I just thought I was playing the right solo. I mean, can you imagine anything else in there? Like, some fucking fast-note thing. Who needs that? It's *rhythm.*

GW: That said, is there any particular song or moment on *Archives* that really captures the essence of Neil Young as a musician?

YOUNG: No one thing. No one thing. It's too big. There's too much information. And you can zero in as close as you like, but then you wind up going too far, and you gotta pull back out. It's big-picture stuff. But it's all there. You know, one day I'm gonna put out a download update, and when you open it up, there'll just be several photographs of kitchen sinks. (*laughs*) That's it.

NEIL YOUNG AND DANIEL LANOIS: LOVE AND WAR

Jaan Uhelszki | January 2011 | *American Songwriter*

Young spent much of 2010 performing solo. During this time he entered the Los Angeles studio of Canadian producer Daniel Lanois to lay down some acoustic tracks and film the sessions. The process soon tipped more toward Lanois's studio atmospherics, with the uncharacteristic *Le Noise* the result.

With Lanois in tow, this September 2010 interview chronicles the duo's working relationship and pushes Young to discuss the full range of his creative processes, from songwriting to filmmaking to energy distribution to architecture. –Ed.

Serious, intense, with hooded blue-gray eyes that always seem capable of pinning you to the wall, Neil Young looks like a man who has forged an uneasy peace with himself and the choices that he's made. Gone is much of that early restlessness and ire; the kind of discontent that found him pitching televisions out of third story windows into southern California canyons, or scowling onstage amid a 15-minute version of "Down By The River," without ever acknowledging his audience. Two months from his 65th birthday, there is an air of quiet acceptance about him as he sits with perfect posture in his smart white Panama hat, trimmed beard and green military jacket. His lived-in features—chiseled and defined—give him the air of an aging leading man, and as you take a step back and squint, he resembles no one so much as Gregory Peck, with the same mixture of obsession and righteousness.

Usually just as tough and stoic as the late actor, Young seems uncharacteristically forthcoming in this unassuming restaurant perched in a redwood grove on the side of a mountain near his rambling Broken Arrow Ranch, the 1,500-acre spread he purchased back in 1970 for the princely sum of $350,000, naming it after a Buffalo Springfield song. Perhaps the reason for the lightened mood has much to do with his new association with Daniel Lanois, who produced Young's latest album *Le Noise*. What makes this new partnership propitious is that according to Young, Lanois is the first person who has told him the truth about his music, since the death of his former producer David Briggs in 1995. But not only that, Lanois was able to coax a whole new panorama of sounds out of the august artist, creating a work that pays homage to Young's storied past, but also looks to the future by using an entirely new sonic palette and hallucinatory echoes without sacrificing his rough edges. If the truth be told, *Le Noise* is like a Crazy Horse record without Crazy Horse. And just as revelatory. Not only does Young divulge his creative process on the song "Love and War," but he has allowed himself to mourn lost friends—specifically, L.A. Johnson and Ben Keith—in the simple eloquence of "I lost some people I was traveling with," on "Walk With Me"—in a way that he hasn't since the Ditch Trilogy and 1994's *Sleeps With Angels.* Young talks to *American Songwriter* about what keeps him up at night, how he knows when it's time to write, the spectral power of the moon and whether there is another ride for Crazy Horse.

You've lived in the United States for so long, does working with Daniel Lanois make you feel more Canadian? I noticed that Toronto turns up in the lyrics of two of the songs on *Le Noise.*

NY: I feel pretty Canadian.

After you released *Living With War,* I thought you might consider running for office, and applying for American citizenship.

NY: No, because I'm a Canadian. I'm born Canadian. You know, you can't change some things. Nothing can change that. Like a piece of paper's not going to change that. So I'm not going to get that piece of paper, because it won't work. You can't become something that you're not just because it's convenient.

You haven't had a producer in some time. Can you tell me about how it was to work with Daniel Lanois on *Le Noise*? What is he able to pull out of you?

NY: It's great, it's fun. I think we get along real well and we complement each other. I got a lot of respect for Dan. I'm a cheerleader for him. I get off on some of the things that he does even though I kept saying to him, "No one knows what the hell you're doing, but keep going. It sounds great. Keep doing it. Go farther. Yeah, let's go farther."

When you heard some of the effects he put on your voice and on your guitar, was it a look back to when music was so much more adventurous in the past? Or did you see it as a look to the future for you?

NY: Actually I think it's a look back. Wouldn't you say that? (To Daniel, who nods "Yes.") What it is, it's a look back but it's done in a very futuristic way because he has a control over all of these things that would have been hard to manage earlier. But the pieces and old records that we used to listen to, man, some of the swapbacks on those early ones, that's where it all came from. And that's just because it was on a fader or maybe they just had it on a tape recorder and then they're doing the take and the guy will just, OK, this word right here, jack it up and record, and then back, and you know, live, as it went down.

DL: I see it as a continuation of some of the adventurous work that was happening in Jamaica back in the day, like early Lee Scratch Perry. They had very little equipment but they really did a lot with it. Like some idiosyncratic detail on a piece of equipment would become like the backbone of an entire production.

I'd heard that you were planning to record this acoustically and Daniel, you convinced him not to. Is that accurate?

DL: Oh, no, there was no convincing. That was the invitation (from Neil): "Let's record some acoustic songs and make a film of the performances." I said, "OK, that sounds great." We did that, and at the end of the first session Neil says, "I got more. Let's try it on electric." And he pulled out "The Hitchhiker." At that point I said, "Wait a minute, I see there's a doorway to another set of tones here we could operate by."

NY: We found another sonic pillar.

DL: Yeah. It's all coming back to me now. There was an early rant from me about sonic pillars. Once you have your sonic pillars in order then you can build a bridge.

OK, do we need a glossary here?

DL: At a certain point we both felt that it would be good to investigate some new material electric, which was not part of the initial invitation. Neil kept coming in with them and they were great. When "Walk With Me" came in, that really opened a door because at that point he had brought in the Gretsch White Falcon, which has a split pickup allowing us to put the bass strings in one amp and the high strings in the other. And as soon as I had that freedom to treat the bottom separate from the top, it allowed me to go even further with this kind of dub technique.

Was there an organizing principle at work with all these songs?

NY: What ties "Hitchhiker" and "Walk With Me" together? Well, they just came to me one by one. When I realized that I was going to use the White Falcon and we were going to explore that area, I brought it in and we recorded a couple of songs on it. One of them had been one that we tried acoustically earlier and another one was a new song, "Walk With Me," and then there was another song, "Sign Of Love," that I had, and for that full moon segment.

But "Walk With Me" was a full-on song. It was twice as long as it is now, and Dan and I worked it together and trimmed it down. Dan took out part of it and said to me, "You're probably going to wonder what happened to this part." I said, "There's only really two lines in that part that you took out that I miss, and I know where to put them, and we already recorded them. So we're just going to take 'em and put 'em in over here, and it's on the same version. You did this but let's just save those two lines and put them in over something else, and that'll work. There's a place where I turned around and don't face the amp, and we can put it right there and then no one will know what the hell's going on, and it'd be like an afterthought."

A lot of it was very creative, with both of us working together, communicating together about what we wanted. I wasn't there when all the mixing and everything was done, when Dan did his thing with all of that. But I was texting with Dan all the time about details and talking about the songs. My job was to write the songs and to perform them so that he had a palate to work with, and then he was free to do whatever he wanted with them for the next three weeks until I got back.

I went somewhere—either to Hawaii or back to the ranch—to write and set up my electric guitar and do what it was that I wanted to do. I don't think I wrote "Walk With Me" at the ranch because that was the electric stereo thing, and I was experimenting with that. So I started going, OK, this is cool. Now we got a big riff, a big sound, a big whole thing, so what can I put on top of it? I've always gone to these weird little tunings that I like and so I said, "Well, I've already used all these tunings. So I'll use 'em again but if I want to, I'll change them even more and make them even weirder than they were before." So I did that a few times and did tunings that I've never used and that I've never heard. That made things different. But really the essence of the songs and where they're coming from was just, it's like it always is. It just happens.

I remember you said you wrote the songs on *Prairie Wind* chronologically because the songs just started coming out as a whole, almost like a suite. Is that usually the way you write or is it never the same twice?

NY: Well, these songs are not presented chronologically on the record but they were recorded as they were written, more or less chronologically. So if you see a timeline of the record you can see the evolution of the writing. But there's really no method other than when I feel like writing, I write.

What makes me feel like writing is the knowledge that I'm not going to create something that's going to be a problem. In other words, if I create something and then there's nothing to do with it, then I have to walk around with this thing. So knowing that I had a guy that was working with me and a great team, that we're going to take the music and go with it, that I could go in there and deliver it and we could have a great time doing that, and then I could just back off and go try to find something else, kind of go hunting, and they could keep all the stuff back in the teepee. Come back, and then "wow, look what you did with that. That's very good. Sounds good."

DL: You know, there was kind of an automatic Canadian curating system at play here. I mean to be honest here, we had an excess of material. Neil came in, it was a nice set of songs and we recorded them all. And then as new songs came in, they bullied some of the other songs and pushed them out into the corral.

NY: Yeah, they did.

DL: And in fact Neil had some very beautiful songs—my favorite one called "For the Love of Man," isn't even on the record largely because I felt that we had the slow songs covered. We had "Love and War" and "Peaceful Valley Boulevard," and if you were to then do "For the Love of Man" or another great one called "You Never Call," now that pushes the record down to a lower tempo. And I thought that these new electric ones that were coming in were offering us an advantage at a better balance. So the direction of the work was largely dictated by the new songs coming in. That's always a tough one because you write a song, you think, well, surely we must put it out. We've done a good job recording it and it's beautiful, so it takes a lot of courage to say, "well, let's just put them aside for now and have a look at this other selection."

So was it more a sonic palate rather than a thematic palate that was the determining factor of what songs made the record?

DL: It was an instinct that we were operating by at a certain point. I think at a certain point, I actually said, "Please consider these eight." It would give us a 39-minute record, and we always talk about how there was something right about the length of vinyl. People's attention span seems much more attuned to that.

NY: We never heard anybody complain about the length of this record.

No one said it was too short? Maybe they were afraid to tell you.

NY: That's a long record in my history. I hate it when they're too long. The bonus track is a bummer. First of all it's an uncontrollable thing. You'll leave the CD on and suddenly you're listening to this other track and you're like, "Where did this come from?" It's not part of that, and it's a bonus. Oh, great. Thanks. Got a bonus track here. How can we handle that? And the hidden track. That's a record company thing. That's all bogus. Seventy-six minutes. Just because a CD can hold 76 minutes, it doesn't have to. Why not make the 40 minutes that it should hold sound better? Anyway, don't get me started on that.

Do you think your creative process has changed much since when you first started out? Working with Daniel Lanois it seems like you have a really good backup support system.

NY: Well, in the old days I had David Briggs and he was great support system, and whatever I did with him and Crazy Horse, I knew it was going to be a certain thing and we were going to be able to go for it, and the Horse was going to do everything they could to provide the beat and there was going to be a process that we go through, and I knew what it was. Briggs and I were completely committed to everything. So really, the process hasn't changed that much. It's just that for a while—for fifteen years or so—I didn't have Briggs. And now that I know Dan, I have someone else who's committed to the music in the same way that I am, and someone who is not scared to say something to me that other people might not. So he can make a concrete observation something like, "You know, the song's too long. It's not right. We're not getting the point. *This* is the point of the song and *this* is superfluous." I'll look at that and I'll go, "That's fine. That's good." That means that I don't have to worry about that part anymore. Rather than be threatened by what Dan says. I'm not threatened by anything like that. People may think that I am but I'm not. What I see it as that having Dan do all this means I'm running lean and mean now. I can just focus on the real meat.

So besides his producing talents, is Daniel's greatest gift being able to tell you the truth?

NY: He has the ability to tell me the truth of how he feels, which is all I ask for. But so many people miss it.

Well, it's back to the idea of your bigger-than-life persona. People are frightened of you.

NY: Those poor people. They were frightened of me? Oh, my goodness. They're frightened of something that they think I am. I think that's in everyone else's mind. It's something that I really haven't been able to figure out. They don't know me. I don't think that people really want to believe that I'm accessible. I don't think they want to believe that they know what they need to know about me.

You've been a celebrity for more than 45 years, so people will always react to that, rather than who you really are.

NY: I'm the same as I was, though. I'm exactly the same. It's just that because I want what I want, and I won't take anything less, and that is the frightening thing. Yesterday this guy from London said to me, "You're quite ruthless." I woke up in the middle of the night because I've been listening to this—it's a bit of a tangent here, but I've been listening to this album called *Treasure*, which I have in the can that was done in 1985. I've been listening to it because I plan on releasing it someday, and it's a great record. But all of the people—the key people—are all gone. I have this history of these people that are playing the greatest music of our lives, playing unbelievably great, and now they're gone, and I didn't continue playing with them. At some point I had to say, "I'll see you guys later. I gotta go do this. I'm gonna go play with Crazy Horse now. I'm gonna do this or I'm gonna do that." In that way I am ruthless, but I'm ruthless for the music. What is ruth? I don't know what ruth is. If I don't have any of it, you know, I'm OK.

It's well documented that you record during full moons. Do you write around the cycles of the moon as well?

NY: No. I just write whenever I feel like it. Sometimes it's the right time, sometimes it isn't. I just do what I feel like doing, so I don't close any door. I'm just open to things. I don't close things off, I don't have a lot of beliefs that stop me from doing things. I'm sure I must have some but I try to be open and follow the muse wherever it goes. And if it's not around, I don't push it. There's no sense in trying to fan a flame if there's no flame. Sometimes we get what we're going to get, and then I stop because I know the moment is gone and I don't try anymore. You've got to rest. And you don't have to go against the grain.

As for the moons, I guess if I track when songs were written, there would be some sort of pattern but I've never done that. When I feel like going in and recording the songs, I like to have them prepared. I don't want to be just writing them right then and there. I have to have them ready—I have to be loaded. And then when the time comes, I'm ready to unload. Then the moment passes, and I don't want to do it anymore. I've tried to make records so that I didn't waste anybody's time. When we go in the studio (during a full moon) to do it and we're ready to do it, the moment is there. I know sometimes it seems like, "What are we doing? What did we wait for? Now we're here and he's not doing anything and we've been here for eighteen hours and nothing's happened." But then when it starts happening, we get two or three things.

It's clear you're in touch with something the rest of us aren't aware of, and recently you said on your website: "I still see the vista and hear the muse, I will continue." Can you talk about that?

NY: I still do see the vista. I feel good. That's my way of feeling good. That's my way of knowing that I can still continue. There's no reason to not continue because I can still see where I'm going. Can't see it clearly but I know it's out there.

Is there any time that you feel more creative than another?

NY: There's no set time. But if I do pick the guitar up in the morning, the first time I pick it up if I haven't played it in a while, whatever I play first is the secret. Now if I'm playing the same thing all the time it's just, not really music. That is just a physical exercise. But there's a difference between that and when you sit down and just start playing something and you don't know why you're doing it. When you do that, that's time to pay attention. And I do. So that's what I do. And then the lyrics, they just all come real fast and I just write them all down. Quite often my biggest struggle is remembering a song. You know, I'll have the lyrics and I'll have the song, but I don't remember how the lyrics go with the song. You can write something at night, go to the studio and not remember it. Then just sit there for a while until it comes back. But you know, it's a very vague thing. You can't box it in, you can't fence it in. If you trust yourself and you don't try to box it in, you'll get it. It's like catching a wild animal. You can't corner it, you can't scare it. You can't be concerned about it though, just ignore it. But you just consistently stay there with it and wait for it to come out.

Yeah, or not scaring yourself.

NY: Yeah, right.

You've said that after *Greendale* it took you two years to write anything.

NY: It was a while. I just feel like, hey, it'll come. And when it comes I'll be ready, and I'll drop everything else I'm doing to do it.

Are you ever worried that another song might not show up?

NY: Well, it always has showed up, so, and I just respect it. I think if they (songs) come in big groups, I'll try to get 'em all. One shows up, I'll try to get it. I won't ignore any but I'm not going to go looking for it. I don't have time to find them. So a song has to knock on the door and say, here I am. But I got my eyes open, so it happens, it happens. I'll be there.

Is the person who makes the films any different than the guy who writes the songs?

NY: The songwriter thinks, but there's more thinking goes into movies. I'm always making songs—it's an instant gratification. The song is there. It's really something that you can express, it's a performance. You sing it and you play it, and the words come out, and an illusion is created of some sort. But a movie's not anything like that. It's much more organized. You have to have a plan. You have to have an idea that's worth spending money on. You really have to think far down the road.

So what would you consider your job to be?

NY: One job that I have right now is that I want to play music. But the most important thing for me right now is creating, or trying to create an energy that can be used, that'll change things. And my goals are very lofty. I may never reach my goals, but I want to try to reach them. I don't think you can't get there unless you aim, unless you try to go there. That's important. So the goal of eliminating gas stations, roadside refueling, with some kind of fuels—people's fuel—something that everybody has access to. And we're smart enough to figure it out. We'll figure it out.

Are you talking about your LincVolt car that carries its own power source?

NY: Yes, It's a Lincoln. Powered by electricity and biofuels and possibly by water. The mission is clearly to eliminate roadside refueling. And your car powers your house when you get home, and the car is the grid after it's finished powering your house, and everything that you need, the car can do it. You put it in your basement and you could heat your house with it. You could power your house and the excess would go out into the grid. All of that way of thinking, distributed power sources instead of power plants with tentacles going out, have distributed power sources everywhere going in, where everything charges everything else. Everybody works out. Everybody's house is charging the grid. Everybody's car plugs in and charges the grid. It's not to take energy from the grid, it's put energy into the grid.

Has doing something like this always concerned you? I mean you live in a very remote area, so has the idea of self-sufficiency has probably always been a concern for you.

NY: Yeah. I've always wanted something like this. In the back of my mind I've always thought that I was a builder and the music was just kind of a hobby. But I've never really been able to get a handle on that. I've built buildings and I love building buildings. I've built a wacky house and I've got studios and I design things. I've designed a house, and here and there did build things. I love working with carpenters and watch them build things. I love drawing things and seeing them come to life. But really, the real challenge is the energy. So to create a system that enables cars to move around and houses to be powered without using the coal powered plants and without using the oil, cleaning the energy, cleaning the planet and eliminating the need for a war.

You're really lucky you're getting to do what you love now. But the music always seems to have been the vehicle for your dreams?

NY: That really seems to be happening, doesn't it? My mom always told me I was an architect. She said, "I know you're going to be an architect. I know that's what you are because when you were just a kid, all you would do was build things." I got my building blocks, got so many building blocks and I was building all these structures, and ways you get in and out, and then building big sand castles on the beach. Trying to figure out how to catch the water, and make the water stay. Then trying to make the water do things. How it would be replenished, keeping things that would never go away when the source would come and go, but the water. This was the kind of stuff that I was thinking about even when I was a little kid. Not much has changed. What I'm doing now at this point, it's along those lines. I looked at everything like it has to do with energy. Breathing, you breathe in, you breathe out.

Do you have any rituals before you record?

NY: Just the timing.

And Daniel, you were OK of just working during the full moon?

DL: Oh, yeah, yeah. I thought, OK, that sounds great. It was a way to narrow things down.

NY: Yeah. It's very organized.

DL: Just one guy with a guitar, and under the full moon. OK, let's go.

NY: Pretty straight ahead. It really took away a lot of indecision or having to figure those kind of things out. Lets you know when you gotta have people there to be able to work with on that, and it just really simplifies everything.

When did you first spot the pattern of the moons?

NY: Well, I saw a pattern a long time ago when I realized that I only recorded when I felt like it. I was used to being very free about that because everybody was there at my beck and call whenever I wanted to do anything. When I had Briggs and the Crazy Horse and we were working that way, things would go for a couple weeks and we wouldn't even see each other. I mean we might play in some bar or something and do this or that, just spontaneously. Then I'd say, "I kind of feel like recording." And then I noticed a couple of, three or four, a lot of sessions, that the moon was full. And I also noticed that I would be recording and we would be doing great, and then suddenly it would go away. I started to pick up on what was making that happen, and what the moon cycle was, and so you can almost predict when you were going to lose the edge. So I started using that as my planning tool.

How did a song like "Love and War" come into existence? It has this self-referential movie-within-a-movie dynamic when you sing, "I sang in anger, hit another bad chord, but I still try to sing about love and war." Did the song begin with those words?

NY: I just started playing A minor in E, and going back and forth and going, well, that's interesting. That sounds like something that's been around for a long time but I've never heard it. Then I started singing, making up the words, you know. "When I sing about love and war, I don't really know what I'm saying." After that it all started coming out.

Your writing on that particular song feels like a conversation. It seems over the past few albums you've dropped a lot of the metaphor and a lot of the poetry and you're really almost reporting on your life. Was that a conscious effort, or is that just how the songs came to you?

NY: Well, that song is pretty plain speaking. It's pretty direct.

Your last few albums have been more autobiographical and less metaphoric than things you've done in the past. What do you attribute that to?

NY: I just started to explore my own beliefs, and it was just a natural thing. I find it hard to talk about those things and generally I don't. Well, I don't like to, and I certainly don't want to judge anyone else's beliefs. Sometimes just stating your own beliefs does that. So I tend not to. All faiths are just stories to me. And I'm a story writer and I look at these and I go, these are classic stories, you know, Buddhism, Christianity, they're all the same story. And I think, "Let's just remember that. Step back, it's a story. It's a metaphor, nothing less, nothing more."

What about on *Le Noise*?

NY: Yeah. I think so. I'm not sure there's some saga. "Sign of Love" is not exactly like that. "Sign of Love" is in a landscape, walking on the land and stuff. It's pretty broad. And even "Walk With Me" is not really very specific. Most of the songs are pretty wide on this record, but the ones you mentioned aren't. There's "Hitchhiker" and "Love and War," they're pretty direct. But "Hitchhiker" even more so. It's about a memory. It's the drug chronicles. Drug chronicles, TMI. That's like a TV show, you know?

So why record it now?

NY: Well, I just finished it.

You mean adding another verse?

NY: Yeah. Finishing was important. The song never could have been done without those verses.

Do you have a lot of things that . . .

NY: Unfinished songs? Yeah.

And you return to them?

NY: Yeah, I'll go back and I'll go, "Well, I never put that out." Why? And I'll go, "Well, it's not done." Then when it's finished it's easy to put it out. When it's not finished, you might try to put it out, you may record it but you'll never release it. So I have recordings of "Hitchhiker" from the '70s but there was never any reason to put it out. I felt like, "Whoa, that's not really a good idea."

For a drug chronicle, it's pretty upbeat at the end. You almost end it on a prayer.

NY: Yeah, it's kind of like that. But it's good that way. I wouldn't have the prayer if I hadn't finished the song.

Especially because if you'd finished it in the '70s you would have prayed for other things. If you'd prayed at all.

NY: Yeah. Where I am now is, it's OK to do that. I never could get there before, so it's all right.

On "Walk With Me" you say, "I lost some people I was traveling with. I miss the soul and the old friendship." Are you thinking about your own mortality because you have lost people this year—Larry Johnson and Ben Keith?

NY: I think it's become more evident. It's in this record a couple places. But it's OK, it's just the way it is.

Do you think that acceptance is the way to deal with things?

NY: Well, you have to. You can't fight some of the things that happen. You can't go, "Well, that never happened." It happened, you know. There's nothing you can do. I'm glad that Dan's journey toward the pavement ended with a happy face.

What do you mean?

NY: Well, you're talking about fate. He was on his motorcycle and he ran into something. So that's what I meant. He might not be here. But he is.

DL: It's not that everybody should know about it. We did four sessions, four full moons. The third one had an intermission.

Because of your accident?

DL: Yeah, a three-week intermission.

NY: Missed one.

There are certain things you don't do after a certain age. One is cocaine, the other one is drive motorcycles.

NY: Oh, try to tell a lot of people that. They won't believe you. Particularly the motorcycles.

DL: The doctor did say that if that had happened when I was eighteen, those ribs might not have broken. He says once you get in your fifties and your bones are more brittle . . . you might do better on four wheels.

NY: Yeah, Dan said he was going to only drive a bus after this.

I spoke to Eddie Vedder recently and he said one thing about Neil Young is that he doesn't care what anyone thinks. He does what he does. But the question really is, do other artists come to you for advice?

NY: Not really, no. Not many people talk to me, actually. I mean Eddie comes to me and we hang out. He's not looking for advice, in fact he doesn't need advice from me. He knows what he's doing.

I often ask people what they do before they go onstage, and I had a run of people telling me they did what Neil Young does. The problem was they all said different things. James Mercer from the Shins said he runs in place; Robert Plant said he does scales like you. And Beth Orton said she meditates like you do. Could they all be right?

NY: I showed Robert the scales. He visited me once and I said, "Go do it with us."

Did he?

NY: Yeah, he did. So did Dylan. He came to one show and I said, "Come on, Bob." So Bob did it but he did it his own way. He was doing harmony parts and going sideways and everything. Everybody does it their own way. But I'm big on rituals. But not so much before I record. Although I do sometimes before I play. I go through a certain thing, which is a combination of meditation and a rehearsal, or an opening. I just go through vowel sounds on the piano, scales. I go through that, and by the time I'm finished I'm oriented. It's just a mindless thing that I do. Just to see what happens.

So you don't run in place like James Mercer says? He'll be disappointed.

NY: I do. There have been times when I've gotten on a treadmill or something like that. I like to do calisthenics to warm up because if your hands get cold and you walk onstage, you might have to play two songs where your hands are freezing. I do whatever. I've been doing different things for a long time. It just keeps changing. Now I warm up my voice and become familiar with the sound of in-tune pianos.

DL: And there are nice vocals on this record. On "Love and War" and "Peaceful Valley Blue," we really had a chance to go hi-fi on those. There's a very beautiful vocal sound on "Somebody's Gonna Rescue You." It's sort of haunting. The only one that gave us a little trouble was "Rumblin'" because we hadn't figured out that technique yet that we used on the later songs. If we'd put Neil in a slightly different spot it would have suited that quieter vocal delivery. So it was a struggle on the mix, a little bit of a struggle.

It's a rougher song, though. It almost seems like a Crazy Horse song.

DL: I love after that little orchestra, when Neil kicks in with a guitar, like other people are playing with you. It's mystifying to me. I'd say, "What's going on in that speaker? Just put it down."

NY: Just put it in there.

It's like there's a band in there with you. Except there's not.

NY: They were able to just focus on me, so if there's nothing else in the way, you can get a lot closer and it gets a lot bigger when you do that. And then Dan had the freedom to add anything. Actually almost all the songs in the album are Crazy Horse–type songs.

I feel like Crazy Horse is there in spirit.

NY: Yeah. Heck, yeah.

You haven't worked with Crazy Horse for some time. Is there still collaboration with Crazy Horse in your future?

NY: Well, you know, there is, somewhere out there. They have to be together before I can be together with them. They haven't been doing anything together, so they need to be able to do it. I don't have the time to support things. I have to go with things that are going to support me. But I think they can do it.

Can we talk about you and Daniel in the studio? Did the two of you fight?

DL: We were thinking of setting up a little wrestling ring, pulling out the boxing gloves. I don't recall any fights. No, so far, so good.

Please don't tell me you guys agree on everything.

DL: Well, I mean I do have my psychological ways of dealing with people and sometimes you have to be patient and—

NY: We discussed a lot of stuff. You have little meetings. Right? Little meetings here, little meeting there. It's good.

What do you think of Jimmy Fallon's impressions of you?

NY: Oh, it's great. I think he's fantastic. I'd like to see him do me now. See what kind of legs he has.

NEIL YOUNG ON

Money

"I spend money as soon as I get it. I don't care how much money I have, I can use it to do something. So I don't save money."

—from an interview with Jaan Uhelszki, *Uncut*, August 2012

NEIL YOUNG ON

American Idol

"Well, I can't imagine *American Idol* in the '60s. It's so different you can't compare it. The idea that there is a contest for who can pose the best. They are all just imitating other people. I don't know what that is."

–from an interview with *Talks*, April 18, 2013

NEIL YOUNG ON

Listening to Music at Home

"I have a lot of McIntosh equipment that I use for listening. My studio is full of different stuff, Tannoy and an old pair of Altec [Lansing] speakers with Mac 275s running them. It's the old Voice of the Theater speakers. They're ridiculous [*laughs*]. Also some reel-to-reel gear."

–from an interview with Spencer Holbert, *Absolute Sound*, March 13, 2014

NEIL YOUNG ON

A Letter from Home's Aural Qualities

"It does sound like it comes from a time before birds. Just because I'm into technology doesn't mean I'll abandon art."

–from an interview by Will Hodgkinson, *Times*, May 28, 2016

NEIL YOUNG ON

Corporations

"We've come to accept a democracy that's really a 'corporocracy' or something. It's not really democracy, because it's controlled, paid for, and manipulated by corporations. Corporations aren't people. They don't have consciences and they don't have children."

–from an interview with Lyndsey Parker, *Yahoo Music*, June 21, 2016

YOUNG AND THE RESTLESS

Mike Greenhaus | January 24, 2017 | *Relix*

Young's work in the six-year gap between the previous chapter and this chapter is well documented in the beginning of this article, save for the 2012 release of Young's first autobiography, *Waging Heavy Peace: A Hippie Dream*. It's a time of diverse, rewarding, and unpredictable creativity that's reflected in this interview's hopeful and at times joyous outlook, even when discussing environmental obstacles, such as the Dakota Pipeline. Young is joined by Promise of the Real. –Ed.

A few years ago, the Transcanada Corporation proposed a section of the Keystone XL Pipeline that was slated to cross the Ponca Tribe's "Trail of Tears." Neil Young didn't like that one bit, so he took action the only way he knows how to when a cause moves him to join the front line—he put together an all-star concert with some of his famous friends.

The benefit show, dubbed "Harvest of Hope," took place in late September 2014 on the Tanderup family's farm near Neligh, Neb., featuring co-organizer Willie Nelson, his twenty-something sons Lukas and Micah and a number of area musicians. Young was about to launch into a round of solo dates at the time, so he asked Willie's sons and the members of Lukas' band Promise of the Real to back him for the second portion of his set. The collaboration clicked, and Young walked away from the benefit with both a new group and enough political ammunition to help convince President Obama to veto the proposed section of the pipeline a few months later.

"They're an amazing band, and they have a great groove," Young says of Promise of the Real, who have grown into his closest musical allies, two years and a flurry of new albums later. "So, when we play together, we can improvise and jam, and they all sing great. They all sing more on pitch than I do. It was about stopping the Keystone (XL Pipeline) from going through a farmer's land. Everybody was there so I said, 'I'll show you a couple songs I want to do,' and we did 'em. 'Who's Gonna Stand Up?' was one of the first things we learned."

Young had already tested the waters two weeks earlier in Raleigh, N.C., during Farm Aid—the charitable show he regularly hosts with the Nelson family—inviting Lukas and Micah to sit in for his final selection of the night, "Rockin' in the Free World." He had recently wrapped-up a European tour alongside his fierce, improv-heavy, garage-rock group Crazy Horse, with whom he had been exploring some new material, including the eco-conscious protest anthem, "Who's Gonna Stand Up?"

It was perfect timing: Despite Lukas' family lineage, Promise of the Real have always been more of jamband than a country outfit or even an Americana act and, less than a month later, Young asked them to back him during his other annual event, the Bridge School's Benefit Concert. Micah—who has his own psych-punk-orchestra, Insects vs. Robots—signed on as something of an "in-residence" auxiliary member of the ensemble. Young hasn't looked back since.

"They're very supportive, and they're a working unit—nothing's in their way," Young says while calling from his Los Angeles home in December. "They love my music, and they actually come to me with suggestions all the time with songs they'd like to do. And I know that whatever song I want to do, they can learn how to play it as soon as I show it to them. So it's given me between five and eight times more songs to play than I've ever had before in my life. That makes it a lot of fun and that's why I keep doing it—because I'm having a good time."

Through Young is famously one of rock's most restless spirits, during the past few years, he's jumped between projects at an even more fervent pace than usual. In 2010, he reunited with Buffalo Springfield for the first time since 1968 for a Bridge School appearance and stuck with the legendary group for a handful of dates in 2011, before putting *that* not-in-this-lifetime tour to bed so that he could revive another long-dormant ensemble, Crazy Horse.

He spent much of the next three years on the road and in the studio with Crazy Horse, but not without some bumps in the road. First, the quartet cancelled a few dates in 2013, including a headlining appearance at the inaugural Lockn' Festival, when guitarist Frank "Poncho" Sampedro broke his hand and, the following year, Rick Rosas subbed for bassist Billy Talbot after he suffered a stroke. In addition to solo dates that recalled Young's early work under his own name, he even found time for a one-off CSNY reunion at Bridge School in 2013.

Young has also entered into one of the most prolific periods of his recording career, releasing six proper albums in the past five years in a variety of configurations, as well as a slew of live and archival offerings. On the studio front, he partnered with Crazy Horse for a set of repurposed traditional numbers and children's ditties, *Americana*, and for the equally hard-rocking *Psychedelic Pill* in 2012. Then there was both the unexpected set of singer-songwriter covers *A Letter Home*—recorded at Jack White's Third Man Records—and the swinging big-band set *Storytone* in 2014, as well as a collection of originals captured at a converted movie house with Promise of the Real, *The Monsanto Years*. More recently, in December 2016, he dropped a stripped-down album, *Peace Trail*, and he's already back in the studio working with Micah, Lukas, and his band.

Though Young laid down *Peace Trail* with noted session drummer Jim Keltner and bassist Paul Bushnell, Promise of the Real's spirit guided the sessions. In fact, Young first heard about Bushnell through Micah, who nabbed the bassist for his upcoming album.

"I have been playing with Promise of the Real and I still am playing with them, but they weren't available," Youngs says of their absence from the record, though they've toyed with some of the *Peace Trail* songs live. "They were on the road and the songs just came to me and I wanted to record them, so I called up Jimmy. We're good, old buddies and we understand how to do it together and have a great time, so I just went for that and we did this record."

Young recorded *Peace Trail* in only four days at Rick Rubin's Shangri-La Studios, and most of the 10 tracks are first or second takes. He produced the album—his 37th—with longtime collaborator John Hanlon, and the swift rollout allowed Young to address some of the day's pressing issues. In particular, numbers like "Indian Givers" rally support of the Standing Rock Sioux Tribe, whose land is currently being threatened by Dakota Access Pipeline.

"Some of these songs are about things that are going on right now," he says. "The First Nations people and the corporations are going at it head to head, and it's a historic moment. It'll probably continue up there all winter long and get bigger and bigger."

He pauses to address how the situation has changed as more musicians and volunteers have lent their voices. "The situation is bigger than it was when I wrote (these songs)," Young says. "This thing is growing, and it's an awareness of a situation that we face in this country and other countries like it so it strikes a chord with everyone. Corporations are controlling our government—and that's what's going on. Now, we have them head to head. Someone says, 'You can't do this,' and the corporation says, 'We're doing it anyway.'"

Other parts of the largely acoustic *Peace Trail* are more closely related to Young's own life. "Can't Stop Working" feels like a direct statement on his reluctance to slow down, despite pushing past age 71, and "My New Robot," is perhaps the first relationship song to feature a cameo by Amazon Echo's voice-activated assistant Alexa.

Young has devoted a lot of time and energy in recent years to launching Pono—a music download service and dedicated music player focusing on high-quality recorded audio. The autotune-colored "My Pledge" is a meditation on how people listen to music in the modern era that namechecks both the Mayflower and Hendrix. (Young, who recently revealed that he even met Donald Trump a few years ago to potentially invest in Pono, went so far as to remove his music from streaming sites a few years ago due to what he considered their poor sound quality. His music has since returned to Spotify, Apple Music, and others.)

"I've made records for a really long time and what I hear is what I want people to hear," Young says of the song. "That's why I make records.

So I fear for the way people are going to hear what it is I create because I know how much that end of it has gone down—I think about that. So when I say, 'I hear Jimi Hendrix' that means I'm hearing something coming off of a MP3 player through some speakers and it sounds like it's (coming from) a bad TV or something. It's very literal. It's a word-for-word description." Most of the songs on *Peace Trail* came to him after his tour with the Nelsons, yet Young is careful to note that they are still elastic enough to live outside any one project. "Each song comes in the room, looks around," he says. "It either comes or goes—sits down or stand—but it's by itself. They're not constructed for anyone else except for themselves. They're not built so they'll fit into what a certain band can play or a certain sound."

In October, Young was one of six marquee acts handpicked by Coachella tastemakers Goldenvoice to play the classic-rock summit Desert Trip. Unlike most of his peers—who relied on radio-anthems and a catalog of older material to connect with their festival-size audience—Young rolled in with a new band, Promise of the Real, and explored both his cornerstone works and selections from the then unreleased *Peace Trail.* He appeared before Paul McCartney both weekends and, since Promise of the Real is comprised of musicians less than half his age, helped bring the event's average performer age down by a few decades.

"It was wonderful playing there," Young says. "We booked a whole bunch of other shows in front of it so, by the time we got to it, we'd just be toasty enough so that it wouldn't matter. We just wanted to be out of it by the time we got out there. We rented this beautiful local place that had a bunch of hot springs and a pool. We had the whole place to ourselves and were together as a band and had a great time. We got through it without it being anything big or different than anything else—but it was still big and different because we were with all these huge bands."

He also offered the dream lineup's only headliner cross-pollination, joining McCartney for "A Day in the Life," "Give Peace a Chance," and "Why Don't We Do It in the Road?" both weekends. ("A Day in the

Life" has actually been in Young's repertoire for years, and he shared a memorable version onstage with McCartney at London's historic Hyde Park in 2009.)

Young isn't sure who made the initial call about reprising the sit-in at Desert Trip but says they rehearsed the song punk-rock style in his trailer backstage. "We were in there just singing, working out some changes and things," he says. "It's great to play with Paul—I've always loved Paul. We've been good friends for a long time and it just grew out of a natural lifetime of things that have happened to both of us, and people that we've known in common. He's such a great musician, and I enjoyed being able to get up there with him and give him something to bounce off of—give him a little bit of something else."

Though his setlists have rarely been static in a traditional arena-rock way, since joining forces with Promise of the Real, Young has dug deeper into his own songbook than he has in years. His recent string of bustouts have included his first performance of "Piece of Crap" since 2001, the return of "Cripple Creek Ferry" after keeping the song on ice since 1997, the unveiling of "Like an Inca" after a 30-plus year break and even the live debut of the tender 1970 *After the Gold Rush* favorite "Till the Morning Comes," among other rarities.

He credits Promise of the Real with unearthing some of this material, admitting that he has "a lot of songs I can play at the drop of a hat" with their insistence. "We sat and learned 80 or 90 songs in the span of five days before we even got to rehearsals with Neil," Lukas says. "Neil was really stoked with the vibe, so we kept going."

Given that Young has taken on several presidents, wars and countless cultural concerns in his music, it would come as no surprise if he revived any of his older tunes in response to the day's current political climate. Young brushes off that question, saying "Well, none in particular. They're all just individual songs—I don't look at them that way. I look at them as individual moments. Some of them stand up and ring true at different times as the years go by, and that's just the nature of it. 'After the Gold Rush' is a song that seems to be having another moment, where there's something about it—I noticed people were relating to it strongly during my last group of shows. It's funny the way it comes and goes, but I'm just doing what I'm doing—writing songs as I feel like writing them and then playing them."

He did, however, decide to capture his instant connection with Promise of the Real on the double-disc, triple-LP live set *Earth*. Far from a traditional concert souvenir, *Earth* is a carefully curated survey of Young's stories concerning the land and living together in this world. It's also something of a studio-show hybrid, buffing up Young and Promise of the Real's raw stage performances with animal sound and effects. He already considers it among his favorite records.

"I put so much love into it and so much care into making it," he say humbly. "We broke the rules of making a live record; we weren't trying to make it sounds live. I think our post-production on *Earth* was about four months—there's a lot of layers to what we did to those live performances, while still maintaining the live mix that came out of the PA. We didn't remix them, but we did add obvious overdubs and used them in ways that were more like a novel than a record. There were all these other ideas happening, like it was a part of something—a bigger picture where, if you zoomed in on it, it was live. But if you pulled back, there were a lot of things going on. It's an Earth story."

The album is also a choice document of one of Young's most exploratory projects yet. Lukas, in particular, has deep ties to the modern jamband scene and has fostered a close relationship with Bob Weir. More than any of Young's bands since Crazy Horse, Promise of the Real have proven to be his ideal improvisational sparring partners. "Neil is one of the ultimate jammers—not many people go as hard as he does, in terms of full-on open jamming and he's never slowed down," Lukas says. "He was a huge part of my roots along with the Grateful Dead, Jimi Hendrix, and Stevie Ray Vaughan. That, along with the great old country music I listened to through Dad, really makes up who I am."

"It's very healthy; you gotta trust yourself," Young adds. "It feels excellent, and there's nothing about it that's not free. It's full of whatever is happening. So there's no way you could compare that to anything. It's not better or worse. It is what it is."

Young's current work in the exploratory realm sits better with him than another relatively recent crossover in the jam scene, when he headlined the second Bonnaroo festival in 2003 with Crazy Horse. Despite a dream setlist that strayed from that tour's complete performance of the *Greendale* rock opera and exposed him to a younger audience, Young is somewhat critical of the gig.

"We played that show and we had a pretty good time, but we didn't really get the high," he says. "The music didn't really take off when we would go into improvisational parts in songs—there's no right and wrong, or even good and bad with that kind of stuff, but it can get to be cosmic and ethereal and powerful and dangerous, not just those words that are only applied to music like sharp and flat. As I remember it, we felt like we came up short for those particular two or three long songs we did where we were jamming."

He pauses and backpedals a bit as he thinks about the many fans who experienced Crazy Horse for the first time that night. "On the other hand, if you've never heard it before—and you weren't living it every second like we were—some people might've really gotten a lot out of it. But my own personal recollection is that we didn't really knock it out of the park at that show."

Young has experienced his fair share of changes off the stage and outside the studio in recent years, too. In 2014, he filed for divorce from his wife of 36 years, Pegi, and moved out of their longtime Broken Arrow Ranch home in Redwood City, Calif., to be near his girlfriend, actress Daryl Hannah. Being in Los Angeles has allowed Young easy access to area studios and placed him back in the public consciousness. The changes in his life have also contributed to his new approaches.

"Really, it all came from having the time and the support of my life," Young says of his increased studio output in recent years. "And the love around me and the ability to do just what I felt like doing."

Young credits his experiments while working on *Earth* with helping his creative juices flow in the studio and for bringing "a lot of other things to the fore for me." He jokes that he felt people were looking at him like he was out of his mind when he started incorporating animal sounds, but that he "felt the freedom to do what it is I thought I knew

I could do as an artist. That's why all these things are happening. I feel good and I feel like I have a gift that I can continue using and enjoying, so nothing's in my way. There's nothing to stop me.

"It just made me more aware of the beauty of working in the studio, so that's why I've put aside some time now to spend in the studio to do some things," he continues. "Some people might think that what I come up with won't be any more on top of it than what I've already done, but there are new things I can do in the studio and I have the tools to do them. It's fascinating to me and it's a lasting document. At however old I am, it's a good idea to make a lasting document, so I wanted to give myself a little chance to do that. I'm just enjoying being in the studio."

Young is currently halfway through a new album with Promise of the Real and, after he canceled a few 2017 Australia and New Zealand dates to continue recording, rumors circulated that he would stay off the road for the rest of the year. "Well, right now, I don't have any plans to tour, but I won't close the door on anything, at any time," he admits. "But I don't have any commitments."

He describes his latest batch of originals as "like movies—like scenes." Though they are topical vignettes, Young says the new material is more "stream of consciousness," tied together with different themes and places.

"You go to one environment and you're looking around, and you end up somewhere else," he says. "You're with somebody who was talking to you very personally, then somebody's yelling at you and rapping and going crazy, and it's a different situation. Then you find yourself drifting on a boat in heaven somewhere, or en route to heaven, or coming back or watching traffic. People are building boxes and houses on the streets everywhere. You find yourself in a place like that."

His other major project is a new, interactive presentation of his extensive archives. He says that the project "is coming in a couple of different ways," but promises that "you don't have to subscribe or anything to get there."

"It's going to be a trip," he says, getting just as excited about this deep-dive into his history as he is about his new works. "You can do it and listen to it and read about it and see different things—find out who played on it and do all that stuff. If you want to buy it, you can buy it on whatever level. If you want high-res, low-res, vinyl, it'll be there."

Young goes on about the project, saying, "We've still never been able to find the technology to give people the sound that we want to give them, but we'll give them Blu-ray because it gets the quality of the sound onto the device that they usually have at their house. But Blu-rays are obsolete now. There's nothing other than hi-res music players and services, of which there are only a few, including mine, and that doesn't involve hardware. So let's change the whole format into something we can use going forward, and we're well on our way to it because we're blending it with a website that's just going to be the archives. We're going to put up about 20 percent of the content (for now) and a lot of things are penciled in. There will be a place where you can go and see everything—a timeline—and open info cards. It's like an old antique file cabinet with file after file after file. Everything we've ever done will be in there."

The process of sorting through his catalog has allowed Young to experience his own material with a unique perspective. "I'll be listening to old songs and I'll heard myself do something and I'll go, 'I remember this,'" he says. "And then it absorbs itself back into my playing because the more you change, the more you evolve, but you leave some things behind. It is worth picking certain things up when you hear them and taking them with you. It's just different skills—different languages to speak with the music. Sometimes you forget one, then you remember it. You can apply that much more than specific songs."

But don't expect Young to reconvene with his old bands anytime soon. Though he admits to having unfinished business with Buffalo Springfield, a rep from Young's camp confirms that he is truly focused on playing with Promise of the Real, whose youthful energy and expert-level knowledge of his catalog inspire him and make him want to rock. Crosby, Stills, Nash & Young are inching toward their 50th anniversary but David Crosby's recent comments about Young's divorce have made gossip headlines and Croz's strained relationship with Graham Nash, who also recently split with his wife, makes even a CSN tour feel far off.

And as for Crazy Horse?

"Someday," Young says of his great backing trio. "When you look at Crazy Horse's past and you look at the frequency of our performances as a band and how they come and go, that's what kept us where we are—so we're right on course."

NEIL YOUNG ON

Retirement

"When I retire, people will know, because I'll be dead. They'll know, 'He's not coming back! He retired.' But I'm not gonna say, 'I'm not coming back.' What kind of bullshit is that?"

–from an interview with Patrick Doyle, *Rolling Stone*, March 15, 2018

NEIL YOUNG ON

Donald Trump

"But my biggest concern right now is not that the guy in charge has no balls and doesn't know how to say goodbye to people and he's a very poor model for our children. That really means a lot to me, but it doesn't mean anything to me compared to the damage he's doing to the environment."

–from an interview with Andrea Domanick and Robert Ross, *Vice*, March 23, 2018

NEIL YOUNG ON

Artists and Algorithms

"All those things, they're weighing on my head, the way these algorithms treat the arts and the fact that there's no algorithm to protect the arts or the rights of artists. There's nothing that really addresses the values that I have, so I'm not overly impressed with the progress in big technology."

–from an interview with Gary Graff, *Music Connection*, August 27, 2018

NEIL YOUNG ON

Writing News for the Neil Young Archives

"When I write for the newspaper I enjoy it because my dad was a newspaper man. We have a lot of freedom. We don't have deadlines. We don't have story counts. We check type, but we don't say that you have to have a headline that's sensational."

–from an interview with Andy Greene, *Rolling Stone*, January 28, 2019

NEIL YOUNG ON HIS 50 YEAR CAREER, MAKING MUSIC AND HIS NEW DOCUMENTARY

Tom Power | October 25, 2019 | *q*, Canadian Broadcasting Corporation

Young reunited with Crazy Horse in 2018, leading to the 2019 LP *Colorado* and film *Mountaintop*. This loose, amusing interview covers this material, recent Canadian elections, and the Neil Young Archives (NYA) website before Power attempts to close the interview by soliciting Young's advice for young artists: "Be true to yourself." But Young doesn't stop there, as he begins asking the questions, leading to extended advice about properly recording music. Young sounds like a man who simply wants to chat with another musician, a fellow Canadian.

And this would be one of Young's last interviews as "only" a Canadian, as he would claim US citizenship in January 2020 hoping to help defeat Donald Trump in the presidential election. Weeks later, the COVID-19 pandemic would force Young to productively hole up at his Colorado ranch for the balance of the year, playing solo Internet Fireside sessions recorded by his wife, Darryl Hannah, sharing his political views on his NYA Times-Contrarion news site, and releasing multiple recordings, including the 10-disc *Neil Young Archives Volume II: 1972–1976*. With more to come in the future. –Ed.

Tom Power: Neil Young, welcome to Q.

Neil Young: Thank you.

Power: Congrats on the documentary. I wanna play a clip from it. Take a listen to this: [*Neil discusses a song take*]. A little Neil Young in the documentary *Mountaintop*, about the recording session to Neil Young and Crazy Horse's new album, *Colorado*. You say there, "Not good—it's great!"

Young: [*Laughs.*]

Power: Which I think is maybe my favorite line in the whole thing. Can you explain that a little bit to me?

Young: Well, it is what it is. I don't know what else to say. Good and great are two different things.

Power: What's the difference?

Young: Good is what somebody thinks is good. And great is something that makes you feel great.

Power: But I think I know what you mean. I'll be honest with you: the reason I'm talking to you in St. John's right now is 'cause I'm here making, making a record right now. I'm here with my band.

Young: Well, good.

Power: Yeah, so we're—I left the studio, I came to the studio here in St. John's to talk to you. And I gotta tell you, that quote's been on my mind all week. 'Cause there are moments we've recorded where things are, maybe, you know, they might be a little bit flat or they might be a little bit out of sync, but, man, they feel good, like, they feel great.

Young: Put those out. We've already got enough perfect records. Everybody's making a perfect record. That's the last thing the world needs is something good. They need something great.

Power: I read that *Mountaintop* is about one of a dozen film projects that you have in the go, and I think it was good for me 'cause I've always wanted to know what it's like for you to make a record with these guys. Why did you want to document the making of the album like this?

Young: So people like you could say—could, could know what it was. So other people could see it. It's something . . . first of all, it's the way people made records for years. And now that everything's been completely made perfect and plasticized and everybody has got—they're all worried about what wire you're using and if it's got, what kind of covering it has on it and everything. It has nothing to do with anything. It's just, you use the best equipment you can and do the best, make the best music you can and get outta there. It's not a way of life.

Power: You decided to document—and how do I put this?—like the whole process, like warts and all. There's moments of tension in this documentary. Why was that important?

Young: Why isn't it important? That's what the documentary is about. It's about making the music. It's the story of the music.

Power: Is that tension important in making things great? But is that necessary?

Young: It is for me. Listen, everybody has to know what the fuck they're doing in there. They're not doing anything else. If you're, if you're playing a song, you should really play the song once and you should be done. Anything that gets in the way of it—if you're running it down for the engineers? Get a new engineer. They should already know how to do it. You can't take time; it's not a way of life, making a recording.

Power: What happens every time you sing 'em after that first time?

Young: Well, usually take one's the best one, if you're ready. And if you're not ready, then you shouldn't have been there. So, you should know the song—everybody should know it. Everybody should know the changes, they should know the melody, they should know what the song's about, before you go in the studio. You never should be running it down or practicing it. You should have the roadies play the equip—play the, play the instruments so that everybody knows it works. And then the musicians go in and play and then they play it once and they're done. If they wanna play it a hundred times to get it perfect, that's fine. That's somebody else's record.

Power: I wanna play some music from the new record. Take a listen to this.

[*Plays "Help Me Lose My Mind."*]

That's a little of Neil Young and Crazy Horse with "Help Me Lose My Mind," a track, a track off their brand-new album, *Colorado*. I'm here talking to Neil Young right now. I'm in St. John's, Neil's in California. Neil, we're both on two coasts, which is very meaningful for me when I listen to that song and a couple of songs on the record. It's about the environment, it's about the world that we're living in right now. This is something that I think we're all thinking about a lot more. Obviously, not new for you, at all. Is there something new you wanted to say about the world and the environment in 2019, or does it feel like a continuation of what you've always been saying?

Young: It's the same thing I've been saying for a long time because it's so obvious. There's not much to say about the environment other than, "We better do something, we better take care of ourselves." But, before you can really start to see the damage, I guess, some people really need to have it come up and hit them in the face.

Power: We just had a Canadian election a couple of days ago and these are things we're talking about here now. We're still taking about pipelines; we're still talking about oil in Alberta.

Young: The whole Canadian system just took a huge hit. You elected the worse, or better of two evils—it doesn't matter. The only good party in Canada is the Green Party. The rest of it's just a bunch of crap. Look at Justin Trudeau. He's running the show now. Isn't he the guy who just put in the pipeline? Isn't he the guy who put the billions of dollars or whatever it was into some pipeline to Vancouver or something?

Power: Yup.

Young: What the hell? Who voted for that? What—who's thinking? Nobody's thinking.

Power: I mean, it's—

Young: Look around. Can anybody tell? What about the climate? What do you think that is? Is that a joke?

Power: I mean, I guess people get worried about their jobs. People get worried about having food on the table.

Young: Yeah, they should worry about their jobs, all right. That's good. Well, they should worry about their jobs. Good idea.

Power: But, you know what I mean? They worry about putting food on their table. They worry about that. I'm just trying—Listen, I'm obviously—

Young: It's the whole thing. You're gonna worry about a job and putting your food on your table, except in a much bigger way. It's like there won't be any food. You won't have a table. There will be people coming up from the equator trying to live in your house. It's getting to the point where you close your eyes and look forward fifteen years: it's a *disaster*. That's what we're giving our kids. That's what we're giving our grandchildren. And people are worried about how the economy is in Alberta. It's just like they got their heads stuck in the tar sands. They just can't see what's going on. I'm not saying that they're wrong. I just totally disagree with it. I think that they're narrow-minded, they're only looking at their own benefit, they're not looking ahead for their children or their grandchildren. And, yeah, it makes them feel bad, so when I say that, they get pissed off. But the fact is that's what they're doing and those *are* their grandchildren and they're doing it.

Power: So what do you do then as an artist? I mean, you're still singing these songs. Is it there that you're trying to talk to more people who may not see things your way, or it just trying to get those emotions out?

Young: No, I'm just expressing myself. I'm saying how I feel. I'm saying what I think. I really don't care so much about people listening to it now as I do about getting it right. I get down there, sing the song, get the feeling out, and do the next song after that—go to the next song.

Power: It's funny to hear you say that you record it and you move on to the next song because I've spent the last couple of months sort of deep in the Neil Young Archives, like, the archive that you put up online. I've never seen anything like it in my life. It's an online archive of most of the music you ever recorded. Now what's it like to look at that archive and look back at everything you've done in 50 years?

Young: Well, I'm looking forward at the next things that I'm gonna put in it. And we're searching through all kinds of stuff that we have from unreleased Crazy Horse to unreleased Pearl Jam to so many things. It's just an amazing amount of stuff. I was going pretty fast for a while there while I was cruising along through the '70s, '80s, '90s, whatever. I made more records than I could put out. And more films than I could put out. And I didn't even have a chance to finish some of them. So, now, that's what I'm doing. I'm going through those projects that were roughed in and sometimes just deciding, well, rough is good enough for those—you got the feeling. Sometimes I have to do a little, I have to do some kind of work to technically make them together, or maybe edit or something. There's just so much to do that's in the future compared to listening to what's there. I'm just creating all of this so that it's a cohesive record of what we all accomplished together.

Power: But it's funny, when you say that you just have to keep moving, you have to keep moving. You're, sure, you listen that because your folks know what's coming up next. But you have an interesting—like, I'm always curious—and I ask a lot of people about this. You're in a curious situation when you get up on stage, 'cause God knows I've seen you an awful lot of times, and you play a lot of really cool new music. You also play your older songs. Like, what's your relationship with that? How do, how do you, how do you make sense of the show like that?

Young: Well, I just wait until I feel like playing an old song and I pick one and do it. But I don't have a list of old songs that I have to do.

Power: But there's lots of people who don't at all. There's people out there who don't ever do 'em.

Young: What? Their old songs?

Power: Yeah, or if they do 'em, they don't sound anything like what they used to sound like.

Young: Well, good for that. Why should it sound like it used to sound? I mean, how long ago was it?

Power: [*Laughs.*]

Young: You already have the record of it. Why not do it like you feel it today? I don't understand trying to re-create what you already did when you've already made a record of it.

Power: I guess so. But, I dunno, I feel like at least when I see you and I hear "Cinnamon Girl," it sounds like "Cinnamon Girl," you know?

Young: Well, you know, maybe the next time it won't. It depends. It just depends. It's not something I focus on. I'm more focused on the last songs that I wrote and the new record that I made or things that I feel like playing just 'cause we were talking about it on the bus. It's a *real* thing. It's whatever you feel like doing. That's what I like to do. And sometimes people go to my shows and I know they want me to play "Heart of Gold" and "Old Man" for, and do—I even had an offer recently to go out and do the whole, the whole *Harvest* album.

Power: Yeah?

Young: And do a tour. And somebody offered me a bunch of money to do that. But I can't do that. All those guys are dead. They're gone. I can't do that. I can't, all I can do is miss those guys while I'm doing it. Or, if I'm playing with Promise of the Real, there's a lot of those songs I can do, but it's doesn't sound like them, it sounds like us. And that's cool. Crazy Horse can't do those songs. It doesn't fit. When I do the songs I do with Crazy Horse, it's because I feel like playing them and we play 'em.

[*"Old Man" plays in background.*]

Power: Yeah, I mean, I get it, man. I get it. I just can't possibly imagine what that's like to, 'cause when we think of artists as these albums, but they don't stop making things. They don't stop making art. They don't stop creating. This new album is a great example. They don't stop creating really cool, kinda amazing things, in my opinion, anyway. I can't imagine what it's like for someone to come up to you and go, "Hey, do you just wanna play all of *Harvest*?"

Young: You could make a fortune doing that, but you'd also have sold your soul and then you'd be done. You might as well just go to bed.

Power: I guess it's nostalgia. Nostalgia is a dangerous thing.

Young: Well, it's OK if that's what you want. Nostalgia makes some people feel good.

[*"Old Man" gets cranked up.*]

Power: I was on the way here and I was texting a couple of friends of mine, and I said that I'm gonna get to talk to Neil Young, and of course everyone was really excited. But the people I was talking to were artists, and I thought about them. I thought about people doing creative work and what an inspiration you've been to them, kind of whether you like it or not, but the inspiration you've been to them or whether that was your intention or not. Do you have anything you want to say to them? What do you say to a young artist making work right now?

Young: Be true to yourself. Just do what you wanna do. The last thing you wanna do is please anybody else. Yeah, just forget about the pleasing everybody. It's the most useless pastime you could ever have. It doesn't make any difference to anything. That's like the most, it's, it's a waste of time.

Power: Neil Young, it's been nice to talk to you, man.

Young: Why did Canada vote for Justin Trudeau? And what did, what *was* that? Can you explain that?

Power: No, I play the banjo; I can't possibly explain that.

Young: OK, good. Good answer. I like that answer. That's a really good answer. I feel enlightened at this point. [*Laughs.*]

Power: Yeah. So my Dad told me one time we went to a hardware store, and he asked someone about picking up a, something for the toilet we were trying to fix back home, and he asked Buddy, and he sent him down the road trying to find something. Dad said, "I wish he had just told me, 'I dunno.'" So that's my answer to you, man: I don't know.

Young: I don't know.

Power: I play the banjo.

Young: Well, that's a great answer. Keep playing the banjo, that's what I say. Do you play anything else?

Power: Yeah, I'm playing, I'm in—

Young: Playing guitar, right?

Power: Yeah, I'm playing guitar in the studio right now, yeah.

Young: Good. You guys all play at once?

Power: Yeah, we're doing it all live off the floor.

Young: Oh, good. That's a great beginning, I think. Not for everybody, but for me.

Power: Accordion, fiddle, bouzouki, guitar, and Irish drum, the bodhran: all at one time.

Young: Nice.

Power: But headphones, not monitors. I can't get over you working in monitors in that film.

Young: Headphones? What are you on headphones for?

Power: I don't know.

Young: Are you living in your own head?

Power: Yeah, I am.

Young: All you can hear is what somebody else sends to you?

Power: Yeah, yeah, it is.

Young: That's no good. What's going on in the room?

Power: The drummer's upstairs.

Young: Put those headphones on and all you hear is those headphones and what the engineer thinks you should hear. Puts echo on one thing. EQ on something else. You put on your headphones and you can't even hear the guy next to you.

Power: I had you until I mentioned the headphones.

Young: Yeah, the headphones really are a drag. Headphones are, headphones are, I won't say who they're for. But they're not a good thing.

Power: To me, it's because you want to worry about bleed. But who cares about bleed if you're just doing everything once?

Young: Bleed! Bleed is where the magic is. Where do you think, what do you think the air is? The air is in the room. When everybody plays together, the magic is in the room. It's not any particular person. And it's not in the blend that the engineer puts together with the producer. It's in the room. That's what you hear when you actually play a song with other musicians is the room.

Power: Neil Young, been nice to talk to you.

Young: Nice to talk to you, too, and I hope you have a great session. Leave your phones in the car. Put them on the floor. Try playing one where like you're playing in a garage, or you're in a place where you can hear yourself because you're getting ready to go on stage. Do you wear phones on stage?

Power: *No.*

Young: Well?

Power: I know people who wear in-ears!

Young: Yeah, you can wear in-ears, but not the kind that plug your ears. You need the kind that, if you're missing some frequency or something, you wanna boost up that frequency. But I use the monitors so that I can hear everybody on the stage. If I wanna hear more drums, I'll move toward the drums. If I want the drummer to play louder, I'll look at the guy. Although Ralph doesn't like me to look at him. He says, "Don't look at me while I'm playing." [*Laughs.*]

Power: Why doesn't he like you to look at him?

Young: He doesn't wanna be bothered. He wants to play.

Power: [*Laughs.*]

Young: He doesn't wanna be distracted by some old fart looking at him. He just wants to play. He's in the groove, too. That's the thing about Crazy Horse: they're all like me. We all feel the same way about playing music. So when you see us playing in the studio, you notice we don't have any phones.

Power: Tell me this, tell me this: was that, was that immediate? You played with a bunch of people before Crazy Horse. When you met them, were you like, "Finally, some guys get me"?

Young: No. We were all doing it together. We started like that.

Power: But you know what I mean? Like you found these guys and were like, "OK, these guys get it."

Young: No, we're just, we just had a good time. Before that, Buffalo Springfield, I think almost everything I played, I overdubbed my vocal. And so we did all the tracks and then we'd sing the song and we'd do this and you analyze it and you do this and you do that. I was so tired of that. Then I got to do my first album. I overdubbed everything on the album. Every instrument we did everything, we did the whole thing, and I got finished with that and I said, "I never wanna do that again, in my life. I hope I've got it out of my system." And then we did *Everybody Knows This Is Nowhere*, which we all played, and I sang some of, myself, live. And then the next records, after that I don't know what it was, maybe *After the Gold Rush* or something, I was just singing live all the time and there were no headphones. So, by *After the Gold Rush*, headphones were gone, and we never looked back.

Power: You know, it worked out for you.

Young: Yeah, it worked for me. Like when I was doing *Harvest*, I got to be, I was about six feet away from Buttrey so I could hear his high-hat, and I sat in a particular place where he could see my right hand. So we did it that way. It was like human-to-human, and that's why we're together on the record, that's why it sounds like it does. It's not because some brilliant engineer used the right wires and then balanced everything. That has nothing to do with it. The engineer's like, like the caretaker at a dog pound or something. He just has to make sure everything lives.

Power: The engineer you got, according the doc I watched, he's pretty great. He seems to get you.

Young: John Hanlon?

Power: Yeah!

Young: He's my partner. He's my coproducer. We work with, everybody we work with is, they're good. They understand what it is we're doing. Some are not as used to doing it as others, but they understand what it is we're trying to do.

Power: Yeah. And I think he worked on *Ragged Glory*, right? He's been with you since then.

Young: Yeah, that was his first record.

Power: Yeah. I mean—

Young: With me and Briggs.

Power: Did he get it right away? Was it a bit of a, a bit of a crash course? Was it a bit of a learning curve?

Young: No, he walked right in there, and I think Briggs told him that if he didn't get it right, he was gonna be in a station wagon heading for the airport.

Power: [*Laughs.*]

Young: So that was pretty well, that's the MO. We saved a lot of time. There wasn't much pussyfooting around out there. We were in the middle of the woods.

Power: No pressure.

Young: No, there is no pressure. There really isn't. It's a perfect situation. You're in there, everybody's doing the same thing, we got all this great equipment, we got the best instruments in the world, we got great recording equipment, a nice place to be, no distractions, and songs, and then when you do the song once, that should be it: you're done, because that was the first take under optimal circumstances. I don't wanna have to fix it. I don't wanna have to change guitar cords or maybe I'll drop a word somewhere or something like that. I don't like to have to do that. Every once in a while I have to. I can point them out to you on records and you go, "Oh, that's right, that's not the same as everything else." But it goes by quickly.

Power: So there are, even though the moment, and the moment is what matters, the pursuit of perfection is bad and wrong, there are still things you'll go back and go, "Ah, maybe I should fix that."

Young: Here's the deal. We do it, we do it and you get the vibe and you hear the song and you feel the song and you see the pictures in your mind that you thought of when you were writing the song. No amount of fixing is gonna change that. Or no amount of unfixing is gonna change that. The thing is you gotta let that be and fix it, or not fix it. But if that vibe is there, then that's the only thing that matters. If you can't get that vibe, you can have a perfect record, but it wouldn't feel like that. So that's the way I do it, because that's what I like to do. I'm not saying anybody else should do that.

Power: No. But I get it. I'm thinking about it now. The only thing is I'm doing instrumental music, right, so I'm just thinking, "God, if I mess up a note" or something like that. But whatever.

Young: Just keep on going. Mess up the note. Hey, you mess it up the same way the second time it comes around, you're probably doing a new part. It's OK.

Power: They say, what do they say, they say make the same mistake twice and call it jazz?

Young: Yeah, but have you ever heard "If you're thinking, you're stinking?"

Power: No!

Young: OK, well that's it. Remember that one.

Power: I will. Neil, man, nice to talk to you. [*Both laugh.*] What a good way to end it.

Young: Have a good time in St. John and keep on rockin' over there. Have fun and good luck with your music.

NEIL YOUNG ON

Preserving Music

"I wish I could do this for Frank Sinatra. I wish I could do it for Nelson Riddle. I wish I could do it for all of the great jazz players. I wish I could do it for all the great songwriters and musicians and everybody who recorded during the time and before the time that I did. But I can't."

–from an interview with David Samuels, *New York Times*, August 20, 2019

NEIL YOUNG ON

Climate Change

"It's the only thing that really matters. People on the streets can't see past next week. They're not thinking about their kids or their kids' kids. I don't fly anymore, except to Europe. I can't do the (Swedish climate activist) Greta Thunberg thing. She's so great."

–from an interview with Edna Gundersen, *AARP*, October 28, 2019

ABOUT THE CONTRIBUTORS

Jeffrey C. Alexander was a Los Angeles–area freelance writer in the mid-1960s.

Richard Bienstock is a rock journalist whose work has appeared in *Rolling Stone*, *Billboard*, and *Guitar World*, where he served as senior editor. His books include *Aerosmith: The Ultimate Illustrated History of the Bad Boys from Boston* (2020) and the coauthored *Nöthin' But a Good Time: The Uncensored History of the '80s Hard Rock Explosion* (2021).

Richard Cook was a writer for the *New Musical Express* in the 1980s before moving on to edit *The Wire* and *Jazz Review*. In the early 1990s, he worked for PolyGram in the UK as a producer and jazz catalog curator. He is the author of Penguin's *Richard Cook's Jazz Encyclopedia*. He died of cancer in 2007.

Jody Denberg has been a fixture on the Austin, Texas, music scene since the mid-1970s. Beginning in 1990, he helped radio station KGSR-FM create its innovative roots/Americana focus. His work with Services Invested in Musician Support Foundation (SIMS), which fund mental-health services for musicians, has raised more than $2 million.

Patrick Donovan spent a dozen years as the chief music writer for Melbourne's *The Age* newspaper. He recently stepped down after a decade leading Music Victoria, a state music advocacy organization, and was chairman of the Australian Music Industry Network. He was Iggy Pop's tour manager in 1998.

Francis Dordor is a French music journalist. He was editor-in-chief of the defunct magazine *Best* (1968–2000) and currently writes for *Les Inrockuptibles*. He is an expert on reggae and is the author of three Bob Marley biographies, most recently 2019's *Bob Marley: Le dernier prophète* (*The Last Prophet*).

Michael Goldman is an American journalist who's covered the entertainment industry for publications such as the *Boston Globe*, *DGA Quarterly*, and *Cinescape*. He was an editor for *Daily Variety* and Senior Editor for the award-winning film journal *Millimeter* for a dozen years. He's written eight entertainment-oriented books, including 2015's *John Wayne: The Genuine Article* and *24: The Ultimate Guide* (2007).

Mike Greenhaus is the editor-in-chief of *Relix*, the longest-standing print magazine dedicated to improvisational and independent music, and Vice President of the Relix Media Group. He also edits the daily newswire for Relix.com and its sister site, Jambands.com. He has written for *Spin*, *Paste*, *American Songwriter*, and other outlets and penned the introduction to noted music photographer Jay Blakesberg's book, *Jam*. Greenhaus hosts and produces The Friday Night Jam (http://www.becausejewish.com/), a meditative, bimonthly speaking series that explores the intersection of spirituality and pop music.

Andrew Hultkrans was the managing editor and a columnist for the pioneering cyberculture magazine *MONDO 2000* in the early 1990s. He was editor-in-chief of *Bookforum* from 1998 to 2003 and is the author of *Love's Forever Changes*, the second volume in the acclaimed 33 1/3 book series.

Alan Jenkins was a writer and editor of *Broken Arrow*, the magazine of the Neil Young Appreciation Society, from the early 1980s to 2001.

Nick Kent is a British rock critic who has written for most of the UK's major publications since the 1970s, including *New Musical Express*, *The Face*, and *Mojo*. He is the author of *The Dark Stuff*, an anthology of his journalistic works, and *Apathy for the Devil*, his 2010 autobiography.

Christian Lebrun was a French music journalist who wrote for publications including *Best* and *Rock & Folk*. His work has been anthologized in *Le rock et la plume: Le rock raconté par les meilleurs journalistes, 1960–1975* (*Rock and the Pen: The Best Rock Writing*).

Greil Marcus is an American music and cultural critic whose work has appeared in countless magazines, including *Rolling Stone*, *Creem*, *Artforum*, and *Spin*. He is the author of more than two dozen books, most notable *Mystery Train: Images of America in Rock 'n' Roll Music* (1975), *Lipstick Traces: A Secret History of the 20th Century* (1989), and *The History of Rock 'n' Roll in Ten Songs* (2014).

Constant Meijers is a long-time Dutch music journalist. His Dutch-language review of a 1973 London Neil Young and the Santa Monica Flyers show was included in the original *Tonight's the Night* album package. His book *Forever Young: de muziek van Neil Young als soundtrack van mijn leven* (*The Music of Neil Young as a Soundtrack to My Life*) was published 2013.

Jas. Morgan was a founding member and editor of the pioneering cyberculture magazine *MONDO* 2000. He has written about techno-culture for numerous publications, including *Spin* and *Exposure*.

Tom Power is an award-winning musician and broadcaster who hosts the national arts and entertainment program *q* on CBC Radio One (https://www.cbc.ca/radio/q). In 2008, Power joined CBC as the host of *Deep Roots*, and, at 21 years of age, was the youngest national radio host on the station since Peter Jennings. In 2011, he became the host of *Radio 2 Morning*, the CBC's flagship daily morning national music program. Power leads his own band, the Dardanelles, who have introduced a new audience to traditional Newfoundland music while playing festivals and theaters around the world.

B. Mitchell Reed (also Reid) was a Southern California radio fixture from the late 1950s to the early 1980s, save for a mid-1960s gig in New York City when he helped introduce the Beatles to America. He was a pioneer in late-'60s underground FM radio and was the first host of the *Rockline* interview program. He was friends with many of the Southern California musicians and at one point had David Crosby, Joni Mitchell, and Elliot Roberts living at his house. He died in 1983 at the age of 56, and in 2014 was inducted into the Rock Radio Hall of Fame.

Mark Rowland was executive editor of *Musician* magazine for a decade and wrote for diverse publications such as *Esquire, American Film*, and the *Los Angeles Times*. His extensive television work includes stints as chief writer for BET's *American Gangster* and coexecutive producer of TV One's *Unsung* music documentary series, as well as work on documentaries for the History Channel, ESPN, and VH1.

Bud Scoppa has worked as a rock journalist (*Rolling Stone*, *Creem*, *Fusion*), music editor (*Music Connection*, *Cash Box*, *Hits*), and for record labels (Mercury, A&M, Sire). He wrote a Byrds biography for Scholastic Book Services in 1971 and published *The Rock People: Interviews with 13 Top Stars and Groups* in 1973. He's also written liner notes for many album reissues and was nominated for a 2001 Grammy for the Little Feat box set *Hotcakes & Outtakes: 30 Years of Little Feat*.

Adam Sweeting is a British music writer whose work has appeared in *New Musical Express, Melody Maker*, the *Guardian*, and *Q*. He has written a number of books, including *Simple Minds* (1988) and *The Complete Bruce Springsteen: The Stories Behind Every Song* (2012).

Jaan Uhelszki was a senior editor and feature writer for *Creem* magazine in the 1970s. She's written for a multitude of rock magazines, including *New Musical Express*, *Spin*, and *Uncut*. She was the founding editor at *Addicted to Noise*, where she won the Journalist of the Year and National Feature Writer Awards from the Music Journalists Association in 1996. She is a regular in music documentaries and cowrote the 2019 feature documentary *Creem: America's Only Rock 'n' Roll Magazine*.

Dave Zimmer is an American music journalist whose work was long featured in *BAM* Magazine. He authored the twice-updated *Crosby, Stills, and Nash: The Biography* and edited *Four Way Street: The Crosby, Stills, Nash & Young Reader*. He currently works at Penguin Random House.

CREDITS

I gratefully acknowledge the help of everyone who gave permission for material to appear in this book. I have made every reasonable effort to contact copyright holders. If an error or omission has been made, please bring it to the attention of the publisher.

"10 Days with the Loner" by Constant Meijers. Published October 9, 1974, in *Muziekkrant OOR*. Reprinted by permission.

"Tonight's the Night: Play It Loud and Stay in the Other Room!" by Bud Scoppa. Published June 28, 1975, in *New Musical Express*. Reprinted by permission of Rock's Backpages.

"Quelque Mots de Neil Young (A Few Words from Neil Young)" by Christian Lebrun and Francis Dordor. Published May 1976 in *Best*. Translated by the author. Reprinted by permission.

"When Does a Dinosaur Cut Off Its Tail?" by Richard Cook. Published October 9, 1982, in *New Musical Express*. Reprinted by permission of Rock's Backpages.

"Legend of a Loner" by Adam Sweeting. Published September 7 and 14, 1985, in *Melody Maker*. Reprinted by permission of Rock's Backpages.

"Blue Notes for a Restless Loner" by Dave Zimmer. Published April 22, 1988, in *BAM* magazine. Reprinted by permission of Rock's Backpages.

"Neil Young: An Exclusive NYAS Interview" by Alan Jenkins. Published August 1990 in *Broken Arrow*. Reprinted by permission.

"Neil Young's New Age Metal" by Andrew Hultkrans and Jas. Morgan. Published Summer 1992 in *MONDO 2000*. Reprinted by permission.

"The Men on the Harvest Moon: Young-Buck!" by Mark Rowland. Published April 1993 in *Musician*. Reprinted by permission of Rock's Backpages.

"Neil Young: Our 1993 Artist of the Year" by Greil Marcus. Published January 1994 in *Spin*. Reprinted by permission.

"I Build Something Up, I Tear It Right Down: Neil Young at 50 Interview" by Nick Kent. Published December 1995 in *MOJO*. Reprinted by permission of Rock's Backpages.

"The *Silver & Gold* Interview" by Jody Denberg. Broadcast April 2000 on KGSR Radio—Austin City Limits Radio. Printed by permission.

"Young and Free" by Patrick Donovan. Published November 21, 2003, in the *Age*. Reprinted by permission.

"Neil Young: 'I'm Not Ready to Go Yet'" by Jaan Uhelszki. Published September 2007 in *Uncut*. Reprinted by permission.

Podcast interview by Michael Goldman. Released January 2008 by *Digital Content Provider* Magazine. Printed by permission.

"Neil Young: Gold Rush" by Richard Bienstock. Published September 29, 2009, in *Guitar World*. Reprinted by permission.

"Neil Young and Daniel Lanois: Love and War" by Jaan Uhelszki. Published January 2011 in *American Songwriter*. Reprinted by permission.

"Young and the Restless" by Mike Greenhaus. Published January 24, 2017, in *Relix*. Reprinted by permission.

"Neil Young on His 50 Year Career, Making Music and His New Documentary" by Tom Power. Broadcast October 25, 2019, on CBC/q. Printed by permission.

INDEX